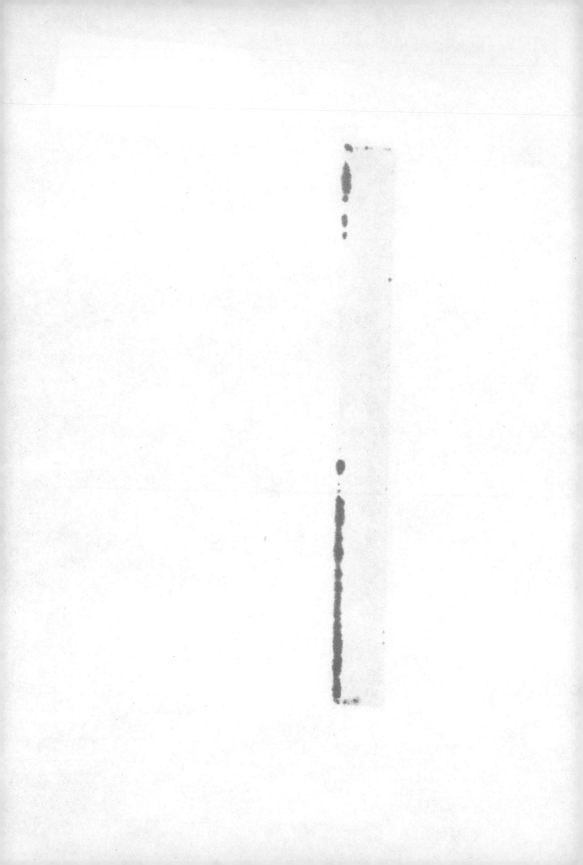

THE CRIME INDUSTRY

The Crime Industry

JOHN A. MACK
University of Glasgow
in collaboration with
HANS-JÜRGEN KERNER
University of Tübingen

SAXON  HOUSE | LEXINGTON BOOKS

Published by
SAXON HOUSE, D. C. Heath Ltd.
Westmead, Farnborough, Hants., England.

Jointly with
LEXINGTON BOOKS, D. C. Heath & Co.
Lexington, Mass. U.S.A.

ISBN 0 347 01074 1
Printed in Great Britain by Eyre & Spottiswoode Ltd, at
Grosvenor Press, Portsmouth

Contents

PART IV   CRIMINAL ORGANISATION RESEARCH

List of tables

Foreword

Originally presented as a report to the Council of Europe, *The Crime Industry* is a discursive study of various aspects of European organised and professional crime, 'business-type' crime, and several extensions of Sutherland's white-collar crime. More particularly, the authors provide discussions of these activities mostly in the United Kingdom, West Germany, The Netherlands, Denmark and Sicily.

Quantitative data are hard to come by in this area of criminological research. The authors readily admit this difficulty but provide some sources from which inferences about the extent and volume of professional crime can be made. Interviews with the police, annotations by persons from Interpol, contacts with social observers in the separate countries constitute the bases for analyses. There are no interviews here with criminals, no participant observations, but there are insights, balanced perspectives, cautiously stated hypotheses, heuristic leads for future research. The survey is not meant to assess organised and professional crime comparatively across countries, and essentially views the drug problem as outside the scope of its inquiry.

There are controversies in the United States about the degree of national syndication that is claimed to exist in organised crime. Donald Cressey focuses on the network, the linkages, the hierarchies, and produces a superstructure of order; while Norval Morris and Gordon Hawkins remind us of our penchant to create conspiracies and raise the issue of the myth of the mafia. Joseph Albini has persuasively described syndicated crime and Francis Ianni anthropologically has shown us, by concentrating on syndicates, how criminal as well as law-abiding behaviour emerge from certain types of Italian families in the United States.

But there appear to be fewer controversies about organised, professional and business-type crime in Europe, and the authors of this volume make their generalisations with little likelihood of serious contradiction. For example, successful crime in this area exists in the gaps between the national law enforcement systems; gangs are not joined together but do render assistance when needed; there is much division of labour and some international teamwork but no international syndicate; there are no systematic international receivers of stolen goods; organised gambling interests from the United States have had no success in invading England, particularly, or the Continent in general; there are no continuing generations of organised families of crime; neither police corruption nor the 'fix' with police or the judiciary characterise European organised or professional crime; most business-type crime is *ad hoc* and short-lived; organised and professional crime in Europe fill no major role of middlemen supplying of powerful economic demands for forbidden goods and services.

The Krays and Richardsons in England provide some exceptions, as do the mafiosi in Sicily. The reader is tantalised by the sketchy descriptions of the activities of these celebrated cases and by the generalisations for Sicily. And despite the disclaimer of comparative assessment, the reader will quickly note the presence of organised crime in Germany and England, with allusions to France and the Italian mainland, as well as the near-absence of such crime in Scandinavia, save for Denmark. The rational planning and preparation, the power of emotional detachment, the practical intelligence and managerial efficiency are attributes of professional crime in Germany and England; the descriptions of these operations are like those that fit legitimate business and remind us of the thin and often unclear line between legal and illegal enterprise.

There is scholarship here that is reflected in the analytical capacity of the authors to use the uneven and sometimes scanty data that were available to them in weaving a conceptual framework and a reasonable classification of organised and professional crime. The bibliography of several langauges, especially the references from Germany, is itself a new and valuable source for scholars. This volume should surely be complimented for its effort to fill a void in criminological analysis and for its implicit encouragement of more multi- and interdisciplinary research that requires economics, political science and sociology in the further pursuit of understanding business-type, professional and organised crime in national and international settings.

Marvin E. Wolfgang, Professor of Sociology and Law, Director, Center for Studies in Criminology and Criminal Law, University of Pennsylvania.

Preface

This book was originally produced as a report to the Council of Europe. The order of the chapters has been altered and chapter 2 has been expanded; otherwise the substance of the work is the same. As in the case of all such Council of Europe research documents, the findings and views expressed are entirely the responsibility of the writers.

The report, presented to and approved by the Council of Europe in 1973, arose out of a proposal by the Council's European Committee on Crime Problems that the theme of the Council's Co-ordinated Criminological Research Fellowship for 1970 should be 'Certain aspects of organised and professional crime'. The material for the report was gathered by a team of four. The report was written by J. A. Mack, director of the team, on the basis of drafts prepared by the various team members. Hans Kerner was a principal collaborator and has advised on the preparation of the report and of this book at every stage of the work.

The team was greatly helped at all points in the study by the secretariat of the Council of Europe. We would wish especially to thank Mr Norman Bishop, who helped greatly in the planning of the survey and in getting the project off the ground; we are also particularly indebted to Miss M. Eckert. We were greatly helped by the large number of consultants in the different countries who gave us freely of their time and expertise, and who incidentally suggested many of the guiding ideas which subsequently shaped the writing of the report. They have asked us not to particularise, so we must confine ourselves to this collective word of thanks, both to them and to the governments of the member states of the Council who authorised and encouraged their co-operation with us.

The special help given to the team by Interpol has not been confined to the items specifically acknowledged in the following pages. We wish to thank M. Jean Nepote and through him his staff for the notable contribution they have made and are making to criminological scholarship, not merely in respect of this report but also over a much wider range of investigative and educational activity.

Acknowledgements and thanks are due to Messrs Weidenfeld and Nicolson, London, and Messrs McGraw-Hill, New York, for permission to quote the passages on pages 26 and 40 below respectively; to the *Sunday Times* for permission to use the material incorporated in the note on pp. 59-61; and to Messrs Stevens, London, for permission to reproduce Mr Mack's paper originally published in the *British Journal of Criminology*, volume XII.

Special mention must be made of the work put in by colleagues in the University of Glasgow Criminal Research Unit; by Mrs M. A. Mack and Mrs Sheila Miller, whose press and statistical analyses have been used in chapter 4 and elsewhere; especially and notably by Mrs Irene Lynch, secretary of the Unit, who has worked very hard and with great accuracy typing and correcting a long succession of drafts of each section of the original report and each chapter of the book.

A word about the layout of the book will be helpful here. Part I expounds the three main discoveries made by the team. Chapter 1 is about the inadequacy of the ideas and the language used by popular writers and criminologists alike to organise what knowledge they have of major rational-economic crime. Chapter 2 is about the largely unnoticed rise of 'business-type crime' to a level of importance and a range of acquisition which is at least equal to the achievement, if that is the word, of the established and accepted 'professional' and 'organised' modes of large-scale criminal activity. Chapter 3 is an attempt to bring out the differences between the North American and European manifestations of what is usually called 'organised crime', what we prefer to call 'syndicated crime'. Part II outlines recent developments in major crime in a number of European countries, as discussed by various consultants in the course of the surveys made by the team. Part III discusses a number of topics selected by the team as requiring special attention; these were researched by Mr Kerner. This section of the book, like the review of current research into criminal organisation in Part IV, is particularly designed to stimulate intensive research into what we discovered to be a largely unexplored territory.

Appendix A outlines the Council of Europe remit to the team and describes the preliminary clearing of the ground and the organisation of the survey. Appendix B is a reprint of a paper on 'The Able Criminal' which helped the team to clarify its objectives in the early stages of the work.

The debt of this book to a large number of fellow-scholars and fellow-researchers is obvious on every page. We would wish especially to thank Donald MacRae for a timely word of encouragement and Marvin Wolfgang for paying us the compliment of writing a Foreword.

PART I

Perspective

1 Professional and Organised Crime

The first discovery made by the Council of Europe team was that they would make no progress on the topic they had been given until they had discarded the terms in which it was framed. The fact is that 'Professional and organised crime' has too many meanings. Do the two words give two aspects of the same thing? European scholars and policemen think they do. Or is the reference to two distinct categories of crime? American criminologists and policemen incline to answer both yes and no to this question. 'Organised' is the villain of the piece. Taken in its dictionary sense, it applies to all activities, criminal or other, which involve more than one person and are not completely spontaneous, not a matter of the impulse of the moment. But 'organised crime' has been used for most of this century in a special sense, to identify the Al Capone type of criminal activity. This usage is also well known in Europe and other continents, but the two meanings are seldom kept distinct. The term 'professional' is less ambiguous. It is used everywhere to signify the Bill Sikes type of criminal activity, with the modification that the Bill Sikes of today is a much smoother operator than his original prototype. But 'professional', the word and the image, has a foreshortening effect, emphasising as it does the front-line executive and understating the background operators in the high-level type of predatory enterprise. The label doesn't fit the facts.

It is not simply a question of linguistic confusion. The things behind the terminology, the things referred to by the terminology, are still largely a matter of guesswork. The continuing practice of criminologists, in Europe as well as in the USA, is to use misleading language in an attempt to describe areas of activity still largely unexplored. There is plenty of knowledge of a kind, knowledge by acquaintance, commonsense rule-of-thumb knowledge, and this is not ineffective for certain practical purposes. It would be astonishing if this wasn't the case, on a subject which arouses such immense human interest and which causes or might cause such immense social trouble. Journalists and special feature merchants produce acres of descriptive material every week, some of it very good, about this or that criminal development. The police on their side show a very real competence in the way they tackle the steady flow of specific events, involving other than petty criminals. But no one, not the best of the crime writers, not the best of the police detectives, has got the matter in perspective. Since they are practical men they get on with the job on the strength of a few generalisations, generalisations which as it happens are quite inadequate for the facts they are supposed to organise.

This is not their fault. Generalising is not their business. As Leroy Gould has pointed out, the good policeman – and the remark is equally true of the good journalist – is master of the *specific* event. (Gould, 1967).[1] The fault – and this is the most startling feature turned up by the research team – lies with the criminologists. Criminologists briefly defined are those persons who act on the belief that the best way to study crime and criminals is to use such scientific approaches and methods as are appropriate to the subject. A basic element in the scientific approach to any subject consists of not accepting existing language habits and ways of thinking. Every scientist has something of the Socrates in him: he queries the assumptions left unexamined in popular discourse. But few criminologists have even begun to examine the conventional wisdom embodied in terms such as 'professional' and 'organised' crime. The present writers have been criticised in quite a number of learned colloquia for spending too much time and energy on 'mere matters of definition'. But the trouble goes deeper. The underlying and usually unspoken criticism derives from a positive dislike of the subject on the part of criminologists. This astonishing fact is not known to intelligent outsiders, who would find it incredible that what common opinion takes to be 'real' crime has been looked at in the past half-century by only a few scholars. But it is well known to the criminological in-groups, and even defended by a number of leading figures. Even the briefest survey of the literature shows up the gap in criminological learning. There is no lack of attention to problems of child behaviour. Learned journals are almost monopolised by papers on penology, which can be broadly defined as what to do about delinquents and criminals once these have been detected and convicted. But little attention is paid to the behaviour systems which the penal systems have been devised to control. There is some continuing study of that sector of criminal behaviour which derives from personal or social pathology; there is only sporadic discussion of the much greater sector of criminal behaviour which is sometimes called 'normal' and which we call 'rational-economic'.

To repeat: the most startling single thing about 'organised and professional crime' is that while there is a great deal of it in practice – not quite so much as is often proclaimed, as we suggest later, but still a great deal – it hardly exists as a subject of serious scientific enquiry. There are a number of good reasons for this, as we point out on pp. 191-2 below. But these are explanatory not justifying reasons. The comparative neglect by criminologists of the study of 'real' crime is something for which there is no justification.

Let us return for a moment to the 'professional/organised' terminology. It is not entirely wide of the mark. It embodies the conventional wisdom on the subject, and the conventional wisdom is never completely mythical. It makes two valid points. It is the case that the entirely heterogeneous mass of people and situations covered by the protean term 'crime' does include a clearly distinguishable category of high-level or substantial criminal practitioners judged in terms of operational scale and operational skill. They are full-time operators. Crime is their occupation, providing them with the economic rewards and non-economic satisfactions which the majority of the population find in the much greater variety of non-criminal occupations. Most of them are known as leading figures in the criminal occupational sub-culture. There are considerable reservations to be made here due to the peculiar conditions and occupational risks of this particular activity. But it is not impossible, given access to the criminal gossip network and to the more systematic knowledge of the police concerned, to trace in this field of socio-economic enterprise the same structure of status system, special values, informal communications network, and other features as is to be found in the more well-defined non-criminal trades and professions.

The second useful point made by the conventional wisdom is the truism that major rational-economic crime is divided into two categories. This goes only some of the way. A growing sector of large-scale gainful crime falls outside both of the rubrics. But the distinction seems to be accurate so far as it goes. There are on the one hand the comparatively well-planned operations of full-time substantial criminal predators of the traditional type − burglars, robbers, confidence men, thieves, and so on. There are also the distinct and different operations of the 'mobs', 'gangs', 'outfits', 'firms', etc., familiar to generations of filmgoers and television addicts. The common and differentiating elements in the two kinds of crime are described below (pp. 172-6). One major difference is that while the first, the Bill Sikes kind of thing, occurs in much the same forms and over much the same range of technical sophistication in all reasonably affluent parts of the world, the Al Capone kind of thing is a distinctively US product. But it has its analogues elsewhere. Something like it is to be found not only in Canada and other territories adjacent to the USA, but also, to a much lesser extent, in Europe and elsewhere. Whether it strictly speaking exists outside North America is a matter of dispute. The activities of the European 'mobs' are primarily parasitical; in USA the main money-making activity is the illicit supply of forbidden commodities. Are these aspects of the same general activity? Or are the two things quite distinct? Our principal collaborator in the USA, Professor Albini of

Wayne State University, makes the distinction absolute. He holds that parasitism — a good example of which is the enforcement of 'protection'[2] payments — is only an occasional and incidental feature of what are essentially supply organisations. It follows that 'syndicated crime', his and our term for 'organised crime', has not yet really taken root in Europe. (With this a principal US authority on the subject, Professor Cressey of the University of California, is prepared to agree, although he differs from Professor Albini on practically everything else.) As we see it these are propositions to be tested by a large-scale historical analysis of this form of crime in the USA and elsewhere of a kind which has still to be attempted. For the rest we devote chapter 3 below to the more general question of the differences between syndicated crime in the USA and in Europe.

The existence of the two kinds of large-scale full-time crime is generally agreed. What is more doubtful is whether the two kinds of crime are practised by two distinct sets of criminals. Our tentative definitions just given assume that they are, and the proposition is supported by our own investigations in the United Kingdom (pp. 38-9 below). But there are many reservations to be made here. The picture differs in different parts of the world, and at different stages of criminal development in the different regions. In the USA itself many leading mobsters have an early history of predatory crime. In many cases, also, the syndicates control and 'protect' groups of straight predators, organise or receive rents from hijackings, monopolise the 'fencing' function, and practise other predatory activities along with the main supply function of the syndicates. The combination is vividly illustrated in the criminal career of Vincent Teresa,[3] who has produced one of the best inside stories yet to appear about syndicate affairs. But it should be noted that Teresa was never a fully incorporated syndicate figure, never a 'made man' (Teresa, 1973, pp. 73-4). By and large we still subscribe to the distinction suggested by one of the Kray twins in the remark that 'only mugs go in for breaking and entering'. As it happens, Reggie Kray was the 'mug' when one compares his probable income and general performance with that of the much more anonymous cohorts of major breakers-in and commando-type robbers of his era (pp. 52-3 below); but the sound point he is making is that most full-time operators take up one line *or* the other, seldom attempt both simultaneously.

We turn now to the principal sins of omission of any criminology which confines itself to the traditional dichotomy. These are that it simplifies (as regards syndicated crime) or ignores (as regards high-level predatory crime) the increasingly important factor of background organisation. There is of course no lack of reference, in discussions of syndicated crime, to the importance of the background operator. But the police studies, the high-grade journalistic studies, even the research studies, lay far too strong an emphasis on the idea of criminal conspiracy, on the all-embracing tentacles of the Mafia or Cosa Nostra, on mighty American oaks growing out of tiny Sicilian acorns, and the like. There is an even more striking absence of studies of the *political* roots of US syndicated crime.[4] Very few American criminologists have co-operated with American political scientists in enquiries into pressure-group politics in the USA from federal down to ward level. Yet to study syndicated crime, for example in Chicago, without incorporating a realistic study of such matters is like attempting to produce Shakespeare's *Hamlet* leaving out the mother of the Prince of Denmark. However, this raises issues going far beyond even the enlarged concept of criminal organisation which it is the intention of this book to advocate.

A more strictly relevant deficiency, criminologically speaking, is illustrated by what we have called the foreshortening effect of the 'professional' image of predatory crime (p. 3 above, p. 177 below). The picture one gets from many of the text-books would almost suggest that the only important operators arc the front-line executives, the people who make direct contact with the victim or his property. This is not only a considerable misrepresentation of what goes on in fact; it is closely connected with an even bigger criminological failure, the failure to pay proper attention to a comparatively new development in major crime: namely the growing involvement of full-time criminal operators – 'professional', 'syndicated', *and other* – in predatory criminal operations consisting in the main of business-type activities and requiring some degree of business skill in the operator. We discuss this third dimension of major crime in the following chapter.

Notes

1 See list of references below, pp. 195-204, for titles, etc. of books and papers mentioned in the text and notes.
2 i.e. in the European meaning of the word. In the USA the word usually means, paying policemen to look the other way; in Europe it is used for the process of making one's unwilling clients pay one for the privilege of not being molested.
3 It is perhaps worth noting that the title of Teresa's book – *My Life in the Mafia* – was almost certainly wished on him by his publishers in accordance with the almost universal disposition to believe that the syndicates in the USA and beyond are held together by a gigantic

Italian-American organisation. But Teresa himself, like Joseph Valachi, had never heard the word used. Similarly, Valachi had never thought in terms of 'The Cosa Nostra'. Valachi himself talked about 'cosa nostra', an inoffensive phrase meaning, in colloquial English, 'our lot', or 'our show'. But Peter Maas, Valachi's editor, gave it capitals, and started one of the most lucrative entertainment and show-business themes of recent decades.

4   See however Daniel Bell on 'Crime as an American way of life' for a good if brief historical sketch (Bell, 1960, pp. 141-50): and Gardiner's recent *Politics of Corruption* for a first-class study of the syndicate-dominated small town of 'Wincanton' (Gardiner, 1970). But when will someone tackle latter-day Chicago, and the major police reforms carried through for Mayor Daley by the remarkable Orlando Wilson, *and the limits imposed on these reforms by the ward political system*?

See for a brief reference Turner, 1968: 'Wilson concedes that progress has been slight, and Virgil Peterson, venerable head of the privately subsidised Chicago Crime Commission and another frustrated foe of the rackets, told the *National Observer* (6 September 1965) that "the department hasn't gotten results in breaking up syndicated crime operations. But there was virtually nothing done in this area before Wilson, and at least we can tell they're now trying" ' (pp. 113-14).

2 The Crime Industry and Business-type Crime

Such impressions as the team gathered on the subject of general trends in crime in Europe were based mainly on developments in the larger countries, those with a population of say 50 million and upwards. The smaller nations — Scandinavia, the Netherlands, Switzerland, Belgium — are not unimportant regarded as stations in a growing continental criminal network (chapter 10), but their internal criminal development is comparatively small in scale. The larger countries of Western Europe — the Federal German Republic, the United Kingdom, France, Italy — have no markedly similar pattern of internal crime, indeed their differences are probably quite as interesting as are such features as they appear to have in common. There is however some evidence in the last decade and more of a general pattern. There appears to be in the first place a fairly steady increase in crime as traditionally defined and measured. Secondly this includes a *disproportionately* greater increase in the activities of the high-level traditional predatory criminal. These developments are more clearly detectable in some countries than in others; the attention of the reader is particularly directed to chapters 4 and 7 below on the United Kingdom and the Federal German Republic respectively. Thirdly, the marked increase in what has conventionally been labelled 'professional' crime has been accompanied by a notable increase in the apparent degree of planning and preparation of the individual major criminal enterprises. Fourthly and lastly, this calls attention to the phenomenon mentioned at the end of the last chapter, that of an increasing organisation in depth, an organisation in which some of the principal figures remain in the background where they are by and large inaccessible although not unknown to the police.

The crime industry

This latter development is the main reason for the title of this book — *The Crime Industry*. The industrial analogy is illuminating in a number of ways. First, it helps to separate out from the mass of heterogeneous activities lumped under 'crime' those which are 'carried on purely for gain by criminals who have chosen that form of activity for economic reasons'

9

(Tobias, 1968, p. 248). 'Purely for gain' is of course a gross simplification. We have pointed out earlier that the criminal occupational subculture, like those of other well-established but law-abiding occupations, also yields non-economic rewards and is also chosen for non-economic reasons. But the abstraction, 'economic man', is a useful one in industry as a whole, as Tobias points out; it is likely to be at least equally useful to the student of crime.

Secondly, the analogy revives a fruitful although recently neglected theme of classical criminology, the relation between crime and economic growth. Ferri puts the matter at its simplest by quoting Lucas: 'Growing civilisation affords more things to be stolen, hence crime should multiply. It is not, therefore, because property is more exposed to theft but because there are more properties exposed to theft.' Ferri warns against pushing the point too far, and is particularly critical of contemporary attempts at comparative measurement (Ferri, 1917, pp. 183-4; Lucas 1828). Certainly the relation between economic growth and trends in general crime totals is not likely to be a rewarding subject of study. But for 'crime' read 'gainful crime', and the idea becomes worth following up.[1]

This puts the crime 'explosion' of the last ten or twenty years into perspective. Since or if gainful crime is part of the economy, its increase can be seen as part of the general economic surge forward since 1945, coming in rather late in the act if anything. This would make a good topic for a combination of criminological and econometric research. There has been a big increase in the bigger European countries in major crime of the traditional predatory sort: van robberies, carefully prepared burglaries, and so on. There has also been a big increase in the less traditional types of crime to be mentioned later in this chapter. Is this increase outstripping or keeping up with or lagging behind the growth of the respective national economies or of the European economy as a whole? It is an open question.

The third contribution of the industrial metaphor to the study of crime seems to us to be its complete justification. Such analogies and metaphors are worth while if they call attention to facts hitherto unregarded, or bring hitherto unnoticed aspects of the subject into focus by opening up new perspectives. And this is precisely what the industrial analogy does for major gainful crime. It shifts the spotlight from the individual operator to the organisation in the background.

All analogies are loose, and much caution is needed in this particular case. The most obvious fact about present-day industrial organisation is the formation of huge amalgamations, conglomerates, multi-national corporations, and so on; and this very real trend tends to marry with the myth, common to crime fiction and to crime journalism, of a large-scale and highly systematic criminal organisation operated by criminal master-minds. Nothing of the kind has been found in any of the few serious attempts at studying the matter. Major acquisitive crime in the London area (chapter 4), and the same kind of thing on a smaller scale being studied in a region of the United Kingdom by one of the present writers, has a considerable element of background goings-on. These have little resemblance to the industrial or business structure in the legitimate sphere. Nor is there much resemblance between the organisation of large-scale predatory crime and the quasipermanent role-systems which sustain the supply activities of the US syndicates.

But there is some kind of continuing supporting arrangement. While the majority of non-petty predatory criminal enterprises are *ad hoc* affairs carried out by small groups, which keep things very quiet before and usually disband immediately after the operation, the entrepreneurs are not entirely out on their own. They are part of an occupational subculture. They sustain and make use of informal systems of communication, information services, supply and equipment systems, marketing systems, and so on. There exists to help them a continuing availability of organisational resources operating on the lines of a loosely structured consultancy network. The principal consultants − or patrons, or senior high-level persons − are almost by definition background figures. But this or that individual may from time to time act as a front-line operator. With this occasional reservation, the background operator usually confines himself to organising; he commands intelligence networks, he prepares in advance for the disposal of the spoils, he sometimes operates an informal welfare and after-care service for lesser criminals and their dependants.

It is almost impossible to write about these background figures, in the present state of our knowledge, without giving a false impression of efficiency, symmetry, comprehensiveness, and so on. The facts are much more ragged, highly complicated, very difficult of access. Take the question of the status of the background operator, for example. There is a powerful tendency in thinking about major crime, strongly akin to the North American compulsion to hypothesise a closely knit Mafia con-spiracy, to think of the background operator as the centre of an elaborate network, enjoying a higher status than even the most skilful of the direct or front-line predators. This is not necessarily the case. The notion of a hierarchy in depth, the idea of the further back the higher up, should not be over-emphasised. All of these criminal systems are informal, work under restrictions much more drastic than those encountered by law-abiding industry. As a result the authority and status of the back-ground organiser, while greater more often than not than that of the direct predator, is comparatively moderate judged on legitimate standards.

The background organisers are link-men rather than tycoons.

The trend towards business-type crime

The prime difficulty encountered in any attempt to indicate the nature of criminal organisation in depth is that people tend to picture it as operating exclusively in relation to one or other or both of the traditional forms of gainful crime. But the people in the background do not confine themselves to providing services for front-line predators; nor are they exclusively concerned with the management of organisations devoted to syndicated crime, whether in its full-blown American form or in the more limited forms to be found in Europe and elsewhere. The most interesting changes in criminal organisation in the course of this century, particularly in very recent decades, relate not to the established criminal techniques, predatory or parasitical, but to a strong increase of activity in the field of what we propose to call business-type crime.

The notion of a crime industry, of an analogy between industry and crime, is again helpful. Consider the nature of organisational change in industry as a whole. The old dichotomy between industrial and business organisation is disappearing. The business element in industry is increasing. By this we mean the office element, the functions which demand some degree, however small, of managerial ability of a generalised kind. The part played by non-manual workers in the primary and secondary industries (the extractive and manufacturing industries) is increasing; not only that, it is increasing in a direct ratio with the level of technological development in the undertaking. The higher the proportion of 'non-producers' (as they are sometimes described) the higher the productivity. It would be silly to attempt a point-for-point analogy with developments in criminal enterprise. But there is a broad resemblance. These things are happening to some extent in major gainful crime.

This is the single most interesting discovery made by the research team. It had not been expected. The team had begun by thinking that their survey would produce a straightforward summing-up of changes in the orthodox and well-established fields of criminal operation: safe-cracking, sneak-thieving, car theft, burglary, the confidence game, bank raids, van robberies, and so on, with possibly an account of new forms of exploitation of criminal opportunity not too different from the older forms. But it became very clear at an early stage of the enquiry that such changes as could be observed within the well-known and generally recognised criminal techniques, while considerable and deserving of record, were comparatively uninteresting when set against certain pointers

12

suggesting an increase of activity in the less familiar territories of business-type crime. This is not an easy thesis to expound, since these territories have still to be adequately mapped, and the definition of business-type crime must consequently remain imprecise. In the note to this chapter we summarise briefly such systematic work as has been done, particularly in Germany, on the concept. Here we propose to do no more than improvise such tentative descriptions as may suit our present purpose.

Business-type crime can be summarily described as the criminal exploitation of business opportunities. It is of the essence of the problem that discussion should not be limited to exploitations which violate only the existing criminal law. Of even greater sociological interest are those more numerous activities which are not plainly and clearly criminal. It is this very broad category in which Sutherland is primarily interested in his treatment of that small part of the field which he labelled 'white-collar crime'. Nothing is more impressive in this celebrated contribution to criminological theory than Sutherland's famous query — 'is white-collar crime really crime?' His answer concentrates on those activities which are prohibited not by the criminal but by the civil law. But the mysterious universe of problematic crimes includes also the utterly baffling category of exploitations without precedent which are technically non-criminal only because the criminal law and the legal process have not yet caught up with them. These are utterly baffling because it is difficult to distinguish, without benefit of hindsight, between innovations in business practice which will eventually be approved by general opinion and innovations which will eventually be stigmatised and punished as crimes. It might be labelled, tentatively, 'business-type crime question mark'.[2]

We now go on to a more precise set of distinctions, referring to the kinds of people who commit business-type crime. Only a few of these have so far been picked out by the criminological spotlight. The literature has been concerned so far only or mainly with those criminal or near-criminal exploitations of business opportunities *which are effected by business men in good standing.* [3] But these white-collar crimes — the term, however diffuse, is now generally accepted — are only part of the picture. Business-type crime is also committed by crooks. There is nothing new in this. What is new is what appears to be its growing prevalence and importance in the field of major crime. This rise into a great prominence of the practitioners of non-white-collar business-type crime merits a close analysis. We offer five tentative classifications, a briefly preliminary sketch towards such an analysis:

1   There are those who begin as white-collar operators — business men of good standing who turn their reputation to criminal advantage — and go

on from that to launch out into full-time business-type crime.

2   There is a second type of business-man criminal, those who could never have been described as being of good repute. These particular 'shady' characters, to use a familiar colloquialism, usually have no connection with or foothold in communication and other networks operated by criminals of the traditional predatory and parasitical types.

3   There is thirdly a distinctive group of 'shady' business men who *are* closely connected with the criminal networks.

4   A small but growing minority of orthodox criminal operators are widening their repertoire and taking to business-type crime. We are referring here not primarily to those high-level predators who already specialise in fraud other than business fraud — the confidence trick, the selling of invisible commodities, and the like, but rather to those predators who are heavily engaged in the organisation and execution of burglary, thieving, shoplifting, and robbery of various kinds. There are also some interesting European examples of the people in the other sector of the orthodox dichotomy, the large-scale mobsters, expanding their income considerably by various forms of business-type crime. This is now such a well-established activity among the US syndicates that it can hardly be described as a very recent development. It is also to be observed that certain forms of business-type crime have been practised by orthodox criminals over a considerable period in a few of the very large metropolitan areas in Europe.

5   The notion of business-type crime helps also to some extent to locate the activities of some of the most remarkable criminal operators of the present day. The term business-type is indeed too narrow for them. They are not simply concerned with shady business deals; their operations extend into rack-renting, illegal immigration, the drug traffic, gold smuggling and gun-running. These people are of interest to a number of governments at any one time and of course to Interpol. They are among those who are described later in this book as finding their more profitable fields of enterprise in the international sphere and in the gaps between the national law enforcement systems.

Examples of business-type crime

We begin with an example of that activity we have labelled business-type crime question mark; in this case white-collar crime question mark. This type of transaction concerns what a man does with what the nineteenth century would have called his own. It is the practice of tax avoidance, currency manipulation, large-scale transfers, and similar operations involving large gains, or the avoidance of large out-payments, for respected industrial and commercial leading figures. The case in question is provided by Sweden: a leading industrialist invested 15 million Swedish kronor in a pension fund in his own name in a small European country, operated by a legitimate small insurance firm, probably owned by him. The point of interest about this investment is that it may have been legal at the time it was done; it appears to have been made illegal by a law which was passed immediately after it was done. Is this kind of thing crime? Or will it be regarded in the future as the invention by a remarkably able tycoon of ways and means, which may well be legitimised in the future, of overcoming narrow national legislation which is clearly unfitted to contain the multi-national or super-national transactions of world business leaders? However that may be it is probable that this type of business activity is increasing. Unpublished police material is proliferating on the subject of large-scale currency transfers.

Next comes a first-class example of the first of our five categories of business-type criminals, those who begin with white-collar operations as a preliminary to launching into full-time business-type crime. The story of the Boss case, as it is called, is to be found in Biilmann and Buchardt, 1970. Five small Danish firms dealing in men's fashions, each of them trading at a loss, had amalgamated, it appears with intention to defraud. The new company began by taking orders from customers and supplying these orders in the ordinary way for about three months. In this way they were reinforcing their already established good repute as small traders who may have been unfortunate but who always had been honest. It turned out later that they had secured the raw materials, which they then went on to make up to supply their customers, without paying or intending to pay the raw material suppliers. Having bilked their suppliers, the new composite firm now proceeded to defraud their customers. This was rendered easy by the nature of the trading system. The system includes middlemen, or Confirming Houses. The Confirming Houses (in this case London-based) pay the suppliers; later the customers, the receiving firms, pay the Confirming Houses. The system worked normally for the first three months, after which the suppliers (the new company) kept on sending invoices and being paid on the invoices, but stopped supplying the customers named in the invoices. After a period of seven to ten months the Confirming Houses discovered that the receiving firms had received no goods. By this time they had paid the combine a sum of about £2 million.

This was only the beginning of a bigger operation. At the point where the defrauding of the Confirming Houses had to stop — at the point of discovery, that is — the combine took over an old company with capital assets of 150 million Danish kroner (D.K.). To get control of this company they required shares to the nominal value of 2 million D.K.; for these the sum of 9 million D.K. in cash was needed. They therefore set about borrowing the money, in the first place to meet a down-payment of 3 million D.K. This down-payment was provided by a German lender, who was given the security he required in the form a declaration of guarantee of property in the company to be purchased. There is an element of sleight of hand in the operation which makes any merely verbal description rather elusive. The series of transactions required was carried out in the space of one hour. But the transactions appear to have come in the wrong order. It is not entirely clear whether the sequence of events broke the law, or whether the sequence of events was such as to require a change in the law designed to ensure that this particular piece of jugglery should be prohibited for all future time. This second operation is of course another example of business-type crime question mark, although the questionable element is much diminished in this case by the preceding series of operations.

From this point on it is difficult, given the lack of research in this field, to establish any exact correlation between the different types of criminal enterprise and the different categories of entrepreneur. Further research may establish that no such correlation exists. But it is not unreasonable to suppose that the new and old types of business-type crime we are now about to describe are attempted for the most part by the two varieties of shady business man referred to above, those who have no connections with orthodox criminals of the traditional predatory or parasitical type, and those who have such connections. It is also likely that our fifth category, the very big fish who seldom surface, have a considerable hand in the more lucrative exploitations.

Exploitation of new types of tax

A big new range of opportunities for sophisticated villainy are provided by those new types of economic legislation and fiscal arrangement whereby governments collect tax on internal and international trade transactions and then refund remissions of tax in specified circumstances. This new type of crime, which might be called 'fiscal fraud', has the same general character as the well-established crime of long-firm fraud, which we discuss later in this chapter. The difference between the two is that whereas the latter consists of the use of spurious or real-life firms to carry through real transactions, fiscal fraud consists in the use of spurious or real-life firms in the fabrication of transactions existing only on paper.

Kerner quotes a number of examples from his discussions with German and Netherlands police advisers. His heading is: 'Dirty work at the government subvention crossroads'. He writes: 'The development started in a small way with the so-called petrol subsidies, which provided tax advantages in the buying of fuel, especially for agricultural machines. It became a bigger operation with the egg subsidies.' But this kind of defrauding gets really big when it goes international. 'International exploitation began in a big way with European Economic Community (EEC) subventions,' he goes on, 'combined with deduction of import profits. In one of the more well-known cases salesmen from France, Germany, Yugoslavia and Rumania sent a large consignment of butter on a European tour, by ship and train. While the butter was being transformed, whether in the course of nature or by a fiscal fiction, to butter-fat, the butter-fat to mayonnaise, the mayonnaise to fat for industrial use, e.g. soap, the industrial fat to seasoning sauce, a series of export or import subsidies was paid for each transformation until 10 million DM (Deutschmarks) compensation money was accumulated on this one consignment.' And finally: 'The pure form of this type of crime is reached when firms are established which have no capital or personnel (i.e. of which the only personnel are the swindlers) and which operate large export and import transactions entirely on paper for the purpose of obtaining subventions, refunds of customs duty, etc. One fraudster got away with over 11 million DM entirely on the basis of fictitious transactions.'

There is also a certain development of the criminal exploitation of the value-added type of tax. A remarkable study in this field is that of Jean Cosson (Cosson, 1971). Most of the European countries have adopted the value-added type of tax only in the last few years. France has had a modified VAT since 1954. It did not have a full VAT until 1968 (Wheatcroft, 1972, p. 5). Cosson describes the criminal exploitation by groups of business men, including our less and more shady varieties, of the opportunities for fraud provided by the tax. The fraudsters, he reports, have made millions of francs out of fabricating large export transactions, completing the transactions as far as paper is concerned, then getting value-added tax rebates on taxes they have never paid.

We turn now to one of the more impressive aspects of the rise of business-type crime − namely, the widening of the repertoire of members of traditional criminal networks. This is to be most clearly seen in the field of long-firm fraud.

Long-firm fraud

Long-firm fraud is the abuse of credit facilities in transactions between big suppliers and wholesale firms dealing in a wide range of goods of a kind which are easy to handle and move and hard to identify as to source. Its precise extent is unknown, since it is very difficult to distinguish between criminal activities and the consequences of incompetence or bad luck in business forecasting. A fair proportion of attempts at long-firm fraud is prevented by trade security arrangements; on the other hand big suppliers and agents take big risks with credit in periods of fast economic movement, and smaller competitors are forced to follow; it is possible therefore to classify part of long-firm fraud under the heading of those crimes in which the victims co-operate, unknowingly or unwillingly, with the exploiters. Another favouring factor is that it is difficult and time-consuming to prosecute long-firm fraudsters, and even more so to convict them. As one police adviser remarked, 'eight out of ten don't show', i.e. are not recorded. Finally the most striking thing about long-firm fraud is that even although it has been going on, with ups and downs, for a long time and is one of the sources of income of the syndicates in the USA, it has been almost completely neglected by criminologists. There are however a number of good descriptions. The *process* is described as early as 1781 (Parker, 1781). The *name* first appears in 1869 (Partridge, 1949). Long-firm fraud has flourished in France for a long time as *carambouillage,* and in Germany as *Stossbetrug.* In the USA it is officially described as bankruptcy fraud, colloquially as 'bust-out' and 'scam' (Cressey, 1969, p. 105). A very good summary description of how it is done, in its simplest form, is given by Sir Richard Jackson: 'it entails starting a business, ordering goods from the wholesalers, and paying for them almost at once. Then, once confidence has been established, the swindler starts giving larger orders and obtaining longer credit. Finally he sells the goods for cash and absconds with the proceeds' (Jackson, 1967, p. 76).[4]

Information obtained by the writer from some trade defence firms suggests a marked increase in the United Kingdom in long-firm frauds in the late 1950s, renewed, after a lapse, in the late 1960s, and continuing into 1971. This increase was checked and brought under control as a result of co-operation between police and trade agencies in or about 1972. As regards the periodicity of long-firm fraud a survey by a well-placed United Kingdom observer — the count being made of all effective frauds irrespective of prosecution proceedings being taken — found that the monthly rate of long-firm frauds, which was running at about 3 per month on a rough estimate in the mid-1960s, increased to about 4-5 per month on a precise count in 1969 and to 8 per month in 1970. A further brief study of the Interpol files indicates an increase in large-scale frauds of this kind in the period 1968-71 (Mack, 1971, pp. 10-11).[5]

The particular interest of the United Kingdom increase is that it seems to have included a considerable contribution from groups of leading established or traditional criminals in at least two parts of the country. In a northern conurbation, beginning in the mid-1960s, a fairly large-scale entry into long-firm fraud was made by a number of people already engaged full-time in traditional criminal enterprises of the more directly predatory type. To the best of our knowledge, this was an incursion without precedent, at least on such a scale, by traditional high-level predators into business-type crime (Mack, 1971, p. 2). It does not seem to have lasted. It was brought under control by the Fraud Squad of the city in question, in co-operation with trade security organisations, by about 1971. It had included a perfect example of that species of long-firm fraud whereby a group of criminals create a number of firms, each of which provides references for the others, and none of which is a genuine trading company.

A more notable widening of the orthodox criminal repertoire, and more successful, at least in the short run, was made by the two London mobs discussed in chapter 3 below, the Richardsons and Krays. In each case the mobs eventually derived a considerable proportion of their criminal income from long-firm fraud and similar activities. In both cases also these frauds could be regarded as primarily an extension of the principal and parasitical activities of the mobs. In some instances the process began in the ordinary way, by purchasing and putting capital into an existing firm. But many of the people put in by the Richardsons or the Krays as the nominal proprietors or 'front men' were working under duress; they were people who had to do what they were told by the mobsters. In other cases an existing firm in good standing was taken over, and its credit exploited, without any cost to the mobsters and without change of proprietor. The inference is that criminals had some hold over the business man con-cerned. (cf. Lucas, 1969, pp. 149-50; Pearson, 1972, p. 106.)

It might be argued that these fairly large-scale business-type develop-ments by the two mobs have brought nothing new into the London criminal scene. Peta Fordham points out that long-firm fraud has long been part of traditional network crime in London, something which the experienced criminal may fall back on when he begins to find that more active forms of crime are overtaxing his strength. But long-firm fraud doesn't seem ever to have been regarded as a *substantial* source of income by the typical member of what Fordham calls the 'underworld'. What the Richardsons and the Krays contrived was an expansion of this type of crime into a major money-making activity by mobs whose predecessors had confined themselves to a more limited range of extortions. Furthermore the longstanding history of long-firm fraud as a sideline for predators of the traditional type appears to refer only to the Metropolis. As far as other parts of the United Kingdom are concerned, long-firm fraud has probably been confined to the type of shady business man who is usually unconnected with local criminal networks. The northern city episode mentioned above is a very recent development; but it is one which is likely to spread in the immediate future, as business-type crime wins an increasing variety of adherents from the ranks of the older Bill Sikes category of villain.

New forms of money

New fields of criminal exploitation are being opened up by new physical and social technologies. Two examples coming immediately to mind are airline tickets and credits cards, developments which are in effect creating new forms of money. The 1968 Symposium on International Frauds conducted by Interpol — one of the most effective contributions to criminological knowledge of recent years — revealed among other things that these new forms of exploitation were being taken up by pre-existing groups of predatory criminals. There is nothing new in this; the ongoing predatory criminal tradition of the last four centuries has consistently shown itself to be capable of a fairly leisurely adaptation to social and technical change. The strikingly new element in the present situation is that the very rapid technological acceleration of the twentieth century has opened up opportunities for exploitation, non-criminal and criminal, which call to an unprecedentedly high degree for powers of organisational manipulation in the exploiters — in a word, for business skill.

Mr Stephens of IATA (International Air Transport Association), contributing to the Interpol symposium, said: 'Criminals quickly realised that airline tickets were an ideal medium for evading exchange control and in one noteworthy case, tickets and Miscellaneous Charges Orders (MCOs) to the value of over 1 million pounds sterling purchased in country X, went into circulation throughout the world. If rapid action had not been taken, the country of original sale would have been faced with an impossible drain on its foreign currency reserves. There are also well documented cases of business men transferring blocked funds by means of airline documents.' He went on: 'I could remain here all day and tell of the different ways in which we have been defrauded by misuse of credit cards; by really clever bad cheque passers; by confidence tricksters actually gaining control of travel agencies together with their large ticket stocks; but we are not here to exchange case histories. However, *I feel it only fair to point out that the true international criminals: the gold smugglers, the narcotic dealers, the currency manipulators, are also the people whose names keep coming to the fore in the context of airline revenue offences'* (Interpol, 1968, Annex 2, p. 5).

Exactly the same point was made by Mr Lipson of American Express. He said 'The call for this meeting was the recognition that a series of problems involving new financial instruments has come to the attention of the police of the world . . . The post-war growth of the credit card has been little less than phenomenal. At the present time engaged in this field are the airlines . . . the car rental agencies, the petroleum industry, the telephone companies, hotels, department stores and even colleges and universities . . . In the early 1950's a new card came into being – the travel and entertainment card . . .' Criminal exploitation seems to have been slow in developing. 'During the first years of credit card existence little attention was paid to them by thieves. They were discarded along with the empty wallets. *But starting some four or five years ago* some of the thieves . . . began a fencing operation.' Perhaps they were slow to come in, suggests the spokesman, because the credit card system has an effective control and prevention apparatus built into it. The crime can be traced back to the criminal. This enables him to confirm the evidence of the airline depredations to the effect that the offenders are mainly those already in the game. *'What I am emphasising is the fact that the thieves whom we have succeeded in bringing to the attention of the enforcement authorities, who prey on credit cards, are professional criminals who, if they weren't attracted to the credit card, would probably be out committing other types of crime'* (our italics) (Interpol, 1968, Annex 3, p. 5).

The financial scene

We turn finally to the most neglected field of contemporary criminal organisation, that of company fraud and general financial buccaneering. This could be loosely regarded as simply a sector of white-collar crime, as described by Sutherland and his successors, since it has seldom been attempted by business men other than those who are at least nominally respectable. But the financial scene is changing rapidly both nationally and internationally. It is not simply that the last ten years or more in Europe have produced a range and variety of financial scandals to match and surpass anything of the kind in the last century and more. It is rather that the business world itself is changing. There is a vigorous proliferation, particularly in the company-promoting sector, of individuals and groups who would not in the past have been accepted or regarded as being 'of good standing' but who flourish in the more permissive atmosphere of recent years. The general deterioration in financial-ethical standards has not been confined to the business institutions; there is hardly a Western country which has not had one or more major scandals affecting high political and administrative figures. This is of course closely connected with the apparently irreversible trend whereby national and local government units have the spending of increasing proportions of national incomes.

This is much too big a subject to be treated adequately in these pages. Here we restrict ourselves to two illustrations of the apparent trend of events.

The first is the rise and fall of Investors Overseas Services. This enterprise, much admired in the period before its collapse in 1970, used salesmen recruited on the chain-letter analogy, and trained in American social group-work methods, to persuade very large numbers of new and unsophisticated investors to invest sums of money amounting in total to no less than two-and-a-half *billion* dollars in a variety of mutual-fund (unit-trust) companies. The entire enterprise appears to have been based on the impossibilist or 'bubble' principle of continuous expansion of sales of units, and the investors lost all or most of their money. The main relevance of IOS as a pointer to future criminal or near-criminal developments is that it was centred in no single country or groups of countries. The story is brilliantly told by the London *Sunday Times* 'Insight' team (Raw, Page and Hodgson, 1971).[6] The managers arranged to register and domicile their funds, and the innumerable companies that managed them, 'wherever in the world they would most avoid taxation and regulation' (Raw *et al.* p. 13).

How did IOS manage to circumvent the regulations and restraints designed to inhibit this kind of development? The answer can be summed up, say the writers, in the single word 'offshore'. 'By working, so to speak, in the interstices between the world's jurisdictions and administrative systems, they were able to do with impunity things that would have been illegal had their enterprise been located in any one place' (ibid. p. 15). There is a very practical moral here for the Council of Europe, for the European Economic Community, and for whatever inter-continental organisations may be shaped in the immediate future to meet the kind of problem presented by IOS.

Investors Overseas Services could conceivably be classified as simply the latest example of the recurring phenomenon of overly sanguine promoters interacting with overly rash investors. Other developments cannot be so comfortably explained. Our second illustration is taken from the United Kingdom in recent years. A similar chronicle could without difficulty be derived from the course of events in the other European national economies. There was a spate of United Kingdom frauds in the late 1950s, the consequences, Hadden observes, of the financial boom of the period (Hadden, 1969). The Mias scandal of 1959, he goes on, 'revealed the open opportunities for fraud in the rash of deposit companies and led to the hurried and not wholly successful Protection of Depositors Act 1963. The more recent scandals in the insurance field . . . the disputes over the management of a number of well-established commercial companies and the general disquiet over the conduct of take-over bids have revived the campaign for reform' (ibid. p. 281).

There is considerable difference of opinion about the latest substantial piece of company legislation in the United Kingdom, the Companies Act of 1967. Hadden's criticism of this Act is that it carried on the well-worn British practice in these matters of locking the stable door after the horses have gone. His comment appears to be borne out by the remarkable sequence of events in the years since 1967. There was general agreement that a new Companies Act was needed to confine or halt an entirely new stable of runaway horses, people of very good standing making very big money very quickly out of gigantic 'take-over bids'. The attempt to get such an Act on the statute book collapsed with the change of government in 1974, but other and temporary measures of self-discipline undertaken by the financial authorities had the effect of moderating the worser excesses of the 1967-71 period.

The years since 1967 have also been distinguished, if that is the word, by some remarkably large-scale orthodox criminal frauds. Some indication of the extent of these frauds can be got from a close study of the columns of the London *Times*. The Glasgow University criminological research unit has made an analysis of *Times* reports of criminal frauds involving an estimated loss or misprision of funds or assets to the value, £100,000 or more.[7] The period surveyed was from 1961 to 1972 inclusive. The count was restricted to company and insurance frauds and frauds on banks. The criteria of selection were: (1) the defrauding, or attempting to defraud, of large numbers of investors or persons insured; (2) in operations which normally would require a considerable endowment of company-promoting skills.[8] In the six years 1961 through 1966 there was a grand total of 2 reported frauds, 1 in 1963 and 1 in 1964; in each the figure quoted is £250,000. In the six years 1967 through 1972 there were 19. Two of these came to light[9] in 1967, 4 in 1968, 2 in 1969, 3 in 1970, 6 in 1971 and 2 in 1972. These included the £600,000 Savundra insurance fraud and the John Bloom affair in which the figure quoted was £1,140,000. In one of the 1971 half-dozen a defaulting insurance company chairman, rumoured to be in South America, was alleged to have fraudulently converted £120,000 of the company money. But he also owed £1 million to various creditors, and the company itself which had crashed four years earlier had losses of £9 million. A second comparatively humdrum case is that of a small building society run practically single-handed by a woman, who got four years after admitting fifteen charges, including the theft of £150,000 of small investors' money over a period of seventeen years. But this particular year's crop also included a huge fraud on the Standard Bank and the Co-operative Bank, involving a minimum loss to these and other banks of about £12 million.

It is not possible, given the present absence of research in these matters, to make a balanced judgement of the significance of all this. But if we were to take the facts at their face value, and to ignore the probability that a certain proportion of this City money is fairy gold, it would leave little room for doubt about the answer to the question posed earlier in this chapter as a problem for future criminologico-econometric research. Is the increase in crime in the period since 1945 outstripping, or keeping up with, or lagging behind the growth of the economy? Taking the criminal financial history of the last two decades into account, the answer favours the first of these hypotheses, at least in the short term. In the long term, setting the recent outburst against the general economic and commercial expansion since 1945, the question remains open.

Reasons for research backwardness

Why should knowledge of these matters be so inadequate? Why should the study of business-type crime, particularly in the financial sector, be so backward?

There is one good general reason. Business-type crime, particularly in the region of fraudulent financial transactions, raises difficulties of an ethical kind which do not exist in the case of the more traditional large-scale crimes. For example it involves no physical violence against either person or property. It is not surprising that a hard-pressed police and judicial system should appear to regard its problems as less urgent than the more dangerous crimes; and criminologists, here as elsewhere, have tended to order their research priorities in line with the needs and demands of the practical world as interpreted by the authorities.

A less laudable answer is that business-type crime is still generally regarded as a kind of crime which is not usually committed by the criminal classes. It appears to be practised to a large extent by people not unlike ourselves, people who give the impression of being law-abiding in all other respects. As a result many of those who set the tone in government circles, in administrative circles, in business and industry, and in society generally, tend to deplore the blurring of the conventional distinction between crime and non-crime that a close study of this subject would appear to involve. In short, Sutherland's doctrine of white-collar crime has to some extent backfired. That doctrine was not simply a theory designed to clarify the facts; it was also and equally a declaration of moral intent aimed at exposing a whole new class of criminal. As such it has been rejected by a considerable proportion of the respectable and law-abiding classes. There is a certain rough justice in this. Criminologists should wear only one hat at any one time. But in the long run the facts are against the respectable citizenry and for Sutherland in his role of theorist. The blurring, such as it is, is simply incidental to the primary obligation on criminologists to re-examine the distinction between criminal and non-criminal behaviour, to redraw maps which are now quite out of kilter with the facts.

A third, technical answer is that criminologists have avoided the empirical study of the company fraud for reasons connected with the historical development of their discipline. This is mildly paradoxical when one considers that criminology, both in Europe and the USA, has developed in close association with juridical studies of the criminal law. But the paradox disappears on closer scrutiny. The alliance has worked out in practice in a manner that allots this sector of business-type crime to those criminologists who are lawyers, or more precisely to those lawyers who are criminologically minded. These in their turn have usually considered that matters of company fraud — and also the even more extensive territory of practices bordering on fraud — are best discussed in terms of company law and in the context, understood only by specialist students of law, of the continual race between company law and the cohorts of company promoters, manoeuvrers, and outright swindlers. The result is that little or no systematic empirical investigation has been made in the field of company fraud, even in those cases where the activities in question are clearly fraudulent and therefore clearly criminal. A recent British thesis on the subject calls attention to 'the almost complete lack of accurate factual information, either on the incidence of the various offences or on the nature of the enforcement process' (Hadden, 1967, p. 323; for Germany see Tiedemann, 1972a). Hadden is writing about the United Kingdom, but his remarks could be made with equal justice about the other European countries and about USA.

Company fraud is only one of the 'black holes' in the criminological universe. Company fraudsters operate on and over the frontier dividing legitimate business activities from the extensive no-man's-land which constitutes a buffer territory between licit and illicit. We are if anything even more ignorant of some of those more versatile criminals who operate on and over the frontier dividing the buffer state from the criminal territories. These include the people referred to earlier in this chapter as our fifth category of business-type criminal, the international operators whose range of operation includes but is not restricted to business-type crime. These operate at a very high level of inaccessibility as far as the criminologist is concerned. The police themselves find it specially difficult to nail them down. They can be 'gated', i.e. kept out of this or that country. It is more difficult to get them behind bars. This is not, decidedly not, a matter of police ignorance. The detective branches of the metropolitan and national police organisations know a great deal about them, and so *a fortiori* does Interpol. But so far this knowledge has not been shared with criminologists.

The general disposition of criminologists in these matters favours getting information from the horse's mouth, from what we have elsewhere called the direct-access approach. But few since Sutherland[10] have attempted this in practice. And the approach is unlikely to be fruitful in the case of these very high-level operators. We know of only one essay at or near this level. John Pearson's book on the Kray twins contains a remarkable description of a treble agent straight from the pages of Graham Greene or Len Deighton, except that this particular agent actually exists, and operates not between sovereign states but between the forces of law and anti-law. Pearson's sketch is a remarkable breakthrough into a hitherto closed territory. Here are two passages:

> Cooper was 36 and rich. He owned a private bank off Wigmore Street, several insurance companies, two Rollses and a Yorkshire Terrier called Sam. Jewish, he had been brought up in England, served with the American Army, been in prison for a while in Germany and travelled on an American passport. He was a mystery man. Some said he was a spy. [He became useful to the Krays, helping them to dispose of certain stolen North American securities. He had impressive connections.]

> Centred on Brussels was Europe's most elaborate forged currency syndicate. In Northern Germany and Amsterdam there was the ring that had virtually cornered the international market in stolen jewellery. Peace-loving Zurich was a centre for international arms deals, Paris and the South of France for stolen major works of art,

London and Geneva for gold-smuggling. There were the drug-runners and the spies. Each of these criminal trades has its acknowledged *virtuosi* and its leaders, who formed a sort of international underground of crime. These were the men Cooper knew. (Pearson, 1972, p. 208.)

The main reservation to be made here is that Alan Bruce Cooper is hardly a representative figure. He differs from other people in his line of life — probably more important figures than he — in so far as he has not bothered to keep his activities entirely secret. A second drawback, as Pearson points out, is that information obtained directly from criminals is almost certain to be *literally* inaccurate. Whether it conveys a reliable *general* impression of the criminal networks is a major problem for the interpreter-criminologist.

It is highly possible that reliable information of the kind yielded in part by Cooper to Pearson — information which the police characteristically refused to confirm or reject[11] — will continue to evade the plodding criminologist. But this is not the end of the matter. There remains the not too remote possibility of a change in the attitude of police detectives to criminological research of a sociological kind. It is true that major, high-level, rational-economic crime presents special difficulties. It is obviously not practicable to study the immediately contemporary operations of major criminals. But it should not be impossible to undertake a semi-historical study, insulated from present operations by an interval of five or ten years. Our own proposals for letting some light in on the subject — mainly through a concordat leading to an alliance between criminological and police science — are to be found in the last chapter of this book.

Note on definition
(By H. J. Kerner)

Sources

Of parallel importance to Cosson's magisterial account of new forms of business-type crime in France (Cosson, 1971) are the discussions of the International Work Meeting of the Gottlieb-Duttweiler Institute in Switzerland. Specialists from many different countries reported on the latest forms and methods of business-type crime (monthly review of the Gottlieb-Duttweiler Institute 11/12, Zurich 1970).

A comprehensive account of methods of business-type crime was given for the first time in Germany in 1963 by Zirpins and Terstegen in their *'Wirtschaftskriminalität — Ihre Erscheinungensformen und Ihre Bekämpfung'* (Berlin, 1963).

Scope and definition

Edwin H. Sutherland in his definition quoted below (note 3 on page 30) emphasised the fact that the offenders involved in such manipulations as infringement of the anti-trust laws, administrative regulations, fiscal legislation, etc. were companies, or to be more exact the managers of companies, which wronged the state and the community to their own advantage. Sutherland's main point was that the offences must be specific to the occupation of the groups and individuals concerned. The more recent practice of describing embezzlement and other classical criminal offences as 'white-collar crime' just because the offenders wear white collars at their place of business, deprives the expression of its sharpness and precision. The distinguishing mark of each form of white-collar crime is that the offender's *main* occupation is *legal,* whereas the illegal activities are performed as a *secondary* occupation.

The factor distinguishing business-type crime of the white-collar variety from business-type crime other than white-collar crime, is that in the latter the criminal activities are the *principal* occupation of the business-type criminal operator. He may also sometimes conduct a legitimate business as a 'cover'. In borderline cases it is often difficult to decide whether the offence is a white-collar crime, or belongs to the other classification. The following tabulation, which is based on the work of Zirpins and Terstegen, presents as precise a typology as can be prepared with our present knowledge. It is suggested that type 1 covers the classical illegal white-collar activities (what Mack describes as prohibited but not prohibited by the criminal law); type 2 covers the classical white-collar crimes, but overlaps with type 1; type 3 covers the activities of business men, working on their own, who commit criminal offences with the object of surviving, if undetected or unconvicted, so as to save their firms or their capital and to continue as legitimate business men; type 4 is in a class by itself and does not apply to our problem; type 5 covers all old and new developments in business-type crime in which the perpetrators are traditional 'professional' criminals; also part-time criminals or dabblers in crime.

28

Table 2.1
Types of business-type crime

Type of firm	Origin	Objective and mode of activity	Remarks
1 Dishonest but not criminal (i.e. not liable to imprisonment)	Non-criminal	Non-criminal	Firms with borderline morals which deceive other involved parties and trap them in an unfair but still legal manner, or: premeditated violation of the civil law; offences against competition and tax laws, etc., which just reach the border of liability to imprisonment but keep on the right side of it.
2 Dishonest and on occasion criminal	Non-criminal	Non-criminal Criminal	Operates on both sides of the line dividing criminal from non-criminal.
3 'Ausweichfirmen' (firms prepared to adopt criminal means to achieve survival as legitimate firms)	Criminal	Criminal Non-criminal	Includes embezzlement in emergency; fraudulent concealment or transfer of capital including bankruptcy; tax frauds — with the object of reverting to legitimacy after the emergency.
4 Camouflage firms	Non-criminal	Criminal	These firms are usually created for the purposes of espionage, usually political espionage; their objective and mode of activity is criminal but not fraudulent, in this differing from 5 below.
5 Swindling firms	Criminal	Criminal	Criminal *and* fraudulent.

(See Zirpins and Terstegen, 1963, p. 533.)

Notes

1   Radzinowicz draws attention to the view put forward by Poletti (Poletti, 1882) that the criminality of a nation was declining if its crimes were increasing less that its legitimate and productive acts. Poletti argued that this had in fact been the experience of the leading European countries towards the end of the nineteenth century. 'Rarely', says Radzinowicz, 'has a criminal hypothesis been repudiated more vehemently. It seemed to run counter to the most cherished beliefs that economic advances and social progress must lead to a drastic reduction of crime. But Poletti's insight has gained in significance as the years have gone by' (Radzinowicz and Wolfgang, 1971, vol. 1, p. 435).

Wolf has a useful passage in which he explores the implications of the 'long-perspective' proposition that 'total crime increases with increasing wealth' (Wolf, 1968, pp. 20-1). See also Wilkins, also quoted by Wolf: '... If a society facilitates the transfer of goods by legitimate means, it seems that, simultaneously, the facilities for illegitimate transfer will also increase' (Wilkins, 1964, p. 53).

2   To the best of our knowledge this class of not-yet-prohibited activity was not discussed by Sutherland. The reader should consult the 1961 edition of Sutherland's *White Collar Crime,* including Cressey's preface.

3   'White collar crime may be defined approximately as a crime committed by a person of respectability and high social status in the course of his occupation' (Sutherland, 1961, p. 9).

4   There are also two good papers by policemen: Baer, Hjr., and Crane, J. W. Both in *Monatszeitschrift des Gottlieb-Duttweiler-Instituts* Heft 11/12, 1970, pp. 53-60 and 61-7 respectively.

A very good inside story has been published by Leslie Payne, himself an accomplished long-firm fraudster, and for some time a background adviser to the Kray twins in these matters (Payne, 1973). See also the brief mimeograph by Mack (Mack, 1971).

5   Interpol files include only operations in which a minimum of three countries are involved.

6   An admirable and comparatively new feature in the British and European post-war scene is the emergence of high-quality financial journalism.

An attempt was made to salvage IOS after the 1970 collapse. A report by the US Securities and Exchange Commission condemns the post-1970 managers as 'being at the centre of the largest scale frauds ever perpetrated' (London *Sunday Times,* 3 December 1972, p. 63).

7   It is perhaps worth noting that all cases of criminal fraud reported in the *Times* are cases in which proceedings have been taken against detected offenders. As regards the scale of frauds selected (£100,000+) see note 1, Chapter 4, p. 59 below.

8   Items excluded were swindles of employers or of individual victims, defrauding of the public by direct dealing, usually by advertising in the press or other media — as for example in the sale of non-existent livestock, non-existent Christmas bottles of whisky, sites for villas in Spain, and overvalued stamps; also numerous cases of forgery; also defrauding of the State, as in evasion of income tax and purchase and fuel tax. These excluded items were greater in total than the company, etc. frauds during the period; the year-by-year incidence was much the same in the two groups.

Tax evasion is a subject in itself. It is a point of great methodological interest as to whether one confines oneself to prosecuted cases or includes also cases detected and admitted, but settled without recourse to the law courts. (cf. Hadden, 1967, pp. 493-4.)

9   The dating has to be fairly arbitrary in this species of crime. The actual fraud and the consequent legal process usually extend over several years.

10   i.e. in *The Professional Thief,* 1937. See also pp. 151-4 below.

11   Pearson writes: 'Quite how much the shrewd old man [Commander John du Rose of Scotland Yard] really knew about Alan Cooper is another of the mysteries of the case. When you ask him he smiles enigmatically' (Pearson, 1972, p. 208).

3 Syndicated Crime in Europe and the USA

Europe is the focus of this chapter, but the US phenomenon must inevitably be included, partly because European ways of thinking about the subject are influenced by the American literature, partly because US syndicated crime is thought to be moving into Europe, on the model of American legitimate business, or even, some would say, of the newer type of multi-national corporation.

To begin with we might venture a rough definition of syndicated crime as that species of moneymaking activity which caters in mainly illicit ways for the mainly illicit economic demand of large numbers of willing and co-operative customers; combined with the extortion of money and services from more or less acquiescent victims, the degree of acquiescence varying directly with the degree of shadiness of the victims' business and other activities; combined with the intimidation or attempted intimidation in different ways and for different purposes of law-abiding citizens and groups over whom the crimesters have no hold other than their reputation for criminal violence.

How much syndicated crime is there in the countries of Europe? How important is it in relation to the more traditional forms of predatory crime? How important is it in relation to the national and international economy? Strictly speaking these questions are unanswerable, since the subject has not been systematically examined either by scholars or by government commissions of enquiry. There is of course a considerable exception to all this in respect of the Sicilian Mafia. But the Mafia is a special study, a part of the history of Southern Italy. Even here it must be said that the literature of Mafia or Mafia-type developments in Europe outside Southern Italy is almost as unreliable as that of its prototype in the USA.[1]

It follows that the location and incidence of syndicated crime activities in Europe and in the different countries of Europe must continue to be a matter of conjecture and speculation until such time as criminologists overcome the existing difficulties in the way of access to information about this and related fields of rational-economic crime (pp. 162-4 below). But a number of points can be made on what information is available. The experience of Interpol is a prime source. The continent of Europe viewed from the heights of St Cloud takes on the appearance of a network of deep-water harbours and international airports, a vital link and power-centre in the considerable worldwide traffic in illicit goods and services which is one of Interpol's main interests. Secondly, certain groups in certain parts of Europe are large-scale growers and manufacturers of heroin and other dangerous drugs. Thirdly, though this may fall to some extent outside the scope of Interpol, and may well be treated by a large number of governmental agencies as a non-criminal and politically convenient activity, there exists an illicit traffic in armaments, and notably in small arms, which flourished strongly from time to time in the post-1945 period and which tends to prosper in times of local wars and insurrections in Africa and elsewhere. These and other forms of smuggling and illicit commerce date back to the beginnings of international and inter-continental trade and will doubtless continue to thrive up to the limits set by effective controls.

All of these activities are part of such international or world-wide criminal organisation as exists, probably in the form of networks. It would be entirely speculative to think of these networks as being organised by some world-wide syndicated crime system. Such arrangements as exist are probably pluralist, *ad hoc,* flexible, and changing. It is not improbable that Interpol and a number of others have a fairly shrewd idea as to who are the leading figures in at least some of the networks; this particular corner of the field is probably comparatively well known to a few.

The same cannot be said of syndicated crime activities within national boundaries. Here there is very little solid information. But from time to time some interesting material is provided by court proceedings following police action; police action in its turn is often a response to a more than usually intolerable outbreak of internecine gang warfare, or some similar eruption of subterranean forces. The processes thus disclosed are no doubt going on all the time, usually on a minor scale, in most big cities. Recent examples are provided by France and the United Kingdom in the main. In France there is the considerable affair of the Guerini brothers and their 'empire' in Marseilles (the Guerinis were convicted in Paris in January 1970). The United Kingdom provides several instances: the trial of the Richardson brothers in 1967, the notorious 'torture' trial; the bringing to book of the flamboyant Kray brothers, convicted in 1969;[2] and some comparatively minor but equally typical cases in provincial cities involving gang murder and intimidation connected with fairly primitive syndicated activities. The information yielded by this handful of cases is biased and episodic and relates largely to British conditions; a more thorough conspectus over a longer period would doubtless include equally inform-ative material from Hamburg or Frankfurt or Brussels or Paris;[3] but what there is suggests a number of useful observations.

The main impression one gets is of a marked contrast with the trans-atlantic scene. Compared with its US manifestations syndicated crime in Europe is small beer. This is not to say that it is of no account. The Guerini 'empire' in Marseilles lasted for more than twenty years. The dominance established by the Krays and the Richardsons in their respect-ive London 'territories' over much shorter periods presented a quite considerable challenge to the forces of law and order. The intimidation of witnesses in cases of this kind is always a matter for serious concern.

Secondly, there is a comparative absence in Europe of the US alliance between syndicates and lawyers. European syndicated crime, and with it the much greater mass of high-level predatory crime, does not constitute a major source of income for any sector of the legal profession. There is a minor reservation here as regards mainly lesser criminals in the United Kingdom. The recent establishment of official legal aid for impecunious defendants has enabled a few lawyers in a number of cities to earn a higher income defending full-time criminals than they might otherwise have obtained. It does not appear that the bigger fish provide any special revenue. The judge in the Richardson trial made an order that some of the costs of the trial should be recovered from the property of the elder Richardson. But the other five convicted persons obtained legal aid, as did all of those charged in the Kray trials (Hudson, 1971, p. 16).

They order things differently in the United States. The Task Force Report on *The Professional Criminal* (Gould, 1967), suggests that perhaps the major activity of the typical high-level 'professional criminal' is the 'fix' — an arrangement by which he safeguards himself from arrest, or conviction, or imprisonment, or (if the worst came to the worst) long-term imprisonment, by the lavish use of lawyers of good standing. Similar defences are provided *a fortiori* for the big mobsters.

It is of course the case that in both continents the lawyers concerned are simply ensuring that the fundamental principle of the Western legal system is maintained — namely that the defendant in any case should be deemed innocent until he is proved guilty, irrespective of his reputation. It should be noted here that US lawyers are troubled by the lack in their legal system of any actionable definition of criminal organisation. It is also to be noted that in both England and Wales and Scotland examinations of criminal procedure have been set in train by the Government.

Thirdly, the same contrast holds for what is conventionally termed 'corruption' in the USA. There is no evidence that syndicated crime in Europe has anything like the power and influence which US mobsters bring to bear on sections of the judiciary, on police, on central and local administrators, on politicians, and on various industries and services through control of trade unions and pressure on entrepreneurs. One recent European episode which might be an exception to the European rule is that of the Guerinis in Marseilles, who were regarded by responsible observers as having considerable influence in police circles. There are also occasional examples in European countries of the corruption of police officers, administrators, politicians, or other persons discharging public responsibilities.

The fourth contrasting feature of European syndicated crime is that its individual undertakings — there is no suggestion in this part of the world that cartels or alliances exist on any scale — are usually short-lived. The most astonishing characteristic of the US syndicated crime system is that it has persisted for many generations through all the vicissitudes of internal and inter-syndicate conflict and in the face of massive law-enforcement mobilisations. Campaigns against the system have waxed and waned; the thing itself has gone on, and many observers hold that the big individual syndicates and groups of syndicates have survived and indeed flourished for two or three or four generations. Not so in Europe. The Richardsons and the Krays were active for a few years at most, coming to the peak of their dominance only for a year or two; then they were cut down. The Guerinis lasted longer in Marseilles, but they had a flying start in the 1940s as resistance leaders — and they were Corsicans. Nevertheless when they collapsed they had become obsolete. 'The word now in Marseilles is "Guerini? — connais pas" ' (Besançon, 1970).

This does not mean that the entire mobster crime potential in the big cities is easily snuffed out. New gangs will come up in London. One interpretation of the Marseilles case insisted upon by counsel for the defence was that the murder for which the Guerinis were imprisoned was arranged by a rival clan which would now step into power in Marseilles. In fact the subsequent lull after each eruption is apt to be quite prolonged. The general inference to be drawn from European experience is that syndicated crime does not possess that capacity to win friends and influence people in power which is the most striking feature of its US counterpart.

The fifth divergence is the most significant of them all. It too consists of an absence of something. We quote below the Task Force Report on organised crime as saying that the core of syndicated crime activities is the supply function (p. 174). This is simply not true of the European brand, such as it is. The mobs may engage in some incidental illicit trafficking, but they fill no major role of middleman supplying powerful economic demands for forbidden goods and services.

This ends the list of things that syndicated crime in Europe is not. What, then, are its salient characteristics? Here one is handicapped by the great lack of dependable information over the European area as a whole. The following notes are based in the main on United Kingdom experience, and refer particularly to the two London mobs mentioned above.

These had two principal sources of income — various forms of extortion on the one hand, and business-type fraud on the other. The Krays operated or attempted to operate a few social and gambling clubs here and there. But their primary criminal activity was parasitical. The *Guardian,* writing on the Kray case on the day the Cornell murder trial ended, said: 'It is ironic that no one will second Mr. Justice Holford Stephenson's vote of thanks to the police after the Kray case more readily than the owners of dozens of more or less shady clubs and businesses in the West End of London' (*Guardian,* 6 March 1969). Both mobs operated mainly at the expense of others who, if not criminal, were at least reluctant to invite the attention of the police. The intimidation they practised was selective in its range: the ordinary law-abiding citizen was only indirectly affected. There are some exceptions to this rule, but by and large the victims of the exploitation, extortion, protection, and general bullying practised by mobs in Great Britain are usually other criminals, or persons operating dubious concerns, or individuals helpless through personality defect or social deprivation.

The Krays were publicity hounds. They wanted to have high status in criminal circles and simultaneously in the easily accessible 'café society' of show business and conspicuous philanthropy. They were in this consciously imitating the more flamboyant of the American mobsters in their brief era of social success in the 1950s. The Richardsons were different. They kept in the background and concealed themselves fairly effectively from the attentions of the police until the last phase of their four or five years' career. They practised a double exploitation on other criminals and on disreputable business men. They occasionally also attempted, sometimes with success, the intimidation of quite reputable business figures. An example of their exploitation of criminals is their moving in on a profitable airport carpark racket. The mob isolated and intimidated the leader of the enterprise. As a result of this cutting-in operation they provided themselves with a regular periodical income. In other instances, where the victim was not necessarily a criminal, they might gain control of a firm, for fraudulent purposes, by making use of knowledge of some weakness in the social defences of one or more of the proprietors, some reason why the latter would be unwilling to call in the law.

The hold thus secured was established by the same brand of systematic violence as reinforced their other activities. But here there is a further and lamentable divergence from the best North American prototypes. In the USA the violence is by and large subordinated to the rational-economic requirements of the undertaking. But the two London mobs could not keep their violence instrumental. The Krays indulged an inordinate appetite for conspicuous murder. The Richardson mob succeeded in avoiding a charge of murder, but the pleasure that one or more of them took in the torturing of their recalcitrant clients, and the varied forms of torture they devised, suggest a pathological history not usually to be found in the top rank of business-like criminals.

The same Achilles' heel is to be found in a smaller Northern example of the same period. In this case a group of mobsters moved in on some small-scale loan-sharking activities. A number of public works, shipyards and factories, have their short-term usurers, unlicensed and illicit money-lenders who supply the financial need of a variety of groups — people making a good wage who have a weakness for gambling or who cannot manage the spending of their income; people addicted to alcohol, usually in the form of cheap wine; and other equally helpless or semi-shady individuals, all having it in common with the loan sharks that they have no desire to get mixed up with the law. A similar business is conducted in a few working-class residential areas. It was formerly a primitive and unorganised business, conducted by individuals and pairs of individuals; the sanctions employed to enforce repayment did not usually include physical violence. These conditions may still hold in other areas. But in this case the local mob moved in by force. They began in a small way by undertaking, uninvited, to act as collectors for their unwilling loan-shark clients; they went on to collect on their own behalf, using violence and the threat of violence to enforce payment of the even more excessive interest now demanded of the customer; finally they took over the business completely, or launched out on their own on a bigger scale and over a wider area than had formerly prevailed. But they turned out to share the London mobs' weakness for uncontrolled violence. This particular episode was brought to an end by the conviction and life imprisonment of one of the mob for a quite gratuitous murder, and by the later incarceration for long periods of several members and accomplices of the enterprise.

A tentative finding to be derived from these United Kingdom examples is that the people engaged in syndicated crime, in its European as in its transatlantic varieties, tend to form a distinct group. The Krays and their followers were members of a rough and violent lower working-class subculture located in East London. But whereas the great majority of their contemporaries had grown up into a comparatively non-violent adulthood, this particular minority had gone on to specialise in full-time violence, putting their skills to extortionist uses. They may have taken part from time to time in predatory crime, but their main line of criminal operation was parasitical. Similarly with the smaller Northern group. They tended to form a separate enclave within a wider system of criminal networks, the members of which are mostly engaged in predatory crime. There is usually some interconnection in this kind of situation: this or that individual takes part with full-time predators in the more direct forms of property crime. But most of the activities of the mobster group tend to fall within its special field.

A second observation to be derived from this latter instance is that the syndicated crimester ranks comparatively low in the status system of the wider network, composed as it is in the main of people engaged in predatory crime, whether as background organisers or front-line operators. There are individual exceptions to this rule: one finds certain individuals engaged in both types of activity, usually from a background position. It is more difficult to make up one's mind about this question of relative status in the London scene. The Richardsons and Krays both certainly gave the appearance of dominating the criminal and near-criminal sectors of the population in their respective areas. But this impression could easily be misleading. The *Guardian* remarked of the defeat of the Krays that this was not the major strategic victory which the publicity might suggest. 'Business-like criminals do not court notoriety like the Krays did, but they are far more of a menace to the law-abiding world than these flashy gangsters were' (*Guardian,* 6 March 1969). The Richardsons' criminal performance judged in terms of financial results — and taking into account also that the elder Richardson appears to have controlled considerable legitimate business interests on the side, so to speak — was a high-level achievement on any method of calculation. But it was only one of a fairly large number, and far from being the biggest. The outstanding single criminal operation in the 1960s was the Great Train Robbery of August 1963; and the main trend in major crime in the twenty years from 1950 onward was the rapid increase in burglaries and armed robberies, conducted by a wide range and variety of miscreants, recorded in the next chapter (at pp. 52-3).

Our general conclusion is that the conditions favouring syndicated crime are to be found in a world-wide variety of settings: it is an indigenous growth in the soil of an urban industrial economy moving into affluence, but retaining extensive pockets of poverty. It is equally true that the North American model of syndicated crime has not developed in Europe — or for that matter in economically well-developed countries in other continents. Is this likely to continue? Or are we to read the European situation as a primitive or embryonic stage in a fairly inevitable organisational development? It is a good question. Cressey has suggested (1972, p. 4) that European countries are simply in the early stages of the same development as the USA has gone through, and that as criminals get wealthier and better organised they will use their increasing resources to buy immunity from arrest and conviction on the US model, so that 'organised crime' in Britain could well come to resemble 'organised crime' in America. This is an altogether too naively deterministic and techno-logical way of thinking. It takes no account of the major social and political differences between Europe and the USA, and between the different European countries. One major difference can be briefly stated. European governments do not make a practice of decreeing prohibitions they are not prepared to enforce: and European populations do not sustain a strong and profitable market for prohibited services on any large scale.

There remains a question of immediate practical or at least topical interest. Are the US syndicates themselves moving in on Europe? Are they moving in on such a scale as to present European governments and police systems with a major new preoccupation? Some observers would answer yes to both questions.

Three lines of activity are most often specified in the accounts given. The first two are narcotics and gambling; there is some evidence of syndicate interest in these fields. The third allegation, that syndicates are taking up *legitimate* business and investment opportunities in Europe, is not so well supported. But it has a special interest for European observers.

The enormously profitable criminal traffic in narcotics falls outside the bounds of this book, partly for logistical reasons – it is too huge and inaccessible a topic to tackle in this survey – and partly on factual grounds. Such impressions as we have gathered from the people who know something about the subject suggest that while some US syndicates have an interest in this traffic, they share it with other and perhaps more important specialist groups. (See note to this chapter.)

As regards gambling, there is fairly conclusive evidence of a major attempt by some US syndicates to move in on the United Kingdom gambling industry in its sudden wave of prosperity in the 1960s. The British gambling boom was a result of the legalising of various formerly prohibited forms of gambling by the Betting and Gaming Act of 1960. A potentially dangerous situation was relieved in large part by the similarly titled Act of 1968, under which licensed gambling of the casino type is allowed to continue on a considerable scale, under conditions of strict control and supervision, exercised by the Gaming Board created by the 1968 Act. The story is concisely told in Gage, 1971. Gladstone Smith, 1970 is also worth consulting. The former's conclusion is quoted:

> American organized crime has established a beachhead in England, but it has not been as successful there as its leaders had hoped. This came about for two reasons. First, late in the 1960's British

authorities made the gambling industry subject to a gaming board. The board was empowered to examine the ownership, finances, and policies of gambling clubs, the prime attraction for organized crime, and to withhold licenses from clubs where irregularities were discovered. The same law that created the board gave the British Home Office the authority to regulate the gaming industry as abuses arose.

These actions cut down the number of gambling clubs and made the climate in England less attractive for the mob. The leaders of organized crime, always an inventive group, have found ways to circumvent many of the regulations, including the employment of respected Britons as front men for their operations. But the regulations have made it more difficult for American gangsters to maneuver, and their initial enthusiasm for England has been somewhat dampened. (p. 155)

This is probably putting it rather mildly. The take-over attempt may have left its initiators considerably more discouraged than this account suggests. The Gaming Board, and gambling controls in general in the United Kingdom, may be doing a much better job than many US (and Canadian) observers are inclined to admit. The present writer's tentative conclusion is that the 1965-70 period saw the decisive defeat of a quite considerable attempt at invasion. The people best qualified to judge the situation will neither support nor dispute this opinion. Perhaps it is wisest to follow the example of the best policemen and keep one's fingers crossed.

So far as can be ascertained no other European country has been made the target of a similar systematic take-over attempt, probably because no other country has recently brought about any change in its gambling legislation at all comparable to the United Kingdom Act of 1960. A minor invasion of a number of European countries has been achieved by those US syndicates whose agents organise gambling parties ('junkets') where the government concerned is prepared to encourage or at least to tolerate casino gambling facilities for tourists. These are well described by the two writers already quoted. It certainly does appear that the US syndicates concerned do operate a virtual monopoly not only in all forms of gambling provision in the USA, but also in casino-type gambling in South America, Europe and elsewhere. But this particular export is mainly by Americans for Americans, like Coca-Cola. The 'junkets' cater mainly for American gamblers. They are flown in at special rates, they are given first-class hotel accommodation, and they provide a handsome profit for the organisers by losing on the average a considerable amount of dollars per head. A big part of this profit may be illicit. There is also a respectable legitimate profit for the tourist industry of the host country. This leaves the government concerned in two minds about the matter. They are delighted to have the tourists; they are troubled by the suspicion that there may be a criminal element in the background of the organisation. It seems on all accounts that these enterprises constitute a minor breach of the European defences against the putative US invasion. But so far it does not seem to have led to large-scale exploitation by USA-based criminals of European gamblers of the respectable sort.

The third alleged invasion point is the legitimate business sector. It is argued that the syndicates are entering into law-abiding industry and commerce and investment on a big scale, and that this is potentially the most menacing aspect of their activities. For this claim there is an almost complete lack of evidence. A recent expert discussion produced little or no data on this subject from the representatives of the European governments present, in contrast to the discussions of narcotics and gaming. There were one or two references to US criminals of Italian origin investing or attempting to invest in Italy, but none to other countries.[4] But it is well worth following up, because it illustrates another kind of invasion, a take-over of European thinking on the subject by American modes of apprehension.

Statements about US syndicated crime fall into two categories; those generally agreed by the bulk of observers, and those which are a matter of continual dispute. The first set of statements is summarised in the definition given in Appendix A below (pp. 173-5). One main example of second is the proposition that the syndicates are invading legitimate business in the USA with criminal intent and with such success as to constitute, at least in principle, a major threat to the political and economic system of the USA. The notion of an infiltration of European business is primarily to be understood as an extension or corollary of the US thesis. The US thesis has powerful support. It was adopted in 1967 as an official finding, so to speak, of the Task Force Report. But it is queried by many serious students of the subject. The dispute is only partly a dispute on facts. It is agreed that the syndicated criminals make a certain amount of money — vast in the official version, moderate as calculated by the critics. It is agreed also that some of that money is invested in non-criminal undertakings. The questions of criminal intent, and of actual criminal exploitation, and of the putative danger to the realm, are a matter of acute controversy.

The heart of the controversy concerns the nature of the organisation that does the investing. Most students of the subject are inclined to agree that the marked decline in inter-syndicate murders in the last fifty years is due to a growing practice of inter-syndicate negotiations; a practice which has now become formalised, so to speak, in a rough and ready nation-wide confederation which negotiates conflicts of interest between the syndicates. The lowest common denominator of agreement on the powers of this confederation — what the bulk of observers might agree to be a matter of fact — is that it operates as a kind of trade association or demarcation dispute conference. But the official or Task Force interpretation is that it has the powers of an industrial corporation — like General Motors or United Steel — and that its ruling body or 'Commission' acts like a board of directors.

If this were to be accepted, and if it were also accepted that the 'vast profits' of the syndicates as a whole constitute one investment fund at the disposal of the board of directors, then it would be in fact arguable that the country was in danger.

It is a most infectious hypothesis. It incorporates the legend of the *Mafia* or *Cosa Nostra,* what may be currently summed up as the 'Godfather' folklore; and it has been backed for some generations by the mass media. But it lacks the bite of evidence.[5] To consider only the immediate matter at issue:

(a)   there is, and can be, no precise estimate of how vast or how meagre the profits are;
(b)   it is fairly clear from the language used in Cressey's expansion of his Task Force Report papers (Cressey, 1969) — and from the absence of any information to the contrary — that the profits are thought to be acquired and invested not collectively by a nation-wide body but severally, by individual syndicates and members of syndicates;
(c)   Cressey, who on the whole favours the 'board of directors' thesis, observes that it is quite possible 'that most of the legitimate businesses owned by *Cosa Nostra* members are operated legitimately, at least most of the time . . . One incentive for entering legitimate business is the hope of becoming respectable.'

There the case must rest. The debate is only in its beginnings. But we are at least in a position to formulate its terms, whether we are considering syndicated crime in the USA or as a possible US export to Europe. The problem is how to explain the remarkable power of survival of US syndicated crime. On the one hand it is ascribed to a vast continent-wide conspiracy. On the other we have the older theory of syndicated crime subscribed to by the bulk of interested US criminologists. Their view is that the thing has so far defied all attempts to suppress it because it is meeting a formally prohibited but actually accepted set of powerful economic demands; and that it will continue to persist until such time as those in political authority in the USA 'face this problem of the over-reach of the criminal law, state clearly the nature of its priorities in regard to the use of the criminal sanction, and indicate what kinds of immoral and anti-social content should be removed from the current calendar of crime' (Morris and Hawkins, 1970).

Comments by Interpol

Two special points were submitted to Interpol, who were so kind as to comment:

Point	*Comment by Interpol*
1 We say on p. 40 above that . . . while some US syndicates have an interest in [drug] traffic, they share it with other and perhaps more important specialist groups'.	1 Traffic in heroin is still in the hands of organised crime, but there is no organic structure of world-wide scope. Those concerned are 'groups' operating separately but having contacts with each other. Also, traffic in cannabis and amphetamines is certainly less structured, and organised crime does not have the monopoly there.

[This Interpol comment relates primarily to the activities *in Europe* of US syndicates. It should be added that the question of the groups participating in drug traffic *in the USA itself* is one that has still to be fully investigated. There may exist a number of specialist one-commodity groups *as distinct from syndicates* — which by definition operate a plurality of illicit trades and criminal activities. A relevant linguistic point is that Interpol may in this paragraph be using the phrase organised crime (without quotation marks) to cover specialised one-commodity groups as well as syndicates. In this they would of course be following orthodox European usage. (See Appendix A below, p. 170.)]

2 Following up a point made on p. 42 above, it is well known that in the United States the large organised crime 'families' have invested considerable sums in legitimate business activities — chain stores, transport companies, nightclubs, etc. What about Europe?

2 In Europe, certain persons engaged in criminal activities sometimes invest in buying a business (nightclubs, hairdressing salons, cafés). This is done more by individuals than groups. In Italy, Italo-American gangsters have tried to invest in the construction industry: these attempts do not appear to have gone any further.

Notes

1 The literature on the Sicilian Mafia proper is almost as unreliable. See our note on Henner Hess, 1971, p. 121 below.

2 For the Guerini trial see the Paris and Marseilles press for January 1970 and after. For the Richardson trial see *The Times* (London), April to June 1967, *passim.* For the Kray trial see ibid January to May 1969, *passim;* also Hudson, 1971. For the Kray story as a whole see Pearson (1972).

3 There is an extensive folk-lore (mainly underground) of the Paris 'milieu': see for a recent spate of disclosures the coverage of the passing and funeral ceremonies of Jo Attia in the Paris press and occasional publications July 1972 and later: also article (title 'When you gotta go Joe') by Nesta Roberts in the *Guardian* (London), 29 July 1972, p. 11. See also Ange Bastiani: Le 'Milieu' est-il mort? in *Le Journal du Dimanche,* 11 January 1970, p. 24.

4 Report of Second International Symposium on International Crime, 1971: reference made by kind permission of Interpol. See also Appendix to this chapter.

5 See also Mack, 1970; Albini, 1971; and Morris and Hawkins, 1970.

PART II

Survey

4 The United Kingdom

The main developments in the crime situation in the United Kingdom since the last war, and particularly since 1955, are: first, the emergence in considerable numbers of well-organised and lucrative criminal ventures, against a background of rapid increase in crime in general; second, a powerful police response, conspicuously effective in certain spectacular instances of the British variety of syndicated crime. This countervailing police action, which has been building up over the period, is also establishing a fair degree of control over some new and old types of predatory crime, but it is confronted with special difficulties presented by new types of criminal organisation and sources of recruitment.

The increase in major crime

The England and Wales crime totals have increased steadily and continuously from 1955 into the late 1960s at the rate of 10 per cent per annum. Scotland shows a roughly similar trend. This remarkable increase is largely a 'real' one. The effects of greater precision of recording, which played a considerable part in the slower statistical increase from 1932 to 1955 (Mack, 1954, p. 230), are probably much less important in the later period.

These national totals are made up to a large extent of minor and indeed petty incidents. But a recent study (Avison and McClintock, 1970) has shown that certain categories of serious crimes have increased at more than twice the rate of the larger less serious sector. For example breaking offences (burglaries) involving property values of £5 and over increased by 209 per cent in the period 1961-69; 'other indictable crimes' (including burglaries of less than £5) increased in the same period by 69 per cent (see Table 4.1 on p. 50). Moreover, it appears that the pacemaker in this increase in the more serious type of offence is the carefully prepared type of operation, a rough indicator of which is the size of the haul: those breaking and entering offences involving the loss of goods and money valued at £100 or more increased by almost 70 per cent in the period 1967-69. A further finding by Avison and McClintock is that the 'carefully planned' type of robbery – category I in the classification invented by McClintock and Gibson (1961, chapter 2) – increased from a third to a half of all robberies in London in the ten years following 1950.

Table 4.1

Number and proportion of selected major crimes in England and Wales, 1961, 1965 and 1969*

Class of offence	1961		1965		1969‡		Percentage increase	
							1969 over 1961	1969 over 1965
	No.	%	No.	%	No.	%		
All selected major crimes	229,787	28.5	375,967	33.2	515,159	34.6	124.2	37.0
Other indictable crimes	577,113	71.5	757,915	66.8	973,479	65.4	68.7	28.4
Total	806,900	100.0	1,133,882	100.0	1,488,638	100.0	84.5	31.3
Selected major offences								
Murder†	147	0.1	171	0.0	182	0.0	23.8	6.4
Attempted murders	193	0.1	207	0.1	332	0.1	72.0	60.4
Felonious woundings	1,913	0.8	2,174	0.6	2,708	0.5	41.6	24.6
Rapes	503	0.2	618	0.2	869	0.2	72.8	40.6
Subtotal	2,756	1.2	3,170	0.9	4,091	0.8	48.4	29.1
Breaking offences (values £5+)	78,708	34.3	132,650	35.3	243,057	47.2	208.8	83.2
Thefts (values £10+)	145,974	63.5	236,411	62.8	261,970	50.8	79.5	10.8
Robbery	2,349	1.0	3,736	1.0	6,041	1.2	157.2	61.7
Subtotal	227,031	98.8	372,797	99.1	511,068	99.2	125.1	37.1
Grand total	229,787	100.0	375,967	100.0	515,159	100.0	124.2	37.0

*Based upon data extracted from *Criminal Statistics, England and Wales,* 1961, 1965 and 1969.
†Including all murders, i.e. also those of children under one year of age.
‡Property offences relate to crimes as defined in the Theft Act 1968.

Table by N. H. Avison and F. H. McClintock, in a paper given in Madrid 1970. See list of references.

The writers go on to say that 'The increase in this kind of offence has also continued throughout the nineteen-sixties although in the last few years (i.e. up to 1969) it has been the less planned sudden violent robbery of the ordinary citizen that has been increasing at the greater rate.' (See also McClintock, 1963; Commissioner,[1] 1969, chapter 4.) The picture may have changed again more recently: we note below that the carefully planned type of robbery – and in particular the large-scale commando-type operation, moves into the centre of the stage again in 1969 and 1970.

These more substantial and therefore more organised types of crime, whether in London or in a radius of a hundred miles round London, are usually connected with London-based criminals. Greater London, which is for all practical purposes co-extensive with the Metropolitan Police District, is the nerve-centre of major British crime. The big provincial cities have a higher general crime-rate, but this is due in the main to differences in social composition. The London area has a greater proportion of the higher income grades, who rate low in the official crime statistics. But London has very much more than its share of substantial criminal operators, and it is probably true that the great bulk of large-scale criminal enterprises in the South and Midlands of England are organised from London, and are carried out by groups which include London-based criminals. The provincial cities have their indigenous substantial operators, some of whom are top-ranking criminals on metropolitan standards, but they usually work on a comparatively small scale compared with their London counterparts (p. 187 below).

The range and variety of activity of the substantial criminal in the United Kingdom — we are referring particularly here to the predatory or traditional property criminal — is much the same as in the past. But what formerly came in single instances, with intervals of months or years between major exploits, now come in large numbers and in quick succession, varying as to *locus,* objective, order of magnitude, and mode of attack according to the changing opportunities provided by the victim community and the methods of resistance and forms of control devised by the police. None of the traditional criminal arts has dropped out. It is not true for example that skilled pocket-picking is a thing of the past. But it is a small, residual activity, and has not shared in the big increase in property crimes in general.[2] The biggest criminal trades in terms of manpower are thieving (including sneak-in activities and shop-lifting) and burglary. (The Theft Act of 1968 retitled 'breaking' as 'burglary and aggravated burglary'.) Large-scale burglaries have not only expanded in numbers. Comparatively new special fields are being opened up: one observer has noted recent successes in the stealing (usually by forcible entry) of new fashion collections before they have been shown to buyers (Gladstone Smith, 1970, pp. 58-9), and Scotland Yard set up a special section to deal with a rapid succession of burglaries of very valuable paintings and other works of art which began in 1969. This police counter-move was immediately successful.[2]

Of the many modes of thieving two are of special interest. One is the theft of motor vehicles; this can now be statistically distinguished from 'taking away for short periods by joy-riders' as a result of a welcome change in recording by the Commissioner of the Metropolitan Police, as far as Greater London is concerned. In 1961 2,531 motor vehicles were not recovered out of a total of 4,743 stolen; by 1970 the figure of vehicles not recovered had mounted to 4,846 out of a total of 8,399 stolen. The fact that agricultural vehicles were a principal target in 1970 suggests that this species of theft, like some others in recent times, is committed with an eye to a specific market: possibly the goods were stolen to order. We have however no hard information to support the thesis that the disguise and disposal of stolen motor vehicles is a highly organised affair in the United Kingdom.

The second example is one of the dark horses of the contemporary crime scene — the hijacking of lorries and other mobile containers carrying valuable loads. One big tobacco firm lost so many consignments sent by rail in the early 1960s that they were compelled to switch to road transport. But this too is a major criminal target. One spectacular case, broken in 1971 after two years of counter-organisation by the Regional Crime Squad, was conducted by at least 83 people, led by a man of 31; they had stolen and disposed of half a million pounds worth of goods up to the time they were stopped. This 'major industry', as the judge named it in sentencing the leader to 18 years in prison, was organised from East London though it ramified over a very wide area. This was part of the results of an effective counter-action by the police and the industries concerned carried through in 1969 and 1970.[3]

The two most spectacular single developments in the major crime explosion of the last decades were a sudden rise in major frauds in the late 1960s (part of this, the increase in company fraud, we have noted on pp. 23-4 above), and a rapid increase over a longer period in the commando type of robbery. This does not mean that the criminal commando bank-raid, or bullion robbery, or wage snatch, has supplanted the well-prepared burglary as the principal money-maker for the skilled front-line predator. The ratio of Metropolitan burglaries to robberies at the beginning of the 1970s remains about twenty to one (see Commissioner's Reports). But that ratio evens out as the estimated value of the spoils rises to £20,000 and more per incident, and the balance has altered considerably at the level of the very big jobs. In the years before 1968 crimes against property valued at £100,000 and over were very few and far between and were usually burglaries — although even in that period the biggest single haul was that of the £2.3 million in used notes seized by the train robbers in 1963. The scene changes in 1968. In that year, of the three incidents involving more than £100,000 in reported value of cash or jewellery stolen two were van robberies and one a bullion burglary.[4] In 1969 there were four commando-type robberies and four burglaries above the estimated £100,000 level. In 1970 the tally of these major direct-action predatory crimes rises to six commando-type robberies and three burglaries. In the two following years the total of high value incidents goes down but the balance remains the same: four robberies and two burglaries in 1971, three robberies and two burglaries in 1972.[5]

Crime control in an epoch of major crime increase

The most troubling feature of the commando type of crime is its combination of low detection rate with high visibility. This is particularly striking in the case of planned robberies of goods and money *in transit* — the first of the five sub-sections of McClintock and Gibson's category I. These include post-office van robberies and wage-snatches directed against vehicles operated by security firms, often carried out in full view of passers-by. This is one of the most vulnerable sectors in the crime control defences, and it also pinpoints a new and particularly baffling feature of the London crime scene — baffling to detectives and criminologists alike. These criminals are quite as technically skilled, in their latter-day co-operative fashion, as was the traditional 'professional' criminal of yester-year. They have all the operational advantages invented and exploited by the war commandos — split-second timing, surprise, disguise (examples are nylon-stocking masks, a criminal innovation of the 1950s, and animal masks, a more recent *grotesquerie*), and controlled violence (coshes, acid, ammonia, guns) used to intimidate more often than to disable. The violence is not always so very well controlled; it carries an undertone of lack of control, if not pathology, in British criminals even of this new type; but it is well enough controlled in many of the large-scale jobs. But these technological advantages, new and old, take second place to a sociological factor — namely, the comparative anonymity of this new generation of criminals.

This anonymity is both individual and social. They are as individuals largely unknown to the police, and they emerge from social groups and locations which lack any distinctively criminal associations. Take first the individual anonymity. A large proportion of these able and skilled criminal operators come in and carry on for a time as criminals comparatively unknown to the police. The orthodox old-type fully committed criminal, making an occupation and a livelihood out of crime, is also a full-time criminal in the sense of being an established member of a criminal social system who has made the grade among the fraternity and is recognised by his fellows as having done so. He is therefore, *because of the communication and information network to which the detective branch of the police have access,* known or liable to be known and traceable by the police.

It does not follow that the substantial full-time member of the criminal network has a substantial criminal record. Very often he has; but such systematic research as has been done in this neglected field suggests that a number of able criminals, front-liners as well as background figures, have a deceptively light record; they are nevertheless known by the police to be continuously active (pp. 188-9 below).

The problem of the new-type criminal is of a different order. The new men, usually but not necessarily young men, may have some kind of official criminal record, but they are not known to the police as *substantial criminals,* able to take part in high-level operations. This element of social surprise is more significant than the physical surprise they exploit in an actual raid. There are various reservations to be made to all this. There is a good stiffening of experienced full-time criminals, as distinct from substantial incomers, in every field of enterprise in the expanding criminal market of today. These do not necessarily assume any major controlling role. 'There is no Mr Big', a senior London policeman is quoted by *The Times* as saying. Nor is there any elaborate collective organisation. 'If one of their specialists is inside', says the same observer, 'they will borrow a specialist from another gang, but the gangs themselves are not joined together.' The unknown quantity in the problem is the flow of new entrants. 'Because of the surprise they will probably get away with it at the time. Although we have success in catching them later, *there is never any shortage of young people coming from under the carpet to take their places'* (Fowler, 1970) (our italics).

Secondly, the entry of comparatively unknown people into the ranks of major criminals is not confined to robbery, nor to the apparently endless supply of able younger men. The December 1968 strongroom theft of £103,000 in bullion, reported by *The Times* as typical of the very big 'breakings' of recent years, enlisted the services of a team of technicians expert in the use of thermic lances. This type of specialist has high prestige and pay; it is recognised by the criminals who organise and execute these jobs that without their expert help certain safes and strongrooms are impregnable. They are brought in at the planning stage, weeks before the crime; plans and diagrams secured from 'inside' are studied and it is calculated to the nearest inch of metal and the nearest degree of heat (5″ and 2,500° in this case) how long is required to burn through the safe or strongroom. This team was thought by the police to have turned to crime 'in the last twelve months' (London *Times,* 17 September 1968, p. 2). Such high-level entrants represent an equally indispensable element in all of the newer developments: the traditional-type criminal needs experts in art, in rare stamps, in insurance, and in a variety of other areas of specialised knowledge and technology.

A brief reference can be made to the factor of social anonymity — the flow of new criminals from 'neutral' special locations. A sharp contrast is observable between London-based criminals — full-time and incomer — and the leading members of a criminal network in a northern city. In the latter the (mainly full-time) criminals are to be found in the Registrar General's socio-economic classes IV and V with the majority in class V (unskilled labourer); likewise nearly all of them were born and brought up in socially deprived and squalid areas. No detailed study has yet been made of able London criminals, but a quick look at the data published in the Press about the individuals known to have taken part in the bigger criminal operations suggests a fair scatter of nominal occupations ranging from class V up to class II — note for example that the term 'company director' now rivals the older favourite 'general dealer' as the description most often proffered in court — and a similar scatter of addresses. That keen observer Hermann Mannheim notes the impression one gets of 'co-operation between mixed strata of society' in contemporary teams of criminals (Mannheim, 1965, pp. 658-9).

The police response

The basic problem raised by these developments cannot be treated in this report. The time is not ripe for adequate causal explanation: the immediate task must be descriptive and typological, establishing precisely what kinds of crime are in question. But a global judgement suggests that two general causal factors are operating, both outside the sphere of the direct crime-control mechanisms operated by the law-enforcement agencies. The first is the weakening of Patrick Colquhoun's principle of 'natural police', the habitual and spontaneous law-abidingness of the community; a weakening exemplified directly in the influx of able criminals from non-typical social backgrounds; exemplified also in the growth of a certain romantic-subversive attitude, favourable to crime, adverse to the police, such as applauded the daring exploits of the train robbers, and later produced a number of remarkable public apologia for some London counterparts of Mack the Knife (Brecht, 1970). The second, mentioned by some classical criminologists and notably by Ferri, is economic growth; more specifically the massive increase in the amount and flow of stealable commodities consequential on the increasing general economic prosperity of the post-war years (see p. 10 above). A broad conception of crime control must embrace these matters. One cannot harness moral values in the service of crime prevention, since moral values are non-instrumental; but one can look at the courts and the prosecution system, study how to minimise the law's delays, at present very considerable, and consider whether the adversary method of conducting a criminal trial is or is not an impediment to a just and effective system of crime control. Similarly the onset of general economic prosperity is not something to be retarded or limited, but the quantity and flow of one eminently stealable commodity, i.e. the 'vast amount of loose cash accessible in banks . . . and in the street' (Commissioner, 1969, p. 8) might be minimised by arranging to pay wages by cheque. This would of course require a big change in the habits of British wage-earners and bankers. It

c

would also, if Scandinavian experience is any pointer, produce a compensatory increase in cheque and cheque card frauds, which have the relative merit of being non-violent — a weighty point in favour of the change.

Preventive measures such as these take time. The age-old police role in crime prevention, that of rapid detection and arrest, has no time dispensation. The police response to the crime rise since the 1950s had to be immediate; given the narrow limits in which it must perforce operate it was not slow in showing results. In the most spectacular single crime of the decade, the 1963 train robbery, all of the front-line criminals were caught. This might be regarded as a drawn game, since most of the stolen money is unrecovered.[6] But Napoleon's dictum holds of this kind of struggle as of war: the moral is ten times as important as the material effect. Over the decade as a whole statistical indications are favourable. The clear-up figure for all indictable offences was 23 per cent in 1960, 35 per cent in 1970. The clear-up figure for robberies was 32 per cent in 1960, 33.6 per cent in 1970; but in the course of the decade it had taken a dive to under 25 per cent in 1966 with a rapid recovery since that year. There are some slight indications of improved crime control in what has already been described as the most vulnerable sector of the defences — that of 'planned robberies of goods and cast in transit'. The only published figure for this category (McClintock and Gibson's I(a)) is the figure they give for 1957 — 8 robberies cleared up out of 43, or 18.6 per cent (McClintock and Gibson, 1961, p. 127). Scotland Yard have kindly provided the writer with figures for the five years ending 1973: these are:

Year	Category I(a) robberies committed	Category I(a) robberies cleared up
1969	359	48 (13.4%)
1970	394	60 (15.2%)
1971	401	62 (15.5%)
1972	373	48 (12.9%)
1973	322	45 (14.0%)

It will be seen that the problem of planned robberies is much greater than it was back in 1957. But the total of robberies committed is declining and the trend of robberies cleared up is in the right direction, however slightly. In any case evidence of operational changes is more weighty in this field than are immediate statistical pointers based on such comparatively small totals. Here there is reported a considerable redeployment of resources to meet the challenge of increasing predatory crime.[7] The reports of the Metropolitan Police Commissioner give examples of effective interception of large-scale planned robberies. More far-reaching, indeed a landmark in British police history, is the establishment of a network of Regional Crime Squads covering Great Britain. No detailed account of the work of these squads has been published, but the Scotland Yard co-ordinator, reporting on their work in England and Wales in 1971, said: 'We have had a wonderful year for catching good-class criminals.' Dozens of gangs have been broken up (the report goes on) and huge quantities of stolen goods recovered. The squads have built up a nation-wide criminal intelligence network devoted to accumulating information about target criminals (the *Guardian*, London, 1 January 1972). This is an extension over the entire country of the principle of the Criminal Intelligence Bureau, instituted in Scotland Yard in 1960. The CID, as it is universally called, is interested more in what criminals are planning to do than in what they have done in the past.

This work of counteracting the sudden uprush of major burglaries and robberies is probably the most difficult long-term task facing the police in the post-war period. Results might have come faster had the CID been able to concentrate their high-level resources on the big numbers of small and mainly unconnected teams of able criminals in this field. Even at that the manpower resources of the police would have been fully stretched. But any such concentration was prevented by a separate and even more powerful, if short-run, outburst in another sector of traditional large-scale crime, the British (and European) variety of US syndicated crime.

The cult of violence

We have noted that the European version of syndicated crime is rather different from its US counterpart. It is usually a low-key development, and ranks low as a revenue-producer compared with the much bigger industry of predatory crime. This is at any rate the broad London picture since the 1920s. There has been an intermittent succession of gangs, exploiting this or that illicit source of revenue — racing, gambling and what used to be lumped under the comprehensive label of vice — but never going much beyond these limits, and behaving on the whole in an unobtrusive manner. The Richardson and Kray mobs presented a more massive threat to the social order. What made them particularly trouble-some was the extent of their commitment to violence. They had other capacities. Both mobs showed considerable powers of innovation: the Richardsons in traditional unobtrusive style, quietly building up their 'firm'; the Krays by a quite brilliant if short-lived invasion of the swinging London scene, in the course of which they acquired a number of influential temporary acquaintances. But they were primarily dangerous because violent: their power in their own 'territories' was based on their known willingness to 'go the whole way'. The tortures inflicted by the Richardson mob, the gratuitous murders committed by the Kray twins, may reasonably be regarded as being indicative of deep-seated personality defect; these crimes can also and simultaneously be interpreted culturally and politically as indicating the arrogance potential, the sheer gall, of the bolder type of syndicated criminal who has insulated himself from the restraints of the public law. Their intimidation and silencing of witnesses was effective for a comparatively short time, but it gave them a relative freedom in defiance of the law which was perhaps the most menacing thing about them. They were tackled and broken by an immense concentration of police manpower and expertise, and intensification on a big scale of the 'special section' technique already referred to. The story of this achievement, and particularly of the smashing of the mobsters' system of intimidation of witnesses and associates, is a notable chapter in the history of police work.[8] The outcome of the affair was not simply the breaking of the two mobs; it was also the destruction of what might have become a powerful cult of criminal violence.

It is important to get the rise in violence in the last two decades into proportion. So far the record is one of a major increase in major property crime. This has not been accompanied by a proportionate rise in crimes of extreme violence against the person (see Table on p. 50). The total of murders has increased; but the murder rate for England and Wales still runs at roughly four per million population, a comparatively low figure. Against this there has been a distinct and significant increase in manslaughter, in attempted murder, and in serious assaults. But the number of murders and the amount of serious violence committed in the course of major property crimes have increased at a comparatively moderate rate. The proportion of London robberies committed by criminals who are armed or who are thought to be armed has risen from 9 per cent in 1961 to 14.3 per cent in 1970.[9] The proportion of cases in 1964 in which firearms carried were actually used was about 1 in 10.[10] In short, many more criminals are carrying guns than in the years before 1955; many more criminals are using guns than in that period; a number of civilians, and an appreciable number of police, have been the victims of murder or homicide committed in the course of major property crime; but the indications are that neither the older type of full-time criminal nor the new wave of substantial incomers have turned to the use of firearms as part of normal criminal practice. By the same token the British police still strongly maintain their preference for the principle of an unarmed police force.

58

Note (1): London *Times* reports

The data on crimes of property valued at £100,000 and over are extracted from an analysis of *Times* crime reports covering selected years by the Glasgow University Criminological Research Unit. Estimates of value of property stolen are of course rough, and indicate the value to the victim, not to the criminal; in the latter case a reduction in the range of 20-70 per cent is indicated accoring to the commodity stolen, excluding ready cash. Press reports reflect editorial policy and other more random factors as well as the facts, but it is a reasonable guess that the *Times* reports anything coming to light at and above the £100,000 or even £50,000 estimate level.

Note (2): Commando-type robbery — police counter-stroke 1974

As this book goes to press in May 1974 press reports of a big trial and conviction of bank robbers provide evidence of a powerful and successful police counter-stroke against the criminal commandos described in the previous chapter. A fascinating account of the case appeared in the London *Sunday Times* for 26 May 1974, written by Roy Perrott, John Ball and Marjorie Wallace. The figures given by them of bank robberies in the period 1968-72 are not limited to the large-scale incidents (£100,000+ in value of stolen property) referred to above. On the other hand this particular group of criminals was responsible for a number of the very large-scale bank robberies of recent years.

In August 1972 (the account begins) Scotland Yard set up a special robbery squad to deal with the bank-raid epidemic in London. 10 August 1972 was the date of the big Wembley bank robbery in which the robbers, some wearing grotesque masks, got away with £138,000 in a lightning raid. Over the previous four years the annual rate of bank robberies in the metropolitan area had risen steadily from 12 to 65 — that is one every five days. After the squad began to make arrests, the number of robberies dramatically dropped in 1973 to 26. In May 1974, at the end of a major trial, the squad's investigation into the Wembley and other robberies produced jail sentences totalling 113 years.

The seven criminals sentenced included two with no previous convictions, one with eight convictions for minor offences, and four with previous prison sentences, including one gaoled four times and one who had served seventeen years for manslaughter. The two leading figures, who each got 21 years, were a 42 year old property developer and golf club captain, two previous convictions, and a 37 year old former greengrocer, later living stylishly in Spain, three previous convictions.

For the law (the writers go on) the capture and sentencing of these men marked the first important crack in the armed-bank-robbery business, the most serious specialist crime of the decade, and one of the most stubborn types of criminal enterprise to unmask. The police success was made possible by the confession and turning Queen's Evidence of one of the former leading figures of the group. This individual is considered to be one of the most successful bank robbers ever, with up to an estimated £150,000 as his share of bank hauls over a few years' work.

His 10,000-word statement confirms the impression shared by most policemen that there is no elaborate continuing organisation behind predatory crime of this kind. A rough estimate by 'a very senior detective who knows the form-book backwards' is that there are about 3,000 criminals in London readily available for bank robbery. These robbers form more of a recruiting pool or fraternity, ready to team themselves up into shifting groups for an assault on a bank or a van. The informant denied that there was any regular leader among the robbery gangs. 'We just talked it over and sorted it out.' The exact composition of each gang is not often quite the same twice running. What has also made these masked marauders difficult for the police to identify is that they were not usually to be found together except during the actual operation. They lived in quite different parts of London and seldom met. Senior detectives also say that the recruiting pool includes many people not 'known to the police', or men with such light records that they hardly arouse suspicion of such a crime. The informant, with 16 years on the Yard's record books, had never been found guilty of anything that warranted more than a three months' sentence.

He gave in his evidence a graphic picture of some of the methods used in the bank raid — bank ceilings blasted with gunshot as an effective form of 'frightener', till-drawers shot open, commando assaults by ladder over grilles, counter doors sledge-hammered down, raids over in a minute or two, mounting hauls, people injured. A decade that had begun with the craftsman bank-burglar working delicately at the vault with a thermal lance had ended with the primitive sledgehammer. Improvement in safe manufacture, fail-safe locks, sonic alarms, and so on had put the old gelignite and lance experts out of business. But crooks had spotted the simple incongruity: banks were less safe in daylight with all the staff on duty than they were at night. In the early sixties the banks were moving towards a more open, friendly look, to win new customers. So it became daylight robbery in which guns were an essential safeguard in hopping over the counter. So counter-grilles went higher in response. Robbers had another think and came back with ladders to go over the top. Grilles built higher again. Enter the sledgehammer to crack counter doors.

Notes

1   Commissioner = Report of the Commissioner of Police of the Metropolis (London).

2   There has been a very recent (1974) increase in pocketpicking in the classical mode. The new practice of tourists, induced by inflation and currency uncertainties, is to carry large quantities of stable currencies, as distinct from traveller's cheques. This has quickly produced a swarm of skilled thieves, working in teams as described by Sutherland and others.

3   See the *Guardian* (London), 2 December 1971, for an account of the trial. The counter-move was aimed mainly at receivers of hijacked goods. The results as reported in *The Times* were as follows: first six months of 1969, no. of hijacks, 25, value of goods stolen, £377,000; first six months of 1970, no., 11, value, £214,000. It is possible that the figures understate the facts: but the trend is probably near the mark.

4   For the source of these and the following figures see end-of-chapter note on London *Times* reports, p. 59.

5   These figures exclude the nine high-value art thefts in 1969 and 1970. If thefts of this kind were brought into the above calculation the balance would swing back to favour burglaries. But art thefts are in a class by themselves: the clear-up and recovery rate is so high as to suggest that this kind of crime is attempted by highly skilled operators only in exceptional circumstances.

6   Also some of the train robbers escaped from prison for a time, and one of these escapers has not yet been recaptured.

7   See end-of-chapter note (2) for a very recent (May 1974) example of this.

8   See Millen, 1972, chapter 15, and Pearson, 1972, chapter 14.

9   See Commissioner, 1970, p. 47. Weatherhead and Robinson (1970) give the 1967 and 1968 figures as 9.9 per cent and 13.9 per cent respectively (p. 25).

10   See Commissioner (1964), p. 10. Weatherhead and Robinson (1970) note that in 1967 and 1968 'only 8 per cent of the (England and Wales) offences of robbery involving the use of firearms actually involved physical injury' (p. 26).

5 France[1]

Main features of crime in France

Immediately after the Second World War there was, as if in reaction to it, a sudden crime-wave, spectacularly illustrated by acts of vengeance, exploits of the American gangster type and the last gasps of the black market. Then, from 1946 to 1949, recorded crime declined abruptly. According to the figures, which were still collected in the same way, crime was in retreat: the number of cases dealt with fell from 745,000 in 1946 to 668,000 in 1947 and 636,000 in 1948. The 1945 crime-wave and the decline in 1946-48 are significant phenomena, and the police statistics, despite their imperfection, constituted an index to them. After this reaction, that is from 1949 onwards, the same departments, following the same procedure and recording in the same way, found that the number of recorded crimes became steady. For six years (1949-55) the annual figure fluctuated around an average of 610,000 cases dealt with. Then in 1956 the police figures show an increase to 645,000. And ever since, the number of crimes recorded has constantly risen. From 1967 onwards the constant increase in the police records suddenly speeds up: 748,000 in 1966, 852,411 in 1967 and 950,555 in 1968. (It should be noted that since 1963 traffic offences have been excluded from these totals.) By 1972 it was clear to the police that crime in France was increasing by 10 per cent yearly.

In 'La Société Criminogène', M. Jean Pinatel points out that 'almost everywhere in the world crime has passed the threshold at which it ceases to be a marginal phenomenon and becomes a political phenomenon'. French crime seems to be changing from a social disease to a normal characteristic of a changing society.

Organised and professional crime

Organised crime[2] has, of course, always been known in France. In *Le crime en France* (Paris Hachette 1959) we described the main kinds of crime recorded during the 1950s: armed robbery, picking pockets, burglaries, multiple outbreaks of theft, hotel thefts, theft of vehicles, pilfering from lorries. These were functional groupings and were in no way fortuitous, and depended on the existence of the wholesaler-receiver, of 'enlightened parasitism', of ever-growing functional mobility and of international criminals settled in a single region. Another chapter described what we called 'the capitalism of crime', an imitation of the lawful economic world, procuring, traffic in human beings, drug trafficking, receiving, and 'laundering' money (bringing 'hot' money back into circulation).

No. 150 of the periodical *Liaisons* (the monthly information bulletin of the Paris Prefecture of Police) gives some very valuable statistical information on crime in the Paris police area.

Hold-ups, defined as 'thefts against establishments having money or valuable objects in their care by teams of criminals, usually armed, equipped with vehicles and prepared to use violence, even to kill, in order to achieve their ends', show a very characteristic graph over a decade. In the five-year period 1957-62 they increased from 10 to 88. Between 1962 and 1966 they decreased. Why? Was police action more effective? From 1966 onwards the curve rises again. Experts believe that this was due to the presence of new gangs, as yet unidentified.

The graph for 'robbery with violence on the public highway' curved downward from 1957 to 1959. But in 1960, 1961 and 1962 it went up sharply. Then in 1963 and 1964 it suddenly shot down well below the level of 1957. Lastly, the increase has been steady since 1964. The graph for burglary reflects the general trend rather better: from 1957 onwards it went up steeply; in 1960 the level remained steady; then there was a decrease in 1963 and 1964, then another increase from 1966 onwards. More and more factories and shops were burgled.

The graph for picking pockets over the same decade provides food for thought, for there was a sharp rise between 1957 and 1960, a sudden fall in 1960, 1961, and then in 1962 and 1963 a huge increase, from 3,903 to 5,611. From 1963 until 1966 there was a gentle fall, and then in 1966-67 another rise. Such an erratic curve, by the very fact of being apparently erratic, suggests that we are dealing with a form of crime which is both persistent and sensitive. As a whole, however, the graph is slowly but surely rising. The variations consist of sudden waves above a steadily rising baseline. This graph fits in very well with the general trend.

Thefts from parked cars show a high and constantly climbing curve without spectacular variations. Such figures give the impression that this is a form of popular crime by which a number of petty criminals made a modest living. Thefts of vehicles also show a rising curve since 1957. Oddly, from 1960 onwards thefts of cars have constantly been more numerous than those of two-wheeled vehicles. In 1968 the sharp increase in crime noted in 1967 continued, especially in the suburbs.

One form of crime in which we may presume that some organisation of criminals is taking place is that of attacks on carriers of cash. In the Paris region between 1965 and 1967 there were 53 such attacks, and this form of attack on property is not decreasing. Old forms of crime survive, and sometimes even come back into fashion. Safe-breaking is a good example, since here refined techniques are being replaced simply by removal or violent forcing.

Another issue of the periodical *Liaisons,* Paris: Prefecture de Police No. 176 for January 1971, summarises police activity in Paris 1970. In that city, the general crime rate increased constantly during the years 1960-70, from 131,537 cases to 216,198. It is noted that

> the different forms of crime are changing and show a tendency to a rapid escalation of habitual offences. Previously criminals progressed in stages leading successively, and sometimes over a long period, from minor thefts to assaults, then to burglary and then to the participation, with others in planned and organised crimes, with the use of advanced equipment, vehicles, and eventually firearms. Now, we see criminals of every sort of social origin moving directly into crime with violence, passing without transition from petty thefts to hold-ups and from car stealing to vicious premeditated crime. (op. cit.)

A very large number of serious offences are not planned and premeditated, but are decided upon spontaneously, upon impulse or as the opportunity arises. A small gang of hooligans will set out together, and may equally well attack either a garage attendant or an aged person at home or a taxi-driver. Or they may assault a small shopkeeper or a chemist or they may rob a bank. The boldness of criminals of this new kind sometimes leads them to kill at random. This is what the experts call a wave of 'robbery on impulse'.

Between 1967 and 1970 the number of hold-ups increased sharply from 20 to 133, and this fits in with what we noted above. Robberies with violence also increased from 1,426 to 2,751, attacks on unaccompanied women from 505 to 892 and burglaries from 16,990 to 36,121. But the figures for picking pockets were steadier, as were those for theft from parked vehicles and thefts of cars.

In order to complete the list of crimes which may involve professional or organised criminals, we should note that the number of cases of bad cheques went up by 178 per cent, of cases of fraudulent conversion by 19 per cent, of cases of false pretences by 40 per cent, and fraudulent bankruptcies by 64 per cent, while the number of breaches of company law and fraudulent company promotions has risen by 43 per cent, since 1966.

Some 'permanent types' of professional crime were listed. First, quite naturally, all forms of larceny, especially armed robbery or the hold-up. But people's opinions of this kind of robbery distort the picture, for robbery with violence is not the most professional form of crime. A gang is not more specifically professional than a team of thieves or traffickers working full-time in less spectacular forms of crime such as picking pockets or thefts from parked cars, pilfering (from lorries, stores, stations or shops), or burglary. New forms of procuring also provide some people with a prosperous living and illicit trafficking in general, in accordance with social and economic circumstances, in arms or drugs, for example.

These are 'new' types of crime precisely because they are offences 'dependent upon exceptional and temporary regulations such as exchange controls, price control, VAT and so on'. This is worth noting, for the conventional professional criminal is hardly ever very active in them. Does this mean that a form of professional crime is emerging here, in an area normally considered the preserve of 'white-collar' crime? May not this neo-professionalism indicate the appearance of classless crime? [4]

'Organised crime' [5]

Many people are acquainted with organised crime only by hearsay or through an image of the American situation which is nothing like what goes on in Europe. If all the replies are collated, they in fact come down to the following.

A few individuals become organised, monopolise a particular kind of business in which it is possible to carry out unlawful or marginal activities, especially all kinds of illicit trafficking. This leads to the control of chains of places of amusement. And this can lead on to the kind of set-up well known to criminology in which there are strong-arm men, with no scruples about taking part in armed robberies or large-scale burglaries, racketeering, corruption and blackmail.

This is not yet very widespread, but it is in itself quite serious. Vigorous repression is called for, to avoid chain-reactions or new movements in the underworld, especially the birth of legends of big bosses who enjoy protection.

Notes

1   This and the following chapter are extracted from the drafts prepared by Mr Susini on the basis of material compiled by Mr Peronaci and himself (see p. 179 below). The drafts were translated by the Council of Europe secretariat and have been considerably shortened, otherwise no alteration has been made (J.A.M.).

2   i.e., 'organised' in the general or dictionary sense of the word.

3   What follows is based on interviews conducted by Mr Peronaci in May 1970 in Paris, Marseilles and elsewhere.

4   Note that these comments by the French police and other experts are in sharp contrast to the views reported in the Interpol conference reported in p. 21 above.

5   i.e., what is defined in chapter 3 as 'syndicated crime'.

6 Italy[1]

Prompted by early militant criminology, the Italian penal code evolved a method of dealing with the question of professionalism in a technical and legal manner.

Thanks to the code the judicial authority is enabled to strike a heavier blow against someone meeting the conditions laid down for being formally and legally proclaimed to have the status of an 'habitual offender', who commits a *further offence*. He can be ceremonially branded by a formal declaration of his status, which is thus legally defined as that of 'professional offender'.

The *further offence* thus plays a radical, qualitative part in this arithmetic of crime. It transfers the person from a condition legally classed as 'habitual' to another, classed also for legal purposes as 'professional'.

This *further offence* is of capital importance because it constitutes a criminalistic unit of quantity, a minimum addition permitting a different interpretation of exactly the same information as that which allows a person to be classed as an habitual offender. In order to class a person as an habitual offender on the evidence of repeated offences, Article 133 is applied. This same Article 133 also operates in the application of the article defining the professional offender. Article 133 obliges the judge to take into consideration the seriousness of the offence *by reference to:* (a) the nature, type, means, subject, time, place and all other features connected with the act; (b) the severity of the injury or risk to the victim; (c) the intensity of the fraud or degree of the offence. These three assessments thus define the seriousness of the act. In addition, however, the judge must also take into account the offender's capacity for committing offences *by reference to:* (a) the offender's motives and character, (b) his past record, his conduct and life before the act, (c) his conduct during and after the act, (d) his individual, domestic and social living conditions.

The same arithmetic applies to methods of behaviour in the matter of smuggling. The professional smuggler is similarly defined in Article 133 of the Legge Doganale of 25 September 1940. This arithmetic of persistent conduct indicators is simple. It triggers off a social reaction defining a status, somewhat as though the law were threatening that 'if you carry on this way of life you will be officially treated as a professional'. How are these formulations applied in practice?

In the *Annuario di Statistiche Guidiziarie* for 1966[2] I counted 2,000 'professional' habitual offenders out of a total of 5,000 habitual offenders, out of a total of 31,943 sentenced to penal internment. 'Professionals' cannot account for more than 6 per cent of all criminals sentenced to penal internment.

In reality judges issue very few of these formal declarations, which are regarded as methods of aggravating the penal reaction. To take into account this professional capacity for crime is to give rise to increased penalties for those legally classified as habitual offenders and the application of safety measures (Articles 109 and 1995). Thus the judges are invited to apply punitive measures.

My informants were unanimous in warning me that a distinction must be made between the professional branded by legal procedure and the offender seen in technical terms. Actually, in the penitentiaries, where those legally classified as professionals should be, we find no more than about 2-3 per cent of the strength, and these have already been sifted out.

It has therefore been impossible for me to assess the importance of the phenomenon through official statistics.

Indirect evidence of the existence of a professional criminal class

In police parlance there is indeed allusion to a professional in the sense of our definition. On the whole, however, the semi-professional being acknowledged as a reality, some place him in more substantial sociological contexts. They regard him as finding expression in the Sicilian Mafia, Sardinian bandits and organised bands of robbers in northern Italy. This is important because it suggests a relationship between forms of crime and regional structures strongly impregnated by new political and economic factors, in which certain forerunners to the European process of criminalisation can be discerned. It ought to be possible to interpret this old criminalistic parlance in modern terms.

According to others, semiological detection of the professional is complicated by the fact that too many amateurs commit acts apparently covered by a kind of criminality that is professional, stable, compounded of ability, trickery and circumspection. Could it be that the well-adjusted professional has found a means of passing himself off as an amateur, so as not to defy social controls and public opinion? What does seem to be constant, in these circumstances, is the existence of crime as an occupation involving a certain amount of technical skill and discretion. Can one proceed from the sociological fact to conclude that there are professional offenders? The majority of my informants admit this, at any rate from prudence and by logical deduction. A clear distinction is made between an ideal professional, who acts without defying fundamental values, imbues his crimes with a kind of private, stealthy characteristic, reaping many small gains (pickpockets), and the chronic underdeveloped person, the unskilled offender responsible for many petty offences, with whom relapse into crime is significantly proportionate to his criminal commitment. My informants think that it is the latter who is more likely to be declared a professional by judicial process.

As may be seen, there is little precision in all this and more systematic research is called for. But might it not be that our question is too weighted and implies a kind of ideological reaction? Those providing the answers may after all be trying too hard to use the model of the professional imposed upon us by general sociology.

The customs authorities, for their part, recognise a professional type, according to the nature of traffic in which he deals — tobacco, coffee, watches. Customs experts are particularly interested in modern methods of smuggling, especially in Europe's new regional networks. Professionalism is thus sociologically implied, since it is found that large-scale smuggling is not a matter of improvisation. It involves financial investment, skill and discretion in handling the traffic, and of course full-time workers of proven ability. The sociological dimension therefore implies semi-professional commitments, so to speak.

It is thought that there is a combination of criminological factors in such a field, and in this connection reference is made to the phenomenon of the Mafia. Without prejudging the essential content of this word 'Mafia', should we not assess the choice of the word in its true light, the need to use it for a better description of the complex development of growing smuggling activities in southern Europe and the western parts of central Europe? This is the expression used to describe the growth in traffic through the intervention of the notorious Mafia which is, as I have just stressed, an assumption based on the possibility that things are rapidly getting more complicated. This may be seen on the spot: traffic is assuming international proportions and is carried on by Greeks, Maltese and French. The existence of a floating population devoted to smuggling is not a figment of the imagination; in the Mediterranean this assumption has been confirmed many times over.

But my informants believe that smuggling is more and more in the hands of *criminals*. Is this not important just at a time when classless crime is making its appearance? It should be noted that the most lucrative traffic has always been monopolised by criminals. Is this not evidence that crime is becoming Europeanised, a new dimension in a growth situation in which powerful factors (profits, large areas, mass crime and administrative incongruities) inevitably come into play?

The police, for their part, regard themselves as the natural antagonists of professional criminals. In service parlance the latter are classified as the 'swell mob', and looked on as socially dangerous because they succeed in protecting themselves adequately. Here we see the reappearance of the stereotyped professional who is clever, discreet, mobile, elusive, evanescent. Clearly, this way of dealing with professionals coincides with a certain concept of organised crime. The same stereotyped view considers the professional to be irredeemable. Thus the concept of specialised crime confirms that of professionalisation. The police amass information on specialised crime and this produces an ideal picture of the professional.

I was given a further criminal model of conventional conduct. In this we find all the traditional notions used for officially describing professional activity of any kind: substantial income, full-time activity, many-sided ability, adaptability, planning and skill in execution.[3] I was also able to discern the existence of a *balance* between criminality and social control. The growing European scale of crime encourages fresh conflicts, thus destroying the balance in question, engendering a defence reaction actually within the social controls. I therefore found professionalism depicted in accordance with the descriptions found in specialist literature up to the period between the two wars.

All the romantic or semi-sociological interpretations at the beginning of the century reflected a kind of *balance* between social control and forms of criminality. We had allusions to the existence of criminal underworlds. Professional theft carried out with knowledge and skill had taken the place of attacks with violence. Then came the notion of a clandestine underworld, seen as consisting of a cohesive body of professional offenders. This stemmed from the kind of life led by the uprooted classes, quite as much as from adaptation to the new parasitic conditions imposed by urbanisation. There was a period when criminal underworlds were confined to towns. There was also, as we have emphasised, a balance between social reaction and the obvious scale of the crime.

Spoils were selected judiciously. The dominant feature so far as criminal underworlds were concerned was a kind of rule of discretion. Concealment of wrongdoers and stolen goods was able to develop without arousing public wrath. We even find a typical form of dress and slang used by professionals. Practical, specialised study of crime should include a study of the forms of speech used by criminals among themselves.

This is, of course, an out-of-date picture of this vision of the professional that was more or less passed on to me.

Trend towards crime

There is no doubt that two portraits of the professional oppose each other in people's minds, the old and the new. Firstly, the conflict between the professional criminal with a peaceable disposition, with a certain tolerance and stereotyped reaction reflecting a stable society well adjusted to its traditional limits; secondly, a new criminality in new specific or criminally amorphous situations. So the factor of Europeanisation appears to me to favour the development of a new *criminal awareness*. In other words, the process of Europeanisation can only be assessed against the epistemological background of a conflict theory. It follows that the corresponding criminality bears the same imprint. For observers brought up on traditional ideas, overclouded by systematic conceptualism, the new forms of lucrative and social criminality assume the form of a challenger.

Many more studies ought to be made of the types of existence led by criminals outside their spheres of activity, as urged in Article 133 of the Italian code. In a general way, in a descriptive perspective, we see a group of fresh interactions, new anthropological combinations clearly indicating the emergence of a committed criminality replacing the old-time professional with his outmoded dress, speech and manner of life. The problem is one of a new generation in a criminal dimension, coupled with an essentially European change.

The idea of a changing society affects criminals of all types, and guiding assumptions can be discerned. Is the nature of crime not changing from that of *trickery* to that of *planning*?

'Violent' forms of crime would tend to change and engage in less spectacular forms of traffic. The act and its return are better calculated. Professionals know each other and are moving towards flexible relationships that are all the more lasting because they are functionally better worked out. Small-time professionals engaged in private crimes were content with small gains. Criminals in the post-industrial Europe now in process of development operate *less* haphazardly and are *more* likely to be clever tricksters obsessed by the idea of a booty that will magically change their destiny.

Specialisation is on the increase and professionalism is becoming more socialised. Professionals live normal lives. There is an obvious trend for crime to go beyond nationalities and we see evidence of activity on a broad European front. Anecdotes and confidential information given outside courts suggest that the police have an untapped knowledge of criminal precursors.

The function of criminal underworlds is more important than ever but is taking on new forms. The concept of the criminal underworld is no longer material, urban, architectural or ecological. More and more it is an imperceptible system of communications and relationships, a means of exchange, passing on information, financial transactions and studies of lucrative elements, for which the fullest possible provision is to be made.

The result is a general change in local 'undergrounds', which are tending to become organised. Side by side with this, ecological, 'wild' crime is also developing. In a community as mobile and dense as Europe, relationships between criminals and victims are changing, and new victims are coming on the scene. Will this not lead to a sort of race between attackers and defenders?

Out-of-date professionalism can be seen wherever it can find expression, especially Calabria, Sardinia and Sicily. In the latter, however, one must take into consideration the geographical situation at a mighty crossroads offering lucrative possibilities for trade and criminal activities alike. We should put an end to romantic talk about the Mafia and rob the world of its mystic connotations, changing it into a specific operational concept, to be put to the test.

Portrait of the Italian professional

It is quite obvious that information must be contradictory, depending on whether it comes from informants concerned with professionals as defined by law, or from others.

The class of professional criminals as seen by the law is not a coherent one. It is a heterogeneous group, composed of persons whose 'anti-social' characteristics would appear to be governed by varied factors.

The only studies relating to them (G. Canepa, 1960; A. Arata and P. L. Bonomo, 1960; see *Medicina Legale e delle assicurazioni,* vol. IX, Facs. 1, 1961) anticipate that treatment will become individual. The effect of branding criminals entailed in the formal declaration of their status dominates such practical studies, obliging them as it were to conform to their classification; at any rate, the combined effects of imprisonment and classification are clinically predominant over any other appreciation of any more anthropological structuration. In a group of 40 persons examined and coming within this legal category there were 7 normal people, 7 of weak intellect, 15 maladjusted persons, 9 psychopaths and 2 psychotic cases. Conclusions based solely on this study and this selection might suggest that most of those legally classified as professional criminals were maladjusted persons.

Combined with the rest of the data, all this confirms that there is an immature 'professional' and an astute, scheming professional type. One feels that the informants are trying to draw a logical picture, a kind of portrait gallery of professionals — the equivalents of the former dangerous classes, prowlers, people torn from their usual surroundings or circumspect gang leaders working for remunerative traffic. One sees the paradigm of those who have come down in the world reinforced through fresh migrations still connected with industrialisation. But already it appears that the distribution of professional crime is following some axiology other than that of industrialisation. An attempt is made to outline the grades of the outcasts of fortune: landless peasants, the unemployed, transport workers. Hence a criminogenic tension in which professional status takes on the air of a reaction. And in the end all this gives us a portrait that is of very little use except in so far as it demonstrates that there is no such thing as a criminal type, only persons who can avoid being noticed, who are not very well balanced, unstable, pleasure-seeking, amoral, extrovert and artful.

What strikes us in all this, therefore, is the fact that there is indeed a criminogenic atmosphere in which traditional concepts disintegrate. Quite obviously the criminological epistemology underlying social controls is full of gaps.

Entry into a professional criminal career is subject to the same uncertainty. We need more systematic knowledge of the conditions of life currently discernible in these days of people moving to northern Italy. Some informants draw attention to the conjunction of circumstances and factors bombarding adolescents overwhelmed by *change supplemented by accelerated migration*. Finally, doubtless because the portrait is vague, and owing to the inadequacy of the contextual sociology of which they are aware, the reaction of informants is dictated by the actual crisis in social controls. And people complain about the evolution of ideas, half-hearted legal repressive measures, the difficulty of securing evidence, the difficulty in intercepting extra-territorial ramifications and the antiquated system of police investigations.

In 1956 a law was passed laying down measures in connection with the committal of persons dangerous to public morals and safety. This law is directed mainly against those who manifestly and habitually engage in unlawful trafficking; those who by their *conduct* and *mode of life* demonstrate that they are living on illicit earnings or are disposed to commit offences; those who by their *behaviour* demonstrate that they are living by prostitution, corruption of minors, smuggling or drug trafficking; those who engage in activities contrary to public morals and morality. This legislation clearly expresses a reaction to *behaviour* and encourages a study of such *behaviour*. The Act of 31 May 1965 introduces measures against the Mafia. It applies to those who appear to belong to Mafia-type associations. As with Article 133 of the penal code, the law appears to take it for granted that the type of conduct against which it is directed is significant, concrete and clearly discernible.

A distinction needs to be made, therefore, between planned crime in over-industrialised areas, and the forms of corruption in the social process noted in Calabria, Sicily and Sardinia. Criminalisation of Mafia processes is apparently obvious, spelling the end of structural 'Mafia-ism'.

European criminality seems to avoid the nationalist stage. Changing conditions already affect large-scale crime, which plans and executes its undertakings in the manner of a criminal technocracy. Changing crime in Europe must therefore be analysed in the light of new and more appropriate concepts, and social controls must rid themselves of their obsession for formal legal branding of offenders. This survey has thus been fruitful if it has shown the urgent need to create a decentralised body for criminological research in Europe. The Italian experts attached to the customs authorities would like to see an administration like their own, with powers extending throughout Europe.

Notes

1   See note at beginning of previous chapter.
2   Annuario di statistische Giudiziarie vol. XVI 1966. Instituto centrale di Statica Roma 1968.

7 The Netherlands

Social and economic background

With its nearly 13 million population, the Netherlands is to be counted among the smaller states of Europe. The nation has long been character-ised by relatively few social class differences, by an even distribution of income and wealth, relative to international standards, and by a marked democratic consciousness. The decline of the colonial power resulted in no irreparable cracks in the political and social structure. The country was badly affected by both World Wars — Rotterdam was very badly bombed in 1940 — but it was not directly involved. As a result the damage inflicted was soon made good.

The economic structure of the Netherlands is based on a modern low-cost agriculture, and sustains a massive foreign trade. Tourism plays an important part in the economy especially in the western regions of the country. Industry is concentrated mainly in the few big towns, particu-larly in the harbours — for example Amsterdam and Rotterdam.

Public attitudes exhibit a high degree of tolerance, open-mindedness, and readiness to use modern methods of social welfare and of aid for socially disadvantaged persons. Particularly impressive to the foreign visitor is the positive attitude of the different government officials as regards not only experiments in law enforcement but also in the therapeutic treatment of deviants.

These and other characteristics tend to inhibit a rapid expansion of crime; long-term crime trends in the Netherlands differ in some ways from those in the larger European nations, for instance the Federal German Republic. Note for example the pattern of imprisonment (see Table 7.1). The Netherlands show the lowest rates of prison receptions (per 100,000 inhabitants) of all the European states, and these rates have steadily decreased from 1945 to the present,[2] without any noticeable effect on major crime trends.

One thing the Netherlands has in common with other countries is the trend of property offences, which is approximately the same as in the neighbouring states: the totals of thefts of valuable goods, including cars, have followed an upward curve for many years. Also mentioned in discussion was an increase in business-type crime and in white-collar criminality, although no outstanding specific instances existed or were quoted. One's main impression was that the Netherlands had a comparatively small, indeed minimal, problem of well-organised or professional crime.

Some criminologists were minded to dismiss the matter as one of no practical importance. Only the big-city police forces and the central criminal police detective agency took a different view. Nearly all of the police spokesmen could cite a number of examples of individual 'professional' criminals, conventionally defined; but they went on to emphasise that the Netherlands have nothing that could be described as a substantial 'crime industry'. The country itself was too small; the existing illegal markets were neither big enough nor attractive enough to encourage the development of a large-scale system of criminal transactions; finally there were not enough specialised criminals to maintain the necessary communication systems.

Many of the professional-type criminals operating in the Netherlands are non-nationals coming in mainly from Belgium, Germany and France. This observation by the police is supported by the results of a survey which divided the country into homogeneous regions and went on to calculate the respective crime rates; the higher rates are to be found in the border regions and in the tourist centres.

The central criminal police bureau lists over 16,000 criminals whose 'working area' covers more than one region of the country. Of these 'travelling' or 'inter-regional' criminals the following were considered by the police to be both specialists and full-timers: 400 safe-breakers, 3,000 burglars, 1,000 fraudsters, and 2,150 other less specialised operators. Only

Table 7.1
The Netherlands: selected major crimes reported to the police, 1960, 1965 and 1969

Class of offence	1960		1965		1969		Percentage increase of rates	
	No.	Rate	No.	Rate	No.	Rate	1969 over 1965	1969 over 1960
Murder, manslaughter, and attempted murder	296	3	378	4	517	5	+25.0	+66.7
Woundings (felonious *and* others)	8,526	94	7,841	81	8,725	85	+4.9	−9.6
Sexual offences (total)	8,358	92	8,751	90	8,837	86	−4.5	−6.5
Breaking and entering	8,388	93	16,138	166	34,234	338	+103.6	+263.4
Larceny (simple theft)	61,706	680	83,302	855	112,046	1,093	+27.8	+60.7
All offences (offences against Road Traffic Act excluded)	128,659	1,418	166,338	1,708	236,544	2,380	+39.3	+67.8

Rate = offences known to the police per 100,000 inhabitants.
Source: Data obtained by personal request from Ministerie van Justitie, OA Opsporingsbijstand s-Gravenhage (Nederlands).

a fraction of those could be regarded as 'professional' and successful.

The Rotterdam police have a special observation squad (or criminal intelligence bureau). This squad keeps an eye on 250 selected full-time criminals. Only 70 out of this number are described as 'real professionals', and of these only 15 are held to be big moneymakers. Altogether not more than 5 per cent of police man-hours (excluding the special sub-divisions mentioned above) are expended on the professional criminal. Nevertheless, the qualitative importance of professional crime should not be underrated. What there is is not usually characterised by elaborate background organisation. The majority of those who warrant the 'professional' label are lone wolves, or work in small groups of two to four, doing their own planning.[3] These are mainly the indigenous safecrackers, burglars and specialists in various forms of theft. When the police come up against larger groups these are in many cases found to consist of non-nationals, particularly the leading figures. It is probably these people who are responsible for the fact that 'crimes on order' (the so-called 'vol sur commande'), crimes which are highly prevalent in other countries, have risen markedly in the Netherlands during the last few years. These non-indigenous practitioners of well-organised crime aim mainly at high-priced and luxury goods. There is a certain amount of well-organised car-theft, although the country seems to be more of a transit area for export to Scandinavia and the USA, and also a market-place for cars coming in from other countries, than an area given to the extensive theft of inland cars. Also on the increase are various forms of fraud, including the use of stolen or forged travellers' cheques; and the illicit trade in weapons and drugs.

The few leading criminal figures in the Netherlands use the same modern methods as are to be found elsewhere; they work inter-regionally and internationally, they repeatedly change their addresses and switch from one type of stolen property to another, they endeavour to sell the products of their enterprise in parts of the world as distant as possible, they plan their criminal operations carefully, they carry through those plans in a businesslike manner, and so on.

We turn now to our discussions of criminal personality. There are no reliable studies of professional criminals in the Netherlands. This is partly due to the fact that there are so few to study. This scarcity of material may have helped to produce the opinion held by some people in positions of responsibility that the so-called professional criminal is a police-created 'myth'. We discuss this remarkable proposition in a later chapter (p. 136 below).

As far as the police are concerned the professional criminal has no psychological peculiarities. On the contrary, he is alleged to have a more stable personality structure than have other criminals. Professional criminals are thought to be of average or above average intelligence; while the top men, especially the business-type criminals, are thought to be outstandingly intelligent. Their attitude towards their occupation is that of the highly profit-oriented businessman, rational and businesslike. They regard crime as an adequate and normal way of making a living. They regard the police not as a hated enemy, but as an antagonist or competitor who has his appropriate role in a conflict which is sometimes won by one side sometimes by the other. Arrest or imprisonment are prudentially calculated as 'business risk'. As a result of this violence is kept to a minimum, particularly in transactions with the police. The level of violence even among the younger 'professionals' is no higher than the general level of violence as measured by the incidence of all crimes of violence. There is one reservation here: in recent years there has been a considerable increase in the carrying of firearms. According to one police observation, firearms have become a status symbol among criminals.

There does not seem to be much of a criminal 'underground' or *milieu* in the Netherlands. Some of the big cities have the usual shady groups and *banlieux* organised round prostitutes, but no connection has been detected by the police between these and the 'professional' criminal category. Nevertheless much of the fencing or receiving of cheap or low-priced goods is carried on in these circles. But the scope and extent of the transactions between the few substantial criminals in the various regions are matters of personal acquaintance and informal business relationship, too slight for the language of 'economic exchange function' to be relevant. Another characteristic of a criminal subculture, namely a status system, has not yet been detected by the police; there are however instances here and there suggesting some kind of ranking system or pecking order among the different categories of persistent offenders, substantial and lightweight.

Expert police opinion is that the lesser criminals are usually quite willing to talk. The relationships which hold between them are not very stable. This does not mean that it is always possible to get sufficient evidence to secure conviction of the detected criminals.

There does exist a category of substantial criminals, mainly background operators, who succeed in avoiding detection in most of their under-takings. So far as can be gathered from evidence obtained in the investigation of a number of fairly large-scale enterprises there are some skilled organisers, working in the background and able to maintain an elaborate system of secrecy, who are specially hard to catch. But this evidence is susceptible of more than one interpretation and one must await more specific police investigation in this area.

The lesser figures who fail to escape detection have still a number of resources left to them. They are usually skilled in the arts of avoiding conviction in court or sentences of imprisonment. They know police methods so well that they often succeed in weakening the evidence brought forward, by the age-old device of admitting only what they cannot conceivably deny, challenging all inferential findings, and suggesting that other unknown persons were responsible for the offences the police cannot prove conclusively against them. As a result of this the police know a large number of near-professional operators whom they connect with this or that *coup*, although they have not enough evidence on which to base a charge.

Notes

1 This account is based on written reports and on interviews conducted by Hans Kerner with police and others in the principal Netherland cities. Among those interviewed were members of the Dutch Rijkspolitie (Afdeling Opsporingsbijstand, Ministerie van Justitie — Central Criminal Investigation Department near the Ministry of Justice) at the Hague, which is the national liaison office for Interpol. Others talked to included the CIDs of the Gemeente-Politie (city police) of The Hague, Rotterdam and Amsterdam; also the Rotterdam Harbour Police. Particular help was given by the members of the Wetenschappelijk Voorlichtings — en Documentatie Centrum van de Ministerie van Justitie (Scientific Centre on Research and Documentation of the Ministry of Justice), and of the University Institutes of Criminology in Amsterdam, Groningen and Leiden. Altogether about 30 individuals — police detectives, other police specialists, criminologists, and other experts — took part.

On the structure of the Netherlands police system cf. A. Vermeij, and F. A. J. van Kralingen: *Kurze Ubersicht über Organisation und Zuständigkeit von Polizei und Justiz in den Niederlanden;* Gemeindepolizei Rotterdam (ed.); Rotterdam, 1971 (mimeographed, 17 pp.).

2 Cf. *Zeventig jaren statistiek in tijdreesken,* ed. by the Central Bureau voor de Statistiek, s-Gravenhage, 1970, p. 164. A slight increase in numbers is observable in 1967 and later years.

3 As far as those types of 'professionals' are concerned, cf. the description given by Van Bemmelen, 1952, pp. 321 ff.

8 German Federal Republic[1]

Social and economic background

There are a number of fairly conspicuous persisting features in the social structure of that Germany which was destroyed by the so-called Third Reich. Even in the Weimar Republic the established class divisions remained relatively undisturbed. Such criminal trends as are observable exhibit a corresponding uniformity. Although the total number of felonies and misdemeanours slowly increased, the increase gave no ground for grave concern (except in particular periods, e.g. property crimes during the first years after the 1914-18 war and, later in the 1930s, during the worldwide economic depression). Likewise the situation as regards juvenile delinquency was not threatening.[2] There were nevertheless signs and forerunners of change; the first corporations of criminals were founded after World War I, for instance the so-called 'Recidivist Clubs' (Vorbestraftenvereine) and the 'Pimp Clubs' (Zuhältervereine);[3] and furthermore, there were a number of celebrated safe-cracking operations, bank robberies and hold-ups on a very large scale in the same period. Police and public alike were faced with the phenomenon of *travelling* 'professional' criminals on an increasing scale, and notably the so-called international criminals, who ranged particularly widely (Palitzsch, 1926).

The general social and economic development after 1945 may be described by the well-used slogan 'americanisation'. The salient features are: to begin with, unstable currency, economic crisis forcing rapid transfers of property and power, the bringing into the expanding economy of millions of refugees, returning soldiers, etc; later on came explosive economic development, the accumulation of large fortunes by individuals, the growing benefits of the welfare state for the general population, political-economic pressure groups and the open negotiation of conflicts in the political market-place — vast social changes which produced equally drastic changes in private and public morality, with corresponding transformations of modes of behaviour, in particular among young people.[4] These are mirrored in the crime scene, which is characterised by a continuing and accelerating increase in property crimes,[5] a steady increase in the proportion of juveniles among the convicted offenders (Göppinger, 1971, pp. 310-28; Kaiser, 1966, pp. 17-68; Kaiser, 1971, pp. 60-87; Rangol, 1959, pp. 365-7) and a conspicuous increase in violence in its various forms.

Types of crime requiring special mention are mainly big hold-ups, bank robberies and serious burglaries, a high proportion undetected, getting away with sums of the order of 1 million DM.[6] In the field of extremely violent crime a number of mass murderers were convicted – notorious examples are Pommerenke and Priegan – and other comparatively new developments are the increase in the illegal drug traffic and in kidnapping. In 1971 alone there were several cases of kidnapping where sums of the order of 100,000 DM were extorted (the biggest single sum paid by the family of the victim amounted to 7 million DM); other cases in which the victims were killed. Finally, business-type crime is becoming a more and more urgent problem (Schneider, 1972, pp. 461-7; Tiedemann, 1972 *a, b*).

Significance of major crime

The German Federal Republic has a relatively large crime industry, the activities of which are not limited to Germany. The police give a high priority to 'professional' criminality; their view is that prosecution of the criminals is becoming increasingly difficult, and may become almost completely impossible if the responsible political institutions fail to carry through big organisational changes. As in other countries, public opinion lags behind police opinion in these matters. The Federal and State Parliaments are busy enough with other legal reforms; and general opinion is preoccupied with the youth revolt, youthful criminality, and the increase in pornography.

It is not easy to establish how many known major crimes are 'professional' in any exact sense of the word. So far there is a lack of reliable systematic data; it is also difficult to differentiate between serious and less serious crimes, as regards quality and quantity; criteria seem to differ from one police agency to another. The police in every area have to contend with such a huge wave of petty and small-scale criminality – the annual total of offences, excluding traffic offences, is more than 2 million – as could easily take up the entire police manhours available. One detective sums up the problem by saying that the police are so overwhelmed by the mass criminality of the average citizen that they lack the time, the energy and the facilities to go after the bigger fish. In fact they do go after the big 'professionals'. This means that in the day-to-day work of the criminal police, investigation of the large-scale well-planned enterprises of the 'professional' type take up the biggest part of the police resources, if one takes into account not the entire police organisation but the single specialised departments such as the Burglary Department, the

Fraud Squad, the Forgery Squad, etc. The fact that these big jobs take several weeks to follow through has the consequence that the bulk of the smaller offences are in the main recorded only, not thoroughly investigated, and mostly remain officially 'unsolved'. The main burden of major crime falls on the police of the large cities in which the incidence of both general and major crime is comparatively high; the metropolis of Frankfurt, with its neighbouring regions, which may fairly be called the economical centre of Germany, has a particularly flourishing crime industry.

According to police estimates the number of large-scale full-time criminals ranges from 60 to 200 in the big cities; there is a much larger number of criminals of lesser stature who exhibit 'professional' characteristics to some degree, but who are much less skilful and successful than the operators of the first rank. The number of these latter − i.e. very successful major property criminals − in the Federal Republic as a whole might be between 1,000 and 2,000. In addition there are a great many more less successful multiple recidivists, who might be given the title suggested by Mack of 'full-time prisoners' (Mack, 1964); for example the files of the German police agencies contain nearly 15,000 so-called 'dangerous and habitual criminals'. Of these the great majority are neither dangerous nor professional; about 30-40 per cent are continually caught and convicted.[7]

Types of full-time criminal activity

The typology of 'professional' crime develops and varies directly with the expansion and ramifications of the economy. The ordinary petty or middle-weight criminal usually takes whatever he finds and goes on to look for a customer after the completion of the crime. The 'professional' plans ahead, taking into account the conditions of the 'market' and the demands of the 'customers' on the analogy of market research and business forecasting. One reservation must be added about the changing varieties of major crime. Fundamentally there is nothing new in the forms taken by high-level crime. There is hardly anything which has not been known to the police on one or other occasion or in one or other period, going back a long time; what is new concerns the method and the scale of criminal enterprises in recent decades.

Since 'professional' crime may be regarded to a certain extent as following the pattern of legitimate business life (it is oriented towards the making of profits, it follows the rules of supply and demand, it is based on more exact calculation and planning, and it seeks to ensure the lowest possible risk and to maintain stable economic exchange relationships) it follows almost automatically that the goods in which it deals are those which provide the higher standards of living, including luxury living, which have come to be regarded as a necessity by the citizens of an increasingly prosperous society. A conspicuous example of such luxury consumption is the automobile. The branch of 'professional' crime which deals with the illegal acquisition and sale of this commodity has grown bigger and more important since the mid 1950s. Basic conditions of lucrative crime are ideally fulfilled by the large expensive motor car: it is of great value, it can be acquired easily, it can be moved quickly away, and it is easy to transform its appearance and so to sell it on the international market with relatively little risk. About 6,000 of the 60,000 motor vehicles stolen every year in the German Federal Republic are never recovered. The majority of the 6,000 are stolen and disposed of by certain well-organised 'professional' groups with good international connections. The amount made away with every year by these groups comes to more than 50 million DM.[8]

A major criminal trade is carried on in the luxury goods of the clothing industry — furs, expensive leather goods, other high-priced clothing. This trade is fed by a highly efficient system of burglary and theft, including shoplifting, which works almost entirely to order. The stolen commodities — at a price of 10,000 DM or more per item — are taken over by a ring of receivers-and-concealers who have close relations with their opposite numbers in neighbouring countries (Schröder, 1970). They have access to factories controlled by other criminal or near-criminal associates where these goods are partially or totally transformed, in the same way as expensive cars are given a 'new look', and finally brought back on to the regular market.

A lesser specialism is that of those highly skilled criminals who make large profits out of the stealing of antiques, sacred art objects, paintings and other works of art. In recent years these specialised groups have systematically burglarised castles and manor-houses (the objective here is historical weapons); others have concentrated on the baroque churches of Southern Germany (stealing statues and wood carvings); others furnish wealthy businessmen with lists of 'original' paintings by well-known artists — examples are Velasquez, Tiepolo, Titian — which are in fact very good imitations, produced to order. Only this year a ring of criminals was detected who had earned about a million DM by these activities. In only very few cases it was possible to produce enough evidence to convict the criminals.

The forgery and counterfeiting of travellers' cheques, bank orders, and other monetary instruments has increased to a striking extent (Hoeveler,

1963, pp. 67-81; Kallenborn, 1960, pp. 131-8; Steinke, 1971, pp. 237-72).

Along with all this the usual traditional forms of high-level predatory crime go on, though these do not have the same rate of increase and, qualitatively speaking, do not present the police with problems of unusual difficulty; examples are safe-cracking, burglary of private residences, skilled pocket-picking, confidence tricks, and sneak-in thieving. What is new and original in these age-old criminal practices can be summed up as the greatly increased mobility of the criminal groups, the systematic international teamwork and the more elaborate division of labour of which they are capable, the elements mentioned above of market research and market forecasting, the system of divided responsibilities and of secrecy between the different levels of the organisation — guarding against the wholesale detection and convictions of the criminals — and, especially, the sophistication and versatility displayed by the criminals in the specific operations, in a wide range of the criminal objectives, and in the lucrative investment of the ill-gotten gains.

Criminal personality and criminal behaviour

There exists little or nothing in the way of scientifically exact knowledge of the 'professional' criminal personality. There are good general grounds for the suspicion — although this is not yet provable — that many of the first-class 'professionals' confine themselves to the role of background director, and are never directly involved in the criminal act itself.[9] This means that they are practically never detected by the police and therefore never convicted. It follows that they are not accessible to police observation. It is also the case that those of them who have been convicted have likewise never been subjected to psychological study by specialist students of personality.

The interviews conducted by the author produced however some useful general police impressions of a psychological kind based on what might be termed single case studies. According to these observations, the successful professional usually displays none of the 'abnormal' characteristics which some therapeutically oriented researchers are disposed to attribute to them. On the contrary, they exhibit a high degree of practical intelligence and business capacity in their chosen field of operation. They have a good grasp of reality, a power of emotional detachment in relation to other people and to the police, a well-developed self-interest enlightened enough to satisfy Jeremy Bentham, and — in strong contrast to the typical recidivist — the ability to use the money they acquire in an economically

D

efficient manner. Terms such as 'psychic disturbance', 'abnormal aptitude' or 'psychopath' seem to be quite out of place in this field of human activity.

The dress and manner of the international specialists, as of the high-level 'professionals' inside their respective countries, strike a new note, incompatible with the usual picture of the traditional recidivist; they dress well and exclusively but without ostentation; they live and comport themselves as to the manner born in the most expensive hotels, they move around in expensive cars or, more usually, by plane, their manners are good, and they often have a fair command of a number of languages (Schröder, 1970, pp. 78-80; Hoeveler, 1966). These observations refer of course only to those who occupy the highest level of the criminal hierarchy: the lesser operators, those who actually commit the crimes, are to be classed socially with the 'blue collar worker'.

The behaviour of the leading 'professionals' is marked by very little in the way of overt violence. The reasons for this are clear. Violence attracts the attention of the public and of the police and so interference with the smooth course of criminal business. In any direct confrontation with the police the use of violence is restricted, and depends entirely on the circumstances of the situation. Most criminals carry a gun as a 'status symbol'. But they only use it when the risk of detection is minimal. A change may be coming over the scene as regards the use of guns; it is said that younger criminals are disposed to shoot without much thought for possible consequences. In general the problem of increasing violence, including the use of firearms, is much bigger in the case of ordinary criminals than in that of the 'professionals'.

Evidence gathered from detected cases of high-level major crime suggests a fairly rapid rise of violence *inside* criminal circles. Some of this centres — the routine is familiar to students of USA syndicated crime — on blackmailing and other rackets within the *milieu,* combined with the intimidation and 'execution' of gang members suspected of treachery.

New types of *milieux*

'Professional' criminals are high-level members of the *milieu* which is to be found in the larger cities. This *milieu* is not to be indentified with the so-called 'Altstadt' (Downtown): those quarters and precincts in or near city centres where all kinds of outsiders and deviants get together. In Frankfurt and elsewhere, the sector of the *milieu* occupied by the outstanding 'professional' includes the international hotels patronised by the wealthy classes (although neither the ordinary guest nor the hotel management may be aware of this). It is usually difficult to distinguish the high-level 'professional' criminal from the wealthy businessman; they have a comparable standard of living and much the same level of income. This use of the term *milieu* is of course a departure from the old territorial concept of 'criminal area'; it is now a network of individuals and clusters of individuals dispersed through an urban region (see Mack, 1964, page 43).

This non-territorial *milieu* has a rather more distinct class structure than that of non-criminal society. The lower levels are occupied by the small-scale recidivists and habitual criminals who work as individuals or in small groups and spend the money they get as fast as they get it. These individuals act without much forethought and as a result spend most of their time in jail. They are dismissed with contempt by the real 'professionals', who call them 'eierdiebe' (egg thieves).

On the next level there are the small-time traditional predators — safe-breakers are a good example — who mix mainly with people at their own level and are clearly to be distinguished from the ordinary petty thief. It is the general opinion of the police that criminals at this level are tending to become employees of their criminal superiors, and are more and more being required to carry out special jobs for agreed payments. This has advantages for both parties: the front-line criminal gets a guaranteed income, and the people who give the orders can usually escape the consequences of failure especially when they use the system of hush-money as a further safeguard.

The highest *milieu* level is occupied by organisers of the big jobs. Their main task is to put up the necessary money to carry out the detailed planning, and to select the control personnel who are responsible in their turn for the selection of the actual operators. In some of the cities the police find it to be the case that these top-level criminals tend to form specialised groups or branches, each branch having its own preferred meeting place, its own distinctive modes of behaviour, even its own special language; they have in common however that they all preserve a certain distance between themselves and the lower categories of criminal. But this specialisation and aloofness is confined to the top level; those who operate in the 'front line' are to a large extent versatile all-rounders who operate in continually changing groups.

It should be emphasised that the organisation in the upper echelons of the criminal *milieu* is loosely structured. It nevertheless holds together quite well with the system of informal business relationships and acquaintances, and leakage of information to the police occurs only very seldom. This does not mean that there is a formal 'code of silence'; even if such a code ever existed, it is adhered to at present only inside small groups of criminals. At the middle levels, occupied by the actual predators, the police find it comparatively easy to pull in all of those directly concerned in an operation once they have caught one of them. More often than not the one who is caught will 'fink' (inform) so as to obtain an advantage in bargaining with his captors; also and mainly because he is certain that any of the others in his position would certainly inform. The top-level 'professionals' avoid the dangers implicit in this looser criminal morality by the system of secrecy referred to above. In this system the operator knows only the people directly above him, and even then he knows little more than the nickname or the appearance of the contact. Consequently there is not much he can inform about.

High degree of immunity?

Many of the policemen spoken to, and also members of the judiciary with whom we talked, inclined to the opinion that not only the top-level criminals but also those in the higher intermediate levels are less easily caught nowadays than in the past. They have learned to plan well in advance, they take measures against detection, they have learned how to cover their tracks to a much greater extent than in the past, they pay more attention to the disposal and sale of the goods they have stolen, they move them over great distances, and so on. Even when detected they 'know their rights' as accused persons; they buy the very best defence counsel; they have studied how to influence the court and the prosecution in their favour.

These at any rate are the impressions to be derived from our discussions. Other social scientists who have the advantage of detachment and objectivity in so far as they have not attempted to study this special subject, are disposed to query the 'fixing' skill of the modern high-level criminal, and to regard the 'uncatchable background organiser' as a myth devised to excuse the low clear-up figures achieved by the police in the field of major property crime. They could be right. This matter is one to be settled only by research, carried out with the same degree of care and skill as goes into the planning of the major criminal operations of the present day.

Table 8.1
Germany (GFR): selected major crimes reported to the police, 1955, 1965 and 1970 (rates per 100,000 population)

Crime	Number of reported offences and rates						Percentage increase of rates		
	1955		1965		1970		1965 over 1955	1970 over 1965	1970 over 1955
	No.	Rate	No.	Rate	No.	Rate			
(1) Murder, manslaughter	371	0.7	482	0.8	779	1.3	+14.3	+62.5	+85.7
(1a) Murder and manslaughter (+ attempts)	927	1.8	1,556	2.6	2,403	3.9	+44.4	+50.0	+116.6
(2) Felonious woundings	26,824	51.4	30,403	51.5	37,895	61.6	+0.2	+18.6	+18.9
(3) Rape	4,574	8.8	5,923	10.0	6,889	11.2	+13.6	+12.0	+27.3
(4) Robbery, forcible extortion	3,685	7.1	7,655	13.0	13,230	21.5	+83.1	+65.4	+202.8
(5) Breaking and entering	136,345	261.3	336,988	570.8	646,325	1,050.8	+118.4	+84.1	+302.1
(6) Larceny (simple)	440,274	834.6	697,969	1,182.2	903,369	1,468.7	+41.6	+24.2	+76.0
All selected offences (1-6)	612,629	1,174.0	1,080,494	1,830.1	1,610,111	2,617.2	+55.9	+43.0	+122.9
Crimes known to the police*	1,575,310	3,018.0	1,789,319	3,031.0	2,413,586	3,924.0	—	+29.5	—

*Road traffic offences: 1955 included, 1965 and 1970 excluded.

Source: *Polizeiliche Kriminalstatistik für die Bundesrepublik Deutschland,* Jhge 1955, 1965 and 1970; (percentage increase calculated by the author).

Table 8.2
Germany (GFR): selected property crimes reported to the police, 1960, 1965 and 1970 (rates per 100,000 population)

	Number of offences/rates/clearing up									Percentage increase of rates		
	1960			1965			1970			1970 over 1965	1965 over 1960	1970 over 1960
	No.	Rate	% Cl.	No.	Rate	% Cl.	No.	Rate	% Cl.			
(1) Breaking and entering												
(a) Banks, post offices, etc.	774	1.4	38.6	1,038	1.8	31.4	1,061	1.7	36.7	−5.6	+28.6	+21.4
(b) Premises, flats, etc.	22,741	40.9	40.5	34,251	58.0	36.1	55,908	90.9	33.8	+56.7	+41.8	+122.2
(c) Factories, stores, shops, etc.	57,712	103.8	35.6	104,928	177.7	31.6	167,339	272.1	31.4	+53.1	+71.2	+162.1
(d) All offences (B.+E.)	195,416	351.6	35.1	336,988	570.8	28.7	646,325	1,050.8	24.8	+184.1	+62.3	+198.9
(2) Larceny (simple theft)												
(a) From department stores	—	—	—	53,344	93.8	95.6	147,315	239.5	96.3	+155.3	—	—
(b) From motor vehicles	—	—	—	131,818	223.3	22.2	212,726	345.8	18.8	+54.9	—	—
(c) Pocketpicking	7,699	13.9	24.6	9,763	16.5	28.3	11,229	18.3	29.3	+10.9	+10.9	+31.7
(d) All offences (L.)	659,617	1,186.9	34.3	697,969	1,182.2	35.0	903,369	1,468.7	39.3	+24.2	−0.4	+23.8
(3) Motor-vehicle theft*	119,433	214.9	26.8	53,270	90.2	33.2	78,782	128.1	35.8	+42.0	—	—

* 1960: all motor vehicles; 1965, 1970: cars only.

Source: as Table 8.1.

Table 8.3
Nordrhein-Westfalen (Germany)*: damages, selected offences reported to the police, 1969 only

	1	2	3	4	5	6		7	
Crime	Number reported	Attempt or no damage	DM 1 - 99	DM 100 - 999	DM 1,000 - 9,999	DM 10,000 - 49,999		DM 50,000 and more	
	No.	%of(1)	%of(1)	%of(1)	%of(1)	No.	%of(1)	No.	%of(1)
Robbery and forcible extortion	3,516	19.8	47.9	27.3	3.7	34	1.0	11	0.30
Robbery in the open street	2,267	17.8	52.8	27.1	2.0	4	0.2	1	0.05
Bank robbery (holdups)	272	36.4	12.5	25.4	15.2	21	7.7	8	2.90
Breaking and entering	135,119	14.4	32.5	46.4	6.2	528	0.4	81	0.10
B.+ E. into factories, stores, etc.	28,036	23.1	27.3	37.3	11.1	294	1.0	55	0.20
B. + E. into banks, post offices, etc.	216	50.0	24.5	16.2	4.6	9	4.2	1	0.50
Car theft	26,369	26.5	4.0	22.9	44.4	427	2.1	22	0.10
Theft from shop-windows (jewels, furs, watches, etc.)	2,229	16.5	25.8	43.6	12.8	26	1.2	3	0.10
Fraud	42,404	3.8	48.6	34.3	11.7	464	1.1	113	0.30
relating to grants of credit, etc.	15,530	2.2	38.3	46.3	12.2	130	0.9	21	0.10
relating to cash, borrowing of money, etc.	9,663	3.7	36.3	31.2	18.7	172	1.8	34	0.30
relating to selling or constructing of premises, flats, etc.	229	11.8	3.9	12.7	37.1	55	24.0	24	10.50

*Nordrhein-Westfalen: the largest federal 'Land' of Germany, population: 17,039,400.

Source: *Polizeiliche Kriminalstatistik für die Bundesrepublik Deutschland, Jhge 1969*; hrsg. Landeskriminalamt NW; Düsseldorf, 1970.

Table 8.4

Germany (GFR): crimes reported to police

(1) (a) All large towns (100,000–500,000 population) (b) German Federal Republic — 1955, 1960, 1965, 1969

(2) Cities (500,000+) 1969 only (rate per 100,000 population)

	1955	1960	1965	1969
(a) Towns				
Total population	17,220,000	18,675,000	19,590,000	19,625,000
Crimes total*	691,704	960,736	928,656	1,135,967
Crimes, rate (per 100,000)*	4,017	5,144	4,741	5,789
Larceny, rate (per 100,000), in part	1,858	2,565	2,945	3,661
Breakings, rate (per 100,000), in part	446	586	995	1,305
(b) German Federal Republic				
Total population	52,189,800	55,576,100	59,040,600	60,840,000
Crimes total*	1,575,310	2,034,239	1,789,319	2,217,966
Crimes, rate (per 100,300)*	3,018	3,660	3,031	3,645
Larceny, rate (per 100,300) in part	1,105	1,539	1,753	2,236
Breakirgs, rate (per 100,000) in part	261	571	571	769

City, etc.	Population	Crimes Total	Crimes Rate	Larceny, in part Rate	Breakings, in part Rate
Berlin (West)	2,135,000	158,976	7,424	4,378	1,699
Hamburg (Land)	1,820,000	124,839	6,859	4,367	1,487
München	1,325,000	84,742	6,506	3,603	1,404
Köln	860,000	49,416	5,733	4,044	1,731
Bremen (Land)	755,000	49,413	6,542	4,213	1,164
Essen	700,000	29,979	4,294	2,674	1,164
Düsseldorf	685,000	33,087	4,845	3,265	1,136
Frankfurt	665,000	55,956	8,389	5,543	2,279
Dortmund*	805,000	33,708	(4,187)	(2,655)	(924)
Stuttgart	620,000	32,760	5,275	3,039	1,358
Hannover	520,000	30,342	5,779	3,872	1,479
Towns (see 1a)	19,625,000	1,135,967	5,789	3,661	1,305
German Federal Republic (see 1b)	60,840,000	2,217,966	3,645	2,236	769

* 1955 and 1960, road traffic offences included in crimes total.
1965 and 1969, road traffic offences excluded from crimes, etc. total.

*Dortmund here includes Lünen and Castrop-Rauxel.

Sources

(1) Population: cf. *Statistisches Jahrbuch für die Bundesrepublik Deutschland*, Jhge 1956 ff.

(2) Crimes: for cities over 500,000 inhabitants, data obtained from local police authorities by personal request; for all large towns and Germany cf. *Polizeiliche Kriminalstatistik für die Bundesrepublik Deutschland*, Jhge 1955, 1960, 1965, and 1969; hrsg. vom Bundeskriminalamt Wiesbaden; Wiesbaden, 1956, 1961, 1966, and 1970.

Calculation of rates: some of the rates given above are as quoted from the official sources; others are as calculated by the writer.

These tables give some comparative data illustrating the general rise in reported crime in the 1960s in the German Federal Republic. It was not practicable to get figures other than those for *all* crimes reported; it is therefore not possible to trace whether the German Federal Republic shows the same more rapid rise in the property crimes above a certain figure as regards value of goods stolen, as that reported for the United Kingdom in the table on p. 50 above.

Notes

1   This account is based upon interviews, supplemented by later correspondence. The interviews held with the Federal Police Agency at Wiesbaden (Bundeskriminalamt), the eleven State Police Agencies (Landeskriminalämter) of the eleven States of the Federal German Republic, the Central Criminal Police Agencies of some of the larger cities, for example Frankfurt, Düsseldorf, Hannover, Köln, München and Stuttgart, and the Police Institute of Hiltrup (near Münster). In all more than fifty officials contributed, including departmental specialists.

Those discussions which concerned the rise of business-type crime in the Federal German Republic, particularly as committed by full-time criminals, have been incorporated in chapter 2 above.

A monograph on the theme of this chapter has been written by Mr Kerner and published by the Bundeskriminalamt Wiesbaden under the title *Professionelles und Organisiertes Verbrechen* (Kerner, 1973).

2   For the long-term trends in crime figures see e.g. Rangol, 1960, pp. 590-6; 1961, pp. 129-43 and 1962, pp. 157-75.

3   Cf. Göppinger, 1971, pp. 374-6. See also Amelunxen, 1967, pp. 22-8; Hoberg, 1958, pp. 143-52; Landmann, 1959, pp. 35-6.

4   On the social structure of Germany see e.g., Claessens, Klönne and Tschoppe, 1965; Fürstenberg, 1967.

5   For the first years after World War II see Bader, 1949; pp. 128-40; Holle, 1966, 1968; Rangol, 1971*a*, pp. 224-8, 1971*b*, pp. 344-51.

6   On robbery, esp. bank robbery cf. Bauer, 1970; Gleisner, Lorenz, May and Schubert, 1972; Polizei-Institut Hiltrup 1966, 1969, 1971; Würtenberger and Herren, 1970. Regarding the 'heavy' repeaters see Ender, 1972, pp. 26-9.

7   See for instance Goedecke, 1962; Hellmer, 1961; Naucke, 1962, pp. 84-97; Weidermann, 1969; Wetterich, 1963. Comparative figures on Switzerland: Brückner, 1971.

8   Cf. Achert, 1969, pp. 119-22; Blanek and Holzenbecher, 1970, pp. 546-50; Lissy, 1970, pp. 339-42; Schröder, 1970. pp. 67-96. On car theft

in France in general see e.g. Robert, Bombet and Saudinos, 1970, p. 629; Rolland, 1970, pp. 787-802. On the American scene cf. Task Force Report: *Science and Technology 1967,* pp. 48-51. See also pp. 109-10 below.

9 This police extension of the term 'professional' to include the background organiser is of course queried elsewhere in these pages (see p. 177).

9 Denmark and Sweden

The main finding of this paper can be put very briefly, following the precedent of the celebrated chapter-heading and chapter quoted by Thomas de Quincey from an eighteenth-century treatise on the natural history of Iceland. The chapter-heading reads: 'Snakes in Iceland'. The chapter itself consists of just six words 'There are no snakes in Iceland'. Likewise with 'Major crime in Scandinavia'. There are certain reservations to be made, which are of great interest for the study of the crime industry in Europe, but by and large it is the case that there is no major organised crime, no highly developed criminal 'profession', in the Scandinavian countries. A 1963 finding to this effect by Sveri and Werner is reported on p. 147 below.

Professor Nils Christie explains why in a recent Council of Europe publication. He points out that the four countries are all rather small, with the following populations (in millions of inhabitants): Denmark, 4.7; Finland, 4.6; Norway, 3.8; Sweden, 7.8; (Iceland, 0.2). They are also, he goes on, easily 'overseen' countries. 'Small and easily overseen countries give reduced possibilities for 'big crime', particularly organised crime.'

Professor Christie mentions also, modestly enough, that the Scandinavian countries combine this lack of large-scale and complex criminality with a considerable development of criminological enquiry – and, one would add, of experimentation in penal practice. The absence of a formidable major-crime problem permits 'a slightly more relaxed atmosphere around the crime question than in countries nearer to the big money. A tradition of non-violence – except in Finland – adds to this, and gives some freedom for at least some experimental *thinking* around these matters. Smallness combined with relatively highly developed systems of social book-keeping creates also some particular possibilities for research' (Council, 1971, pp. 255-6).

Admirable accounts of Scandinavian criminological research are available in a number of publications, including Council of Europe publications. Current research into 'crime industry' topics are referred to elsewhere in this study. The present paper is based entirely on discussions held during a brief visit to Copenhagen and Stockholm in the summer of 1970. These discussions were with police detectives actively concerned with the pursuit and arrest of criminals, prison governors, central government administrators, and criminologists. Doctor Preben Wolf of the

University of Copenhagen, and Professor Sveri of the University of Stockholm, gave valuable guidance based on their own original studies into aspects of the crime industry.

Discussion in both countries centred on two main themes; first, the comparative absence of major predatory crime, and a similar absence of syndicated crime *except in the shape of a thriving smuggling industry;* and second: the emergence of some striking examples of newer types of property crime — one being an increase in cheque and cheque card frauds; also some larger-scale instances of business-type crime *practised by businessmen.*

No successful major crime

Our Danish advisers were certain that Denmark has no professional crime in the ordinary sense of the word. They remarked particularly on the absence of *successful* major crime. The only people who approximate to the description of the professional criminal are those who, when they come out of prison, take to crime again to keep going. There are no known examples of background organisers or skilled front-line operators who continue to engage in criminal activity on a more or less full-time basis while avoiding imprisonment. (The avoidance of imprisonment, as already observed, is the only *verifiable* mark of criminal success.)

Current instances of aggressive predatory crime in Copenhagen were comparatively small in scale, and consisted of smash-and-grab attacks and armed robbery of banks and shops, conducted either by casual offenders or by the type of more persistent offender who is in and out of prison all of the time. As regards non-aggressive predatory crime, there was very little real trouble with pickpockets. There was some shoplifting, mostly practised by amateurs. On the other hand there was some evidence of a sporadic kind of organisation behind some of the shoplifters.

The impressions derived from discussions in Stockholm gave a rather different picture. It is broadly true of Sweden as of Denmark that there are unlikely to be many examples of full-time major criminals who stay out of prison most of the time. But there was a recognisable group of substantial 'heavy' operators — armed robbers and burglars — who had gained sufficient notoriety to be named in the Stockholm press that week as the 'Swedish Crime Company'. The Company, such as it was, was headed by a smallish group of 'top criminals' — a term used by each of my police informants — estimated variously as consisting of 10 or at most of 25 operators. (Here as elsewhere the calculation depends on the grading system used.) Seven of these distinctive figures had escaped from prison in that particular week.

In Stockholm, as distinct from Copenhagen, there were rather precise indications of a rising trend in property crime. In contradistinction to serious assaults, which had shown a downward trend since 1968, bank robberies were increasing — 524 in 1968, 545 in 1969, 325 in the first six months of 1970. Some of the bank robbers carried real guns. But in most cases in which guns were brandished the weapons were a fake. (The same was true of Copenhagen.)

A point made about Copenhagen was that while there was no successful *indigenous* major criminal there was a possibility that big international criminals might touch down there fairly regularly. In Stockholm the position was similar. An example given was shoplifting which here was conducted on a professional scale. But the 'real' professionals are foreigners, from Austria and Germany in the main, who may have a special organisation in Germany for receiving the proceeds of shoplifting in Sweden. This is not an outstanding feature of Scandinavian crime. Sweden like Denmark is outside the main current of international crime. But there was one export-import business of a criminal nature — that in stolen cars. One police informant estimated that about 20 or 30 persons in Sweden were involved in this trade. He held that Hamburg as well as Frankfurt was a German centre for stolen cars. A car could be stolen in Hamburg, moved to Lübeck, shipped to Sweden and sold there, reported to the customs and sold again, all very quickly.

Smuggling

The nearest Danish approximation to US-type 'organised crime' (which we have opted to call *syndicated* crime) is the smuggling of cigarettes and liquor. The term 'syndicated' is perhaps misleading. The smuggling industry was there before the syndicates and will doubtless outlive them, even in the USA. On the other hand *one* of the essential marks of syndicated crime, indeed its chief characteristic, is the illicit provision of forbidden or controlled commodities for which there is a strong economic demand; and this is the *whole* of smuggling. It is one of the more remarkable features of Scandinavian criminology that it has so far failed to include direct studies of smuggling in its unusually wide range of research activity. Failing such studies one must guess a little; for example, that the smuggling groups on the whole do nothing but smuggling as far as habitual criminal income-earning is concerned; they may be involved in some of the leisure activities of the Copenhagen or Stockholm *milieux,* such as these are, but they don't normally interact closely with practitioners of thieving and 'breaking' and the other traditional criminalities.

There are exceptions which prove this hypothetical rule. When on occasion the sea is frozen, so that the smugglers' ships are icebound, the result is an extensive increase inside Denmark of thefts of tobacco and alcohol. The smugglers still have their regular customers to supply so they turn to thieving when they can't get their supplies in the ordinary way.

The power-centre of Scandinavian smuggling is fiscal and political. Cigarettes and liquor are very heavily taxed in Denmark, less so in Sweden. The same goods can be bought cheaply in East Germany and Poland. Moreover these two countries do not subscribe to the familiar West European convention whereby cigarettes sold to ships' crews and passengers are strictly limited. Any such goods carried by the ship over and above the quota 'for selling on the voyage' must be listed on the cargo manifest and duly inspected and checked intact at the journey's end. Not so in East Germany and Poland: any ship can buy there as many cigarettes as the ship will hold without counting them part of the cargo.

Why do East Germany and Poland do this? The answer is that they don't — they allow it to be done. The smuggling industry is run mainly by Danes and Swedes who buy in Poland cigarettes made in Scandinavia and elsewhere and sold in Poland at a low price. They then transport them back to Denmark and sell them there at about half the Danish retail price. The profit on the deal is roughly 300 per cent. In Poland in 1970 500 DK bought a box of 10,000 cigarettes. In Denmark this box is sold, illicitly, at about 1,750 DK. To simplify the calculation: they buy the cigarettes at 1 DK for twenty and sell them at 3½ DK for twenty, which is just over half the legal price.

These are purely fiscal matters. The political angle is suggested by an answer to my question — why do the East German and Polish governments allow this to happen? Partly, I was told, because they want the Danish money, partly because in the long run the smuggling might damage the capitalist economy in Denmark and through Denmark the European capitalist economy. This latter is certainly a point, though hardly a strong one.

There was less interest in smuggling and less mention made of it in the Swedish discussions. Mainly by foreigners, said one policeman, and not important, mainly smuggling of liquor and cigarettes; some smuggling of gold and diamonds; a more recent development was smuggling in furs. One centre specially mentioned was the island of Gotland, which had a large-scale trade in spirits with East Germany.

There is a final point of interest to criminologists and sociologists of law. It was raised vigorously in the Danish discussions but caused little interest in Sweden. It concerns the relation between import and excise duties and indirect taxation on the one hand, and crime, particularly smuggling, on the other. Could and should the system of indirect taxation be organised so as to diminish the possibilities of criminal exploitation? Denmark finances its elaborate welfare services very largely out of indirect taxation, concentrated on those luxury commodities like liquor and cigarettes which public opinion permits to be heavily taxed. The answer was, emphatically, No. It is not desirable to alter the taxation system so as to catch more criminals. If one were to give top priority to an anti-criminal policy one would spread one's indirect taxation over a wide range of commodities and not concentrate on liquor and cigarettes. But this is not the kind of criterion by which taxation and social welfare policy are or should be determined. Sweden, as it happens, tends to demonstrate the relevance of the proposition. The Swedish indirect taxation system is much more evenly spread over the various commodities. While this is a result of quite other considerations it lessens the incentive to smuggling, and consequently Sweden's smuggling problem is less than that of Denmark.

A footnote to the magnitude of smuggling in Denmark is provided by the statutory penalties imposed. The top penalty is two years' imprisonment, the average sentence is six to eight months; most of the smugglers serve their six to eight months at more or less regular intervals.

All of the foregoing relates to smuggling of commodities other than drugs. This report is of course restricted to only a peripheral mention of the drug problem. But it is necessary, in any discussion of Scandinavian crime, to record that traffic in drugs is one of the more considerable issues requiring the attention of the law enforcement authorities.[1] A recent discussion of the matter observes as follows:

'Europe's pill smuggling is, in fact, concentrated almost entirely on Denmark and Sweden. The manufacture and distribution of pills in Scandinavia has long been rigorously controlled and the black markets of Stockholm, Gothenburg, Malmo and Copenhagen are unable to get their supplies locally. Moreover, these two countries have the most serious problem of drug addiction in Europe; Sweden has over 10,000 addicts . . . Denmark, has, according to a special report published early in 1969, 4,000 addicts, the majority of them dependent on amphetamines. The crossroads of the traffic to supply this Scandinavian black market is Copenhagen, because it is the best communications centre. Its airport handles nearly ten times as much international traffic as Stockholm's . . . Apart from the local Danish trade, 90% of the illegal drug supplies for Sweden pass this way.' (Green, 1969 p. 88).

Business-type crime

The Scandinavian countries may have little to offer in the field of major conventional crime. The picture as regards business-type crime is very different. The increase in cheque frauds and in cheque-card frauds in these countries in the last two or three decades is a matter of first-class police and criminological interest. In the deeper reaches, where the bigger fish swim, some of their more versatile businessmen have produced remarkable instances of fraud and/or currency manipulation on a large scale. We have quoted two examples above (pp. 15-16). This is not in any sense evidence of a colossal plunge into crime by large sections of the business leadership of the Scandinavian countries. The precise relative magnitude of the phenomenon is still to be estimated. But even as things stand, these northern latitutdes have provided some very good textbook examples, from Ivar Kreuger to the present day, of criminal ingenuity in this comparatively recently opened-up field of enquiry.

Copenhagen and Stockholm have also some instances of large-scale business-type crime practised by full-time criminals, persons with long-standing criminal records. An Englishman and an Australian, both based on Stockholm, had been profiting in the 1960s by the gullibility of investors, using a number of ingenious devices. But this is common form in all capital cities.

Cheque fraud

In the last twenty years or so it has become the rule to pay wages by cheque in both Denmark and Sweden. This is now the practice in all national and local government employment and in the majority of the big private undertakings. One result is that cheques and cheque-books are themselves a commodity in the 'grey market', and are bought and sold, enabling a large number of people to go in for cheque frauds in a small way. Another consequence is a considerable change in the criminal status-system. The big safe-breakers used to be the criminal elite. But their skill has been devalued by the change from cash to cheques, so that the safe-breakers have turned to cheque frauds: they now steal and forge money orders and cheques.

No systematic estimate of losses through cheque frauds was available. A steady increase in Denmark over the past 15 years had been accentuated only in the last year, coincidentally with a new arrangement in the banks whereby any bank in Denmark will cash cheques for any other Danish bank up to a maximum of 300 DK per cheque. A loss figure of 2½ million

DK was mentioned for 1969. A more precise measure was given for Stockholm by Professor Sveri, who had made a survey of internal cheque forgeries for the two months January and February 1965. In that period 209 forged cheques had been passed involving 600,000 Swedish kronor.

Cheque stealing and forging have developed also on an international scale, part of a wider movement of international currency fraud and manipulation.

Note on smuggling: changes since 1970

The Danish smuggling scene has undergone a marked change since 1970. The kind of smuggling by small fast boats described above almost stopped some time after Foreign Office discussions between Denmark on the one hand and Poland and East Germany on the other. It is also a fact that the availability of the same kinds of contraband, especially cigarettes of the same brands, has not decreased on the black market — at least not much and not for long.

It is now revealed by the police that groups of the same well-known smugglers who formerly used the small fast boats now do this smuggling by sealed lorries or trucks allegedly carrying other goods for transit. The contraband comes over the border by land (the Danish—West German border and prior to that the other West German borders) or by ordinary ferry boats across the Baltic from West Germany to Denmark, in trucks supposed to carry and sometimes actually carrying legal cargoes of building material, machine parts, etc. It comes from Poland, East Germany or Czechoslovakia, and the cigarettes are the usual Danish-manufactured and exported cigarettes that are thus illegally re-imported and sold on the black market in the usual places by the same people. [*Dr Preben Wolf, personal communication.*]

Notes

1 We have just received a copy of an important paper by Esbjörn Esbjörnson entitled 'International criminality in Sweden', which we understand will appear in vol. III of *Scandinavian Studies in Criminology* (edited by Nils Christie, forthcoming). This paper includes an authoritative statement of the drug situation in Sweden.

10 International Criminal Networks[1]

It has been said that in present-day Europe 'He who desires to win the acknowledged status of a good "professional criminal" must be able to prove, to the satisfaction of the criminal community in his own country, that he has "worked" several times in a foreign land.' His achieved prestige is demonstrated, for example, in his being allowed to meet 'prominent persons' in certain places; and he along with them can look down on the lesser fry (known in Germany as *Eierdiebe* or 'egg thieves'; and in the Netherlands as *Kartoffeldiebe* or 'potato thieves').

The definition given here is slightly off-centre. It is certain that more and more criminals are tempted to cross frontiers to commit offences abroad. But (a) there are big criminals in Europe who confine their activities within their own country, and (b) it would be an exaggeration to call anyone who has committed a crime abroad an 'international' criminal. Here at Interpol it is held that a criminal becomes 'international' when three countries at least are affected by his activities: e.g. an Italian living in France and who has committed a crime in Spain; a Swiss who has committed crimes in Germany and in Belgium. Similarly, the title of international criminal is given to those who take part in criminal activities which by definition have international consequences: manufacture of spurious foreign currency, illegal drug traffic. (See note 1, p. 112)

'International operation' as such is a phenomenon well known to police departments. From 1923 onwards, the central police authorities in the European countries joined the International Criminal Police commission (ICPO-Interpol) to try to find better methods of prevention and better methods to fight against the so-called itinerant offenders. These were practitioners of traditional property crime. Examples are specialised pickpockets, who are to be found in all the large congresses, conferences, trade fairs, etc.; confidence men; hotel swindlers; sneak-thieves; and lastly counterfeiters (Lindenau, 1906; Palitzsch, 1926). These specialists were usually lone wolves and to a certain extent marginal men, exotic flowers in the large garden of everyday crime. They were well known to the police authorities of the different countries through the Interpol machinery. The numbers remained fairly constant over a long period. There are still such offenders going about today, and they give the police a lot of trouble from time to time. One example is that of certain lone-wolf burglars originating in Austria and working in Switzerland, Germany and the Netherlands. But the broad picture is changing. The number of offenders has become considerably larger, they come from all European countries; the operations they conduct are more varied in comparison with former times, most striking of all, the miscreants are no longer marginal men but are often central figures in a business-type and profit-oriented criminal enterprise. The salient point is probably the increase in numbers and the increase in organisation. (The term 'organisation' here is used with reference to predatory as distinct from syndicated crime.) More and more groups and gangs are springing up, showing on the one hand new methods of joint operation and on the other a more intricate division of labour.

The greater ease of travel and the increased facilities for international contacts offered by modern life have benefited the criminal no less than the law-abiding sections of the community. The internationalisation of business and the absence of formalities at the frontiers have also served to increase the international activities of criminals.

There is a big range of types of group. The following classifications are not intended to give a fixed or rigid impression, but only to bring out significant differences. Here are five main classifications; the number could be increased.

1   Closed national groups, who occasionally cross the border into neighbouring countries, perform planned offences, and then return to their own country.
2   Closed national groups and gangs who have several contact-persons in neighbouring countries working as leaders or providing information. Typical operations are burglary of all types, car theft, smuggling. Of special interest are the tobacco smugglers of Denmark (chapter 9) whose contact men and accomplices in Poland and Eastern Germany do not violate the law, and are therefore neither 'criminal' nor 'professional'.

We have no information about this Denmark–Poland etc. traffic. As far as we are concerned the smuggling of cigarettes, which is very important, is centred above all in Italy.

Of special interest are the settled criminals operating mainly in such cities as Cologne and Frankfurt in Germany and Paris and Marseilles in France. We are informed that these people have an extraordinary attachment to their native city — they cross into other countries only for short periods of time, carry out one job at a time, avoid close contact with the criminals of the other country, and get back home again as quickly as possible.
3   Mixed groups in which one nationality is dominant. Depending on which country the group is operating in, it uses the appropriate indigenous

106

number as guide and adviser. This type of group is widespread and works in many fields of crime, especially in burglary.

4   *Ad hoc* groups, well mixed as regards nationality, and chosen for their complementary skills. These get together for a particular operation only and break up afterwards. There is some circumstantial evidence that these groups are recruited in part from a numerous and changing flow of transitory individuals, and in part from a kind of general reservoir of European experts which has a somewhat limited range, but which supplies different selections of operators for different operations.

This concept of ad hoc *groups is generally valid. Forged currency operations are conducted by two sub-groups: on the manufacturing side — the actual forging process — the qualifications required are technical. As regards the putting of the forged currency into circulation — the qualification here is more general — the circulation groups comprise a great diversity of nationalities and also of criminal trades: e.g. a burglar or a thief will augment his income by circulating spurious currency. The only thing the members of these groups have in common is the source of supply.*

5   Groups of itinerant offenders (tricksters, sneak-thieves, counterfeiters of travellers' cheques, 'picture-handlers', etc.). These are often non-European. They arrive, for instance, by plane from South America, rent an expensive car and go quickly through several countries, getting out very speedily at the end of the operation with their loot, also by plane. They are usually of elegant appearance, they are well versed in languages, and they are good judges of people and situations.

We offer here a note on negotiators of travellers' cheques, stolen or counterfeit. These divide into two categories: (a) groups conducting important negotiations: these sub-divide into teams of two persons; (b) individuals. The big teams of past years came from South America and Europe (Italy above all). The former confined their fraudulent activities almost entirely to the European countries, while the latter extended their operations to the Middle East, the Far East and certain African countries.

The 'peak period' for these ventures used to be the holiday or tourist season. This is no longer the case; they are evenly spread nowadays throughout the entire year.

This traffic is no longer mainly in travellers' cheques stolen from tourists; it is now much more a matter of stolen blank cheques or counterfeited cheques. This enables the operator to dispense with the risk involved in having to forge the signatures required by the stolen cheques and to assume the corresponding identity in the actual transaction: he can instead make up a signature for himself at his convenience. (See also Aube, 1958; Hoeveler, 1963; Kallenborn, 1960; Steinke, 1971).

As a general rule none of these groups and types of groups is elaborately structured. They are rather loosely connected collectives which get together for particular projects and for a limited period of time, separating soon afterwards. This is to some extent a matter of personality — rivalries, jealousies, quarrels play a part — but it also has objective grounds. The organisation of the criminal business system exhibits the same powers of rapid adjustment and adaptation to the changing needs of the market as does its law-abiding counterpart. The ordinary run-of-the-mill criminal is like the law-abiding craftsman or businessman in one respect: if he is to achieve an adequate economic return he must specialise in one form or another of income-earning activity. The skill of the organiser consists in solving the problems of choosing, for each series of crimes, the most suitable specialist to form a functioning team. It often happens that he is not in a position to select particular individuals, but he knows where to go to get the information which will enable him to get the right kind of person without much delay. The general picture is one of continuously changing small groups of specialists, drawn from a relatively firm ground stock of offenders forming a large informal system of networks.

This is generally the case. However, it has been observed in certain fields, such as drug traffic or currency counterfeiting, that there are groups of rather stable composition, or which at least have a hard core which rarely takes in new elements.

What we have here in fact is a special type of 'European Community' which works on the whole more effectively (of course on a smaller scale) than the official European Economic Community (EEC). It is not, however, to be described as an organised system, with a firm hierarchy, precise rules and regulations, or an established method of settling disputes and keeping order. It is not a crime syndicate on the USA pattern, but rather a loose network of mutual acquaintanceships and friendships, informal connections, and local contacts. In the majority of cases this is quite sufficient for the tasks involved, and it has the additional advantage of providing a considerable measure of safety from police investigation. To give a clearer picture, an analogy with ordinary legal commercial affairs may be useful. International trade in vegetables, for example, functions very efficiently. There is a big turnover in goods and money and contracts are usually concluded punctually. This happens even though the 'organisation' is not firmly structured. There are a few firms with strongly regulated relationships amongst themselves, but otherwise the circle of people involved is often made up of persons who have little more than a writing table with a telephone as their office from which they make their contacts.

The criminal economic network is of great importance in the rapid

108

disposal of goods and realisation of assets. The hauls are often so extensive and the single items so valuable that they cannot be sold within their country of origin without fear of immediate discovery by the police. An exception to this rule is jewellery, which is very often taken out of its setting before being resold, especially extremely valuable items. In general the rapid movement of stolen goods over national frontiers is expedited by the deficiencies of the present system of teamwork between the law-enforcement agencies of the European countries in respect of the following-up and prosecution of crimes. They feel, with good reason, quite safe when they can quickly disperse the goods into another country. With especially valuable items they go outside Europe altogether. The German police authorities have traced contact-lines to South America.

The deficiencies concern the courts more than the police. In fact, current systems of police co-operation make it possible to send out a general and almost immediate alert to European police forces. The procedure allows rapid contacts and the sending of police officers abroad. Criminals obviously take advantage of the distance which they put between the scene of the crime and the place where they take refuge, but police co-operation at European level greatly minimises this type of advantage.

For some goods definite 'trade-trails' have been developed. These naturally differ in durability and have no set passage. Everything is done according to the requirements of the market and the estimated degree of risk of police interception. These trails extend over a wide area. Recently the German police succeeded in discovering a group of more than fifty offenders, with many additional accomplices; this outfit had established bases which stretched from Stockholm to Istanbul via Frankfurt, Brussels and Milan.

Car theft is especially well organised. A widespread division of labour prevails; there are specialists for each single step. These specialists, who are residents in and nationals of different countries, act on precise orders from outside. The car theft system needs planners, document counterfeiters and forgers, technicians, motor mechanics for the alteration of vehicles, scouts, burglars and lorry drivers. The stolen vehicles are moved over big distances. Up to a few years ago the route from Germany through Austria and Yugoslavia into Turkey and the Lebanon was very popular. There are other routes between Sweden and the Netherlands as well as between Sweden and the German Federal Republic — these are two-way routes. The latest route to be developed is by ship to the USA. The teams who handle transport into the Middle East or into Scandinavian countries sometimes transport narcotics and firearms as well (Lissy, 1970; Schröder, 1970).

Agreed. This point is particularly well illustrated by a criminal enterprise which lasted through 1968 and 1969. There were involved 74 individuals belonging to three brands of car thieves and merchants, of German and Italian nationality, operating in Austria, Federal Germany, Italy and France. They were interested only in luxurious and very expensive cars. The thefts took place in the majority of cases in Kitzbühel (Austria), Munich, Rome and Paris. The cars were disguised in garages operated by accomplices of the thieves. The necessary papers were manufactured by two teams of forgers; vehicles supplied with these new documents were driven into other countries, offered for sale to certain wholesale car traders and sometimes even to individuals by means of newspaper advertising. The arrest of a garage proprietor in Kitzbühel led to the identification and then the arrest of the smaller operators. The growing mass of information obtained and exchanged between the national central offices of Interpol made it possible for the various services of the national police forces to identify and then to arrest the majority of the members of the three groups of thieves. A large proportion of the stolen vehicles were recovered, including 30 Mercedes, 38 Porsche and 7 of other makes, the Jaguar E model notably. This particular network was thus completely smashed.

In the case of jewellery, furs and other similar goods there appears to be a 'trade-trail' which leads from Germany to Brussels, from Brussels to Antwerp, and then via Spain to Italy, where special 'factories' have been set up in which the objects are processed and new articles manufactured which can then be sold legally. The best organised routes appear to be those of the drug trade. Here Germany is not only a 'user' country, but also a reloading point for imports from the East and export into neighbouring countries — above all to Scandinavia (via Munich, Frankfurt, Berlin and Hamburg). A large amount of amphetamine manufactured in Germany, the Netherlands or Italy goes to Scandinavia.[2] The German police recently discovered almost a thousand kilograms in a single consignment.

The receivers of stolen goods have always played an important part. The big receivers have established themselves in a central and almost entirely decisive position. This shows among other things that those thefts and burglaries which are planned to acquire specific properties ordered in advance, and other crimes which are carried out under precise orders, are becoming more and more important in the criminal enterprise system. This is indicated by the increasing frequency of cases where criminals, operating over a short period, and in different European countries, break into fur shops and steal particular pieces leaving other items of equal value untouched.

110

These remarks are not altogether clear. If the reference to receivers refers to the illegal traffic in narcotics, a more complete analysis would be necessary. Apart from this, as regards stolen commodities, there are certainly receivers, but these are usually local receivers, working in and with the local criminal market. But this does not mean that they are not carrying on any business with foreign criminals who are introduced or already known to them. We are not aware of the existence of receivers operating — in the full sense of the term — on an international scale.

Lines of communication between US criminals and above all the US syndicates on the one hand, and European crime on the other, do not appear to exist, or at least not on a large scale or permanently.

Agreed with one single exception. There are evidently from time to time connections between certain American criminals and certain European criminals. The impression one has is that these connections are temporary and occasional, a product of changing circumstances and of the individual situation of the persons in question. One simply cannot say that American organised crime (including here not only the syndicates but also the major predatory organisations) has powerful connections and exercises an important influence on European organised crime. The single exception? — the illegal traffic in narcotics.

The question of the possibility of the development in European countries of the US type of syndicated crime is dealt with elsewhere in this book, as is the question of the Sicilian Mafia. Here it may be permissible to mention the suggestion made by several informants that the Mafia might be trying to gain influence in other countries by blackmailing Italian migrant workers. On this, as in most questions about the Mafia, there is as yet no reliable information. But a relevant point was made by Mr Susini in our team discussions, concerning the situation which is developing at the present time in the large towns of Northern Italy. Here thousands of uprooted men from the South, searching for work, settle without permits, form a large proletariat and could — given a general failure to solve the consequent social problems — quickly furnish the material for the establishment of an 'ethnic bound' organised crime system of the US syndicated type. This could be on a small scale to start with, but might grow very quickly into something quite formidable.

The 'Mafia' phenomenon in Italy is in the main a very local affair which has spread outside its own part of Sicily, to develop a number of ramifications in the great cities of the Italian mainland, Rome and Milan. This is a typically Italian phenomenon which, up to the present time, had had no repercussions in other countries (except in the United States and to a small extent Canada).

111

Notes

1   This section has had the advantage of generous and precise annotation by Interpol. These annotations are inserted in italics at the appropriate points.

The examples and illustrations given derive mainly from the Federal Republic of Germany and from the Netherlands, but occasionally touch other countries as well.

2   See Bejerot, 1970 for amphetamine-addiction in Sweden; Fridberg, 1970, for the trade in amphetamines; Robert, Bombet and Saudinos, 1970, p. 638 ff., for heroin in France.

PART III

Special Topics

11 The Sicilian Mafia[1]

A main source of confusion in 'mafia' literature is the increasingly strong tendency, amounting to obsession, to attach the 'mafia' label to any example of organised criminal activity involving violence, intimidation, extortion and corruption. This tendency is to be found even in Italy itself. In fact, the authentic Mafia[2] is one particular phenomenon, originating and mainly located in the western regions of the island of Sicily.

This restriction is practically never observed. The mafia, strictly so-called, is usually confused and distorted by the nebulous mass of conceptions and misconceptions surrounding the so-called (American) Cosa Nostra. This is very well dealt with by Albini (1971). Albini's findings are broadly similar to those of Hess. The main confusion arises from equating the term 'mafia' with the notion of a huge organisation of international scope. But the word, in its indigenous sense, so to speak, stands not for an organisation but a certain form of conduct or mode of behaviour: 'mafia' is a synonym for 'mafia'-like behaviour. And that behaviour originates, as Susini stresses, in certain political and historical features peculiar to Sicily. It is a great mistake to discuss the mafia phenomenon without taking into account the structure of the society in which it appeared and appears; but it is a mistake that is almost universally made. The history of Sicily has been shaped by highly idiosyncratic factors — a long sequence of changing foreign dominations, the survival into modern times of a peculiar feudal structure and mode of exploitation, an exceptionally weak governmental bureaucracy through the centuries, producing in the last two centuries a profound distrust, amounting to hostility, on the part of the people towards all organs of the state. Hence the general acceptance of the mafia way of life with its informal anti-political system based on clan relationships and on patronage.

In so far as 'mafia' has a specific semantic content, it refers to the particular combination of aptitudes and achievements which make Sicily unique in Italian and indeed in European history: aptitude for managing the informal anti-political system, ability to maintain independence and self-government in the teeth of the opposition of the organs of the state, and above all the capacity to defend one's own dignity ('honour') at all costs. The chief ingredient of the concept is therefore a very special psychic attitude: a proud consciousness of the supreme value of the self-sufficient 'Ego', joined indissolubly with a feeling of chivalrous solidarity with the clan. It is to quote Susini, *uno modo di essere, di sentire è di operare* (a mode of being, of feeling and of behaving) closely linked with tradition deep rooted in Sicilian thinking and feeling.

One crucial consequence or feature of this special psychic attitude and moral code is that it is always and without exception incumbent on an *uomo d'onore* (man of honour) to seek revenge by his own efforts in any situation in which his personal integrity has been violated, or is considered by him to have been violated. This usually if not invariably means that he feels bound to use violence. Violence has a closely linked and equally important role: it is used to achieve and to uphold status. As Hess remarks:

> An essential constituent of mafia-like behaviour is the capacity to use power. The act of violence opens up the way to power. Failure or incapacity in this vital respect makes it impossible for a man to meet the other conditions for the carrying out of mafia-like functions. He cannot command the respect which comes from fear and so he cannot compete successfully with his rival *mafiosi* . . . The statement that every *mafioso* must have demonstrated the capacity for effective violence by no means implies that everyone so capable becomes a *mafioso*. The career of the *mafioso* is distinguished from that of the bandit by the events which ensue from the act of violence. Both *mafioso* and *bandito* are necessarily in conflict with the legal standards of the state. For the bandit in conflict with the law, the typical solution of any confrontation is the escape into the mountains . . . The *mafioso* achieves a stronger solution: the failure of the legal system to prosecute his violations of the law indicates that he has the qualities of a real *mafioso*. The typical end result of the confrontation in his case is the acquittal in default of evidence (Hess 1970, pp. 53, 55).

The development of the *mafioso* type is best understood in terms of the resolution in his favour of the conflict between the norms of the bureaucratic state and the subcultural modes of conduct which govern his actions: the maintenance of the mafia ethos is determined by the failure of the physical power deployed by the state's jurisdiction in the face of the physical power exercised by the non-political organs of the clan.

The term *mafioso* carries with it also a 'criminal' nuance. Nevertheless one must make a clear distinction between the *mafiosi* and the mere criminals, like the *banditi* or *briganti* already mentioned. There is however a kind of symbiotic relationship between the *mafiosi* and the *banditi*, for in Sicily, and in the so-called Mezzogiorno of Italy, *banditismo* and also *brigantaggio* are traditionally regarded by people as the natural modes of

116

social revolt of the individual and the group. A different and more fundamental interpretation is provided by sociological analysis: this shows that *mafia* on the one hand and *brigantaggio* on the other are essentially antagonistic social formations. *Brigantaggio* is a form of criminal deviance and also a form of pure individual revolt; *mafia* by contrast represents a special mode of establishing and maintaining positions of social power and political influence. The *mafioso,* commanding power and influence as he does by his personal use or threat of force to violate the codified law, is and remains nevertheless *'un uomo di rispetto',* a respectable citizen in his village. His conduct is legitimised by the morals and folkways of his people and by his functional necessity within the social system. He himself regards his activities as being in no way criminal but rather as normal *comportamento sociale* — modes of conduct which maintain the equilibrium of Sicilian society. The peculiar strength of the legitimacy accorded to him by the society arises from the fact that his activities do not serve his own needs only but are also functional for the whole subcultural system. The principal functions he discharges are those of protection, mediation and negotiation. Throughout his career he maintains a successful endeavour to legalise his position. He is successful in this because he has at his disposal a *partito,* a close network of connections which ranges widely and includes a large number of those individuals and groups, *mafiosi* and other, who occupy positions of institutionalised power in the bureaucratic state system.

This *partito* is maintained by the performance of continuing mutual services. The *mafioso* finally attains the position of a *padrone,* a protector of the people in a given territory. Moreover the *mafioso* sets up a so-called *cosca,* a clientele closely connected with him, serving to legalise his supremacy, and mainly dependent on him. This *cosca* consists partly of ordinary law-abiding citizens — or as law-abiding as is required by Sicilian standards — and also of a number of violent criminals, strong-arm men who enable the *padrone* to maintain his power without personal recourse to violence. The *cosca* augments the power and influence of the *mafioso-padrone*; but in contrast with the *bandito,* who enjoys the conspicuous exercise of power, he prefers to conceal his power under a veil of secrecy.

The *cosca* or (plural) *cosche* expand and complicate the definition of *mafia. Mafia* is primarily a mode of personal conduct; it is also and essentially an associational fact: a cluster of groupings of *mafiosi* for the purpose of common action: these are the *cosche.* These have no resemblance to the clearly structured organisations so prevalent in the literature. There is no one unified organisation. As far as the Sicilian evidence is concerned, one is compelled to conclude that there are many groupings, small clique-like entities led by a *capo,* existing independently, in contact with each other, supporting each other, sustaining loose combinations for specific purposes, acting together in a unified manner when necessary, but also capable of entering into bloody internecine conflicts, in short the relationships which hold between these *cosche* vary considerably and are not strongly controlled.

There is no evidence for a more or less strongly codified system of norms. To quote Hess: 'There is no need for the student of the structure of mafia-groupings to posit a codified system of law which provides norms of *mafioso* conduct. There are no initiation rules or ceremonies, since no formal organisation exists. Passwords are unnecessary, since the *mafiosi* who work together know each other personally. Thus the modes of interaction of the mafiosi are regulated only by pre-existing subcultural norms' (p. 111). Again: '*Mafia* is neither an organisation nor a secret society: it is rather a method' (p. 135). Similarly as regards *omerta*: this is often defined by scholars and regarded by laymen as a rule of absolute silence, maintained by sanctions of violence. The silence which conceals all mafia-like activities is a function of common feelings and values, not a product of the mere fear of violence.

The vital role of *omerta* is that in which it effectively frustrates all police activities of search and seizure. Peronaci considers this problem, and particularly the profound difficulties of securing adequate evidence, to be particularly urgent and serious in Italy, where the police are greatly restricted by the difficulties put in the way of gathering evidence by the rules of law. A recent complication of this kind dates from 1969, since which year the police are forbidden to undertake direct interrogation of individuals and groups suspected of law-breaking; all such interrogations must be performed by a magistrate in the presence of an attorney for the defence. But even without such legal restrictions on evidence problems would remain. The *mafia* rule of silence is observed not only by *mafiosi* but also by ordinary citizens in the areas concerned. Once again it must be insisted that this is not primarily a matter of fear or of intimidation: the heart of the matter is the general feeling that it is not the state's business, and even more emphatically not the business of the police, to know what goes on within these territorial areas. With the development of the gangster-like operations of the 'new' mafia of today there seems to be coming about a greater readiness among ordinary people to co-operate with the public power. But the traditional situation has not greatly changed: the *mafioso* enjoys, now as in the past, the advantages of that freedom which is termed in the theory of guerrilla-warfare that of the 'fish in water'.[3]

To proceed. A close study of the illegal and overtly criminal activities

118

of the *mafiosi* reveals above all the fact that their power is used to further their economic interests. Historically speaking an especially important role has been played here by the *gabelotto,* the large-scale landlord, who achieved by gradual stages a quasi-feudal position of power in relation to the mass of dependent peasants. This is the primal source of the exploitation exercised at a later historical phase by the mafia itself. As a result the *mafiosi* finally became defenders of the established economic system.

They are part of that system. Their social and economic roles are legion. They are industrialists, middlemen, they carry on a great number of occupations and professions in the economic area lying between the rich landowner and the farmer: corn merchants, cattle dealers, butchers, brokers, etc. They are also to be found in the ranks of the lawyers, the doctors, the pharmacists, and so on. In each of these branches of activity they follow a common aim: the monopolisation of resources within the particular occupation or profession. The classical function of the *mafioso* was that of go-between between the *ladri* and *banditi* on the one hand and their victims on the other; a role which was most conspicuously useful in the numerous cases of cattle-stealing. But they have assumed other and more varied roles: the practice of usury, the ordinary financial usury and the more locally relevant water-usury, the inflationary increase of prices for all the types of goods in which the mafiosi deal: monopolisation of market gardening: the illegal occupation of the best places in the market: the monopolisation of building contracts or of licences for the sale of petrol.

All things change — even the Mafia and its hold on Sicily. But in what direction? There is no certainty. The popular version of the decline of the system in fascist Italy and its recovery in the war years has been roughly handled by Albini and other researchers. The popular version is that the Mafia sustained a profound setback at the hands of the Mussolini regime, and that the regional police, led by Cesare Mori, had them on the run and could conceivably have suppressed them (Mori, 1933). But they survived, greatly weakened, to make a spectacular comeback in the war years. The occupation of Sicily by the American armies in World War II was made easy by Mafia help (arranged by the notable American Mafia leader Lucky Luciano); in return the older *mafiosi* were reinstated in Sicilian positions of power with the support of the US Army, or so the story goes (Lewis, 1964; Pantaleone, 1966). Such is the generally accepted version, but it is suspect.

Albini remarks, with reference to their near-suppression by the fascist regime, that there is no evidence of their having lost their major source of power — the large landed estate — in the inter-war years. Using data

E

regarding landed property for the period 1929 to 1947, Anton Blok found that, in Contessa, the *latifondi* throughout that time had remained intact (Albini, 1971, p. 140; Blok, 1969, p. 167). As regards the alleged US Army reinstatement of the Mafia, Albini argues that the main thing the war did was to remove Mussolini enabling the *mafiosi* to resume the functions they had performed in the years before fascism – as mediators of violence, as vote brokers, and as suppressors of peasant unrest. The basis of the continuation of Mafia power in Sicily must again be found in the Sicilian social structure (Albini, 1971, p. 142).

Whether we regard the Mafia of today as restored or as simply re-emerging, it is becoming something very different from anything that went on in the past. The younger elements are no longer continuing the old traditions. They are overtly criminal. Their range of operations is moving from the Sicilian countryside to include the cities of the mainland. They follow the traditional criminal trades of thieving, robbery, blackmail and protection. They do not aspire any more to be *'uomi d'ordine'*, nor do they play any vital role within the political (or anti-political) system. They are losing the support of the people, in whose eyes their activities are no longer regarded as functional or as deserving of support. Recent reports indicate that the pressure of the State police has been powerfully renewed. The full story of this has still to be told; it lies outside the scope of this study. Finally, it appears that what might seem at first sight to be reinforcement of Mafia strength is in fact a source of weakness. This is the demographic and cultural 'blood transfusion' from the USA, producing a mixing and mingling of Sicilian and American-Italian manpower and modes of behaviour. As Hess says (p. 165): 'This new type of *mafioso* (if the term *mafioso* is any longer applicable) is the product of a process which has four phases: the emigration of millions of southern Italians to the USA, the development of a specific sub-culture within American society, the adaptation of the sub-culture to the new social-economic and technical conditions of the USA, and finally the return to Sicily; in short, a process of extensive cultural exchange.'

The big question is whether indeed the term *mafioso* is any longer applicable. And other modifications of Hess's statement are needed. The extensive cultural exchange referred to covers a great variety of people and modes of behaviour, non-criminal as well as criminal. But even confining ourselves to the criminal behaviour of the criminal minority, the break with the past is obvious. Consider the range of criminal activities now developing in Sicily and on the Italian mainland: these range from the smuggling of alcohol, tobacco and jewels, through gambling, prostitution and drug trafficking, to attempts to control sections of the market, the building and construction industry, and so forth. These developments take us quite out of the orbit of the authentic Sicilian Mafia and into some of the central themes of this report. It could be that the two major new factors in the situation: the movement of the younger element into outright crime, merging in the process with similar elements on the mainland and even in northern Italy; and secondly the increasing authority and power of the Italian state and particularly of the police, in Sicily itself and elsewhere, spell the end of the Sicialian Mafia as it has hitherto existed, and its assimilation into an international and even intercontinental crime industry which can lay no claim to historical uniqueness or to the peculiar non-political virtues of the older Sicilian tradition.

Notes

1   Reports on the so-called 'mafia' are usually lacking in direct knowledge of the facts. A notable exception is a recently published study by Dr Henner Hess (Hess, 1970, English translation 1973; see also Manopoulo, 1967). For whereas other writers on this subject have made do with secondary material, Hess spent two years in Sicily — mainly in Palermo — making an exhaustive study of the first-hand material collected by the police authorities, and to be found in the local archives along with material relating to government and administration, judicial proceedings, transactions affecting land tenure, etc. This material (to be found in the Archivo di Stato di Palermo) *had not been studied by any previous writer on the subject* (Hess, 1970, foreword).

This chapter presents only a brief summary of Hess's argument; a close study of Hess's own work is recommended. Use has also been made of other material contributed by the team, and of the Report of the 1971 International Symposium on Organised Crime held by Interpol (Interpol, 1971).

2   Mafia (capital M) is used in the chapter to refer to the Sicilian Mafia and to the Sicilian Mafia only.

3   Cf. Ianni, 1972, p. 40: 'Like Chairman Mao's archetypal guerrillas, *Mafie* are the fish who require a supportive sea of oppressed partisans around them in order to survive.'

12 Legal Controls[1]

Legal concepts of the 'dangerous habitual criminal'

Most of the European penal codes have a special law, or at least special sections in the code, pertaining to the so-called habitual criminal. The Federal Republic of Germany, for instance, used the term 'dangerous habitual criminal' until 1970 in paragraph 20*a* of the German penal code before it was altered in that year. The word 'dangerous' in this context does not necessarily imply that the offender in question is violent, or excessively violent; the usage, which is common to most of the penal codes, implies rather 'major', 'serious', 'heavyweight' persistent criminal. Offenders so designated are normally sentenced to preventive detention. A few of the heavyweights are detected and dealt with in this way − but only a few; likewise many of those who are so labelled − indeed the majority of them − are not in fact the type of offender aimed at by the relevant parts of the code. This is partly a result of court practices which express a natural and probably unavoidable response on the part of the court to the circumstances of the offender. In this century at least, and indeed ever since the legal reforms which resulted from the Enlighten-ment, the Courts of Justice have been of the opinion that a mild sentence should be given when an offender is still, so to speak, at the beginning of his 'criminal career', and that heavier sentences should be imposed only after further convictions, the length and weight of the sentence being determined by the severity of the offences, the intervals between them, and similar indicators. It can take a long time before the court catches up with those persistent offenders who have managed to avoid arrest and conviction for a number of years. It therefore happens frequently that an offender who is newly classified as an habitual criminal may in fact have almost reached the peak of his criminal career.

A second difficulty in the way of the efficient operation of the penal code is the fact that legal and court proceedings are the last stage in a long process during which agencies of law enforcement have been concerned to identify the offenders, and to link them with their offences. It is the firm opinion of policemen, and of those criminologists who have studied the subject, that the intentions of the penal code as regards major persistent offenders are nullified in most instances at a stage long before the court appearance, and therefore before the penal code itself applies − that is to say, it is at the police investigation stage that the clever criminal contrives to cheat the law. It is difficult to see how matters can be improved by a more precise formulation of the penal code. Any formulation, however precise, is rigid and comparatively inflexible, in contrast to the patterns of behaviour of the criminal which adapt themselves very quickly to changes in law enforcement practice.

Individual liberty *v.* effective law enforcement

General opinion in western Europe, without exception, tends strongly towards imposing and maintaining constraints and restrictions on the agencies of law enforcement, with the object of protecting civil and individual liberties. This comes out clearly when one studies penal law, procedural law, judges' rules and all such regulations governing investigative and arrest procedures. A characteristic restriction, to be found in the majority of state legal systems, is that which affects the gathering of evidence. The courts are restricted to admitting the validity of only such evidence as the police have obtained by 'permissible methods strictly defined'. It is indubitably the case that these rules impose a severe restriction on the work of the criminal police, especially as regards experienced-offenders. Contemporary criminals are fully aware of their legal rights, and they also know how to make use of the law to obstruct police access to evidence.

Peronaci considers this problem to be particularly urgent and serious in Italy. (It is also of course central to the struggle against syndicated and 'professional' crime in the USA.) The most difficult problems arise in connection with the Sicilian Mafia. These are referred to in Chapter 11 above. The Mafia-dominated territories and sub-cultures regard the central state power as the 'enemy'. The ordinary citizen, who in other parts of the world is usually called the law-abiding citizen, will in these territories protect and cover up for the *mafioso,* even in the cases where the citizen may object to the particular practice or operation in which the *mafioso* is engaged, and even when the citizen himself is the sufferer. This is not a product of fear, or of fear only, it arises from a profound feeling, referred to in the previous chapter, that the state has no business – and *a fortiori* the police have no business – with what goes on inside these territories. We have noted that this is a principal constituent in the traditional concept of *omerta* in so far as this concept still holds. Peronaci writes:

> A number of the difficulties in combating professional crime are the result of the criminal underworld, which has been described rather

picturesquely as a 'highly criminogenic culture medium' made up of the physical and mental environment in which the criminal lives. By its very nature and constitution, the underworld protects its members. It provides them with all sorts of help, such as hiding places, shelter, papers, contacts, perjured testimony, alibis, and so on. Sometimes it even manages to spirit an arrested person out of the hands of the police, or, at the very least, to help him escape.

But the underworld's principal means of baffling the police is *omerta*, i.e. passive assistance to a suspect or wanted person and especially absolute silence about eveything relating to the purpose of a police investigation. The first thing to be done to solve the problem is to identify the true nature and psychological causes of *omerta*.

There are two main types of *omerta*: the *omerta* directed subjectively to helping the criminal and the *omerta* which is due rather to hatred of the police. The first type must be placed in the context of the general theory of crime and so is outside the scope of our study. It is the second type that is of interest to us here.

What, then, are the psychological causes of this second type of 'omerta'? By and large, they are to be identified with the underworld's suspicion and contempt of the police. In specified cases, the criminal wanted by the police is certainly not the man they are interrogating, and may sometimes even be an enemy of his. If so, why does the underworld refuse to collaborate with the police? First of all, because it is suspicious and contemptuous of the State, which it does not trust in the slightest, and, secondly, because in its eyes the police is the principal representative of the State and uses unorthodox, or even illegal, methods. *Omerta*, in other words, is one form – and the most ancient form at that – of primitive protest against society and the State.

The history of the long struggle maintained by the Italian police against the Sicilian Mafia and its outposts is so marked by difficult and usually hopeless situations that Peronaci is minded to suggest desperate remedies. He points out that the only solution in the long term must lie in the direction of socio-economic and humanitarian improvements leading to major changes in relationships between the citizen and the state. In the short term, however, he thinks that it would not be inappropriate to adopt extraordinary tactics to deal with these extraordinary situations. But desperate remedies, like hard cases, make bad law. The Commission on Human Rights of the Council of Europe, surveying the whole European scene, sees good reason for keeping state and police authorities within tight leading strings. It is also the case that sufficient experience has been built up throughout the world to cast considerable doubt on some of the newer methods recommended for the breaking down of the powerful criminal defences. It is of course possible that such devices as lie detectors, 'truth serums' and similar devices may eventually be put to good use, and operated in such a way as not to violate individual rights, as for example under the condition that the person involved should agree of his own free will. But such reports and experimental evidence as are available suggest that by and large these procedures are usually unreliable. One must also take into account the strong likelihood that use of these methods may be expanded beyond legitimate limits; 'freely given consent' is often obtained by various more or less subtle procedures which effectively exclude genuine acquiescence on the part of the subject or victim.

The system of informants

The ruling out of these 'applied science' contrivances does not necessarily condemn the law enforcement agencies to continued frustration. Outside the few territories and cultures dominated by the Sicilian Mafia a principal police method of crime control — which operates not only through outright arrest but also in many other ways — is the system of informants. This particular subject is bedevilled by ancient myths, and a great deal of research will be required before one can even begin to see clearly. One such piece of research in the United Kingdom suggests that there is no such thing as a particular class of informants; the great majority of people engaged in full-time crime, heavyweight and lightweight, are capable of informing more or less frequently. The reliability of the information given, and the purpose for which it is given, varies infinitely; but these are matters which the experienced policeman is accustomed to handle with moderate success. There is no fundamental problem about the so-called 'rule of silence'; it is primarily a matter of the personal dexterity of the police officer in question, combined with the variable factor of the comparative cohesiveness of the *milieux*. In old-established neighbour-hoods, criminal and other, there are a great many informal ties binding the police to the community. Recent police organisational changes, including those produced by motorisation, have not entirely destroyed the informal communication systems of which the police are a part.

There is one partial blind spot, or rather deaf spot, in the informant network. The criminals in the front line, big fish and small fry alike, generally give little away about the receivers of stolen goods with whom they deal. The same is true about the other people who work behind the

126

scenes. This is not reciprocated by the receivers, who inform quite a lot, and generally with ulterior motives — sometimes to discourage novice thieves (see Mack, 1964, p. 49), mostly to divert police attention from their own current receiving operations. No doubt the thieves themselves keep quiet about the receivers and background organisers because the thieves' own livelihood and future criminal career depend on the continuing inaccessibility of these individuals. Another safeguard devised by the people in the background, already mentioned in this report, is their system of restricted access to information, restricted according to the ranking of the individual; this prevents the individual front-liner from giving away essential information should he weaken, since he cannot tell what he does not know.

A frequent police complaint is that their technical equipment is inferior to that of the good 'professional', who as a general rule has the most modern equipment at his disposal. There is a good deal in this; the responsible authorities might be well advised to give a higher priority to the equipment of the police than to the planning of major law reforms, at least in the short run.

The sentencing practice of the courts

We had repeated complaints from many of the people we interviewed, mainly on the police side, about the mildness of the sentences handed out by the courts. Many believe there is a direct causal relationship connecting the alleged decrease in the harshness of sentences and the increase in crime. If there is a causal relationship, it is certainly neither direct not simple. The Netherlands, with the lowest prisoner-index in western Europe, has *comparatively* little crime and little in the way of an increasing crime trend. It is also worth pointing out once more that the court comes in at a fairly late stage in the contest between the offender and the law. It is certainly true of a number of countries that measures to make arrest less difficult would give better results, both in the short and long run, than a change in sentencing practice in the direction of longer or harsher sentences. This is illustrated in a negative way by recent happenings in the Federal Republic of Germany, in the course of which the laws affecting arrest, which were held to be biased in favour of the police, were revised. The number of reasons for arresting a person, and the maximum period of custodial holding, were both reduced. This change, which was generally approved, has had some unexpected and unfortunate effects. Broadly speaking the new regulations benefit neither the ordinary citizen nor the average offender; the people who benefit are the so-called 'dangerous', i.e. major, criminals for whom the concessions were not intended. The police point out that in many cases major offenders who have been caught with much difficulty are freed immediately after the hearing, thanks to the fact that they can satisfy the judge that they have a 'fixed place of residence'. The formal notice which meets the judge's requirements is provided by local authorities to any applicant who fills out a simple residence registration form, without having to provide any substantive proof of residence, a procedure obviously open to abuse. Criminals can get away with this not once but many times; as a result a number of major offenders, when finally they do come to trial, are able to confess to a large number of previous offences in the hope, very often fulfilled, that they will be given all the more lenient treatment as a result of their 'coming clean'.

The police in the Netherlands are not entirely happy about court practice in their country, but at least they have the help of a special regulation, operated by specially trained senior officials, under which the police and the public prosecutor may hold a suspected 'dangerous' criminal for a period of up to twenty days. This gives more time to complete the gathering of evidence; and enables the judge to deal the more faithfully with flimsy evidence, since shortage of time cannot be pleaded as an excuse.

Problems of police organisation and communication

There are also major problems of internal police organisation. In many countries there is much room for improvement in the way the police carry out their duties; it should be added that this opinion is shared by the police. The distribution of police functions among the different police departments, and the system of territorial divisions within national and regional police forces, are very often such as to make it easy to bungle any specific operation which crosses the functional and territorial boundaries. This is not just the old debate about centralisation and decentralisation. In France the police are strongly centralised; nevertheless the problems set the police by the 'professionals' are hardly less complicated than in other countries where the police system is more decentralised. The nub of the problem is intercommunication, whether between decentralised forces or between divisions of a centralised force. Necessary information about big criminal operations does not move fast enough between division and division or between department and department. There is a lack of co-ordination in the general process of crime prevention and crime repression (in other words the system of pressure and vigilance with which the police force, and particularly the detective force, maintains a continuous control over the activities of known major criminals even when they are not obviously engaged in some particular enterprise). Last but not least there appears to be a good deal of overlapping, and of time spent by one branch of the police on exercises which have already been carried out by another branch. The police, both on the higher executive level and on the operational level, find it difficult to carry out their work in a rational-economic way because of the large number of regulations and bureaucratic controls which hinder them. All of this is very well known to the majority of the more serious and high-level criminals; they know only too well the advantages of travelling, not only hopefully but rapidly, and of carrying out their jobs in quick succession in a number of separate and distinct police districts.

A special set of additional difficulties arises in some countries through the lack of clarification of the relationship between the police and the public prosecutors in their daily work.

Practical short-term and long-term solutions to these problems are not far to seek. New methods of organisation, and new types of response to the problems set by high-level criminal innovation, are being attempted in a number of countries. The United Kingdom and the Federal German Republic, for instance, provide examples of new departures in police work which should be closely studied and evaluated by police research agencies and by independent researchers. Examples of these new responses are the Criminal Intelligence Bureau, established in New Scotland Yard in 1960 (and in Glasgow in 1963), Observation Squads, and Interrogation and Search Commissions.

International police co-operation

As regards international police organisation, considerable progress has been made; at the same time there is still a great deal to be done in this direction. The writers of this book were not in a position to attempt a detailed study of Interpol, and in any case it is impossible to do the subject justice in a summary statement. We give here only some impressions gained from discussions with the various police forces. These tend to suggest to us that the recent expansion in rapidly executed international criminal operations has opened up new problem areas, and that there is a case for a special study of contemporary developments with a view to action.

It may not be known to the man in the street that Interpol is concerned almost entirely with communication of information, and that international police operations designed to counter specific international criminal enterprises are carried out on an *ad hoc* basis. There is no strong demand for a change in this respect, but there is a universal complaint by police forces that even the simplest matters arising out of the crossing of national boundaries by criminals must be dealt with, in the greaat majority of cases, through formal diplomatic channels, instead of being settled directly between the national police forces themselves. This is particularly the case where some kind of court action is in question. This of course slows up considerably possible action by the respective police forces, it also slows up communication. This particular weakness in international law enforcement is greater than any of the weaknesses to be found in internal police organisation. There are cases known to the team where it took over six months before a simple request for the hearing of an important witness was answered. It is unnecessary to point out what this kind of delay implies, especially where high-level criminals are involved. The national police forces are meeting the problem in a small way and in an informal manner. The members of the team became aware of several cases of so-called *'kleinen Grenzverkehrs'* whereby the police authorities concerned have developed an informal system of communications and contacts so as to overcome, at least in part, difficulties set them by political and diplomatic barriers. These informal frontier activities may serve to point the way to future adjustment designed to make for more effective police co-operation.

Problems of combating business-type crime

Economic crime has been the problem child of law reform for some time; there has been much deliberation about it, but little has been done and it has become a more urgent problem from year to year. Such intensive research as has been made of legal procedures has disclosed at once that the general rules of the various penal codes make prosecution of these offences very difficult and complicated. Where it is a matter of business-type crime, the criminals concerned prepare and carry through their offences so cleverly that it is practically impossible, in the majority of cases, to prove 'felony with criminal intent'. This is particularly true in the case of fraud. There is a striking absence of special laws designed to cover business-type crime activities in a comprehensive manner in all of the countries visited.

It is also generally true that police organisation is still far behind the newer developments in business-type crime. It is true that here and there the fraud squads are catching up, but they have still a long way to go.

There is an equal if not greater lack of skill and training in those government departments — those which control the police themselves — and those other departments which are concerned with trade and business. The higher officials are often of that remarkable omnicompetent breed who can move from department to department with ease, and who by very virtue of their general ability are therefore unqualified to understand the technical and social problems set by the high-level business-type crimester. The lower-level civil servants (like the Police Fraud Squads) might have a better grasp of the realities of the situation, but the decision in the big cases has to be made by the higher official. It is usually made on those broad political grounds which are his special area, it is usually a 'safe' decision, and it can only too often be a wrong decision. But changes are at hand. There are a number of examples in the different countries of very senior officials who are not only omnicompetent and generally intelligent but who are also specially experienced and learned in this or that economic or technological field.

Changes are also coming about in the area of the administration of justice. In the Federal Republic of Germany the states (*Länder*) are now establishing specialised *central* public prosecution offices to deal with major complicated cases of suspected business-type crime. The public prosecutors who work in these offices are responsible for a whole region, are specially trained, and deal exclusively with business-type crime including white-collar crime. It is not yet possible to evaluate these new departments: they are still at the stage of settling in.

Comment by Interpol

As mentioned above, it was realised in writing this chapter that the reference to Interpol on page 129 was too brief to do justice to an increasingly complex situation. Comment was invited from Interpol, who were so kind as to prepare the following remarks:

1   It is an exaggeration to say that the area in which Interpol is allowed to work is rather restricted, as it includes all ordinary law criminal acts having international implications: thefts of all kinds, assassination, drug traffic, offences against morality, all forms of swindling, fraudulent imitations, fraud, counterfeiting, taking of hostages, etc. Interpol can intervene in connection with almost any act punishable under criminal law.

2   It is important to remember that through no fault of the police, States will not relinquish their sovereignty, and that the police are accordingly

bound by the law of their own country. The limits of police intervention in all matters of co-operation are set by each national law.

Furthermore, in many European countries, when the police do not act *in flagrante delicto* (as is usual in cases involving international co-operation) they are essentially ruled by orders from the court authorities which are their superiors, and in some instances the courts themselves cannot give such orders unless cases have been referred to them through diplomatic channels. It is certainly true that this leads to delays which the police are often the first to deplore: but they have no choice but to put up with them.

3   It is both true and not true that Interpol is 'concerned almost entirely with communication of information'. True, it is composed of national central offices and a general secretariat, forming a vast permanent network for the exchange of information. But it must not be forgotten that information is centralised as well as exchanged, and although this other aspect of the work is perhaps not fully understood by the ordinary policeman, it is becoming increasingly important.

Lastly, one of the goals of the Interpol co-operation system is to permit certain police operations (arrests, etc.) and to facilitate direct contacts between officials investigating a case.

4   In addition, it is perfectly natural for action relating to particular criminal activities to proceed on an *ad hoc* basis. It is only reasonable that persons familiar with all the ins and outs of a case should continue the investigation themselves by means of direct personal contact with colleagues who can assist them in other countries. In a large-scale police investigation of any given case, appropriate tactics must be worked out at international level and must be suited to the way of life, personalities and activities of the suspects. It is far from certain that the efforts of some international super-officer would make any useful contribution. On the contrary, it is to be feared that in his international investigations he would only encounter, on a larger scale, obstacles identical to those facing central police officials when, as occasionally happens, they involve themselves in local matters.

5   Of course, much remains to be done to improve co-operation within Interpol, and we are the first to say so. For example, we are constantly striving to save time, and are therefore setting up a teletype network to accompany our European telegraph network. With this same end in view, we are proposing that every country should take steps to combat the 'unwieldiness of bureaucracy', and in the interests of improved co-ordination, we are going to see whether an 'international computer' can be used.

The truth is that, whatever desires or whims may arise, international police co-operation will always raise thorny problems (differences in language, procedure, freedom of action, etc.) *because* it is international. One passage in this chapter gives cause for alarm, namely the statement that 'police authorities concerned have developed an informal system of communications and contacts so as to overcome, at least in part, difficulties set them by political and diplomatic barriers'. We would very much like to know precisely to what the author of the document is referring. Interpol has always acknowledged unofficial cross-frontier contacts but where they exist they must be confirmed, above a certain level, by an exchange of information following traditional channels. Otherwise, an unfortunate gap would be created for which the ordinary police officers themselves would be the first to be blamed.

6   Another difficulty in police co-operation is the technical impossibility of restricting it to a particular geographical area. The best illustration of this was the recent attempt of the six Common Market countries and the United Kingdom to co-ordinate their policies in the field of drugs. The moment problems of punishment were touched upon it became clear that efforts restricted to those seven countries could not be effective, as in crime (this holds true for all types of crimes, not only those relating to drugs), the modern offender is heedless of distances or political frontiers.

The problem of international police co-operation is actually very considerable, and what is remarkable is the degree of success achieved.

Note

1   This chapter is based on: (*a*) a report prepared by Mr Peronaci entitled 'Difficultés qu'on Rencontre dans la Repression de la Criminalité Professionnelle'; and (*b*) a paper by Mr Kerner. These documents refer in the main to Italy, the Federal German Republic and the Netherlands. The text incorporates also notes made during team discussions in Strasbourg.

13 The Penal System and the 'Professional' Criminal[1]

'Prisoner production' in different countries

Any specific statement about professionals in prison makes sense only when one knows something about the history and background of the institution and its inmates. It will therefore be useful to look at the different rates of 'prisoner production' in the different countries.

The larger European countries are well known for their large prisons (some prisons have up to 1,000 and more inmates), with a correspondingly large turnover of prisoners up to and beyond 100,000 per annum. Countries with smaller populations show on the whole a different pattern, especially in the Netherlands. Here the system was changed decisively after the Second World War: a radical reduction of institutional size was carried through together with a decreasing use of confinement as a mode of disposal. This is illustrated by a particularly interesting table prepared by the Ministry of Justice in the Netherlands (see Table 13.1).

These figures might well suggest that the Netherlands locks up only the hard core of offenders and that there must consequently be more 'professionals' amongst the prisoners than in other less rigorously selective prison systems. Our visits and questionings produced a rather different picture. There were a number of individuals in almost all of the institutions who had committed a series of major property crimes, some of them highly profitable, at least in the short run. But inmates and prison staff alike were of the opinion that there were no prisoners to be found in prison at that particular time who could be said to rank as 'high-level professionals'; also that this type of criminal was only infrequently to be encountered in prison at any time. An exception to this rule was Breda, the only maximum-security prison in the Netherlands. Here the prison officers stated that they came across this type of offender only now and again: only three out of the eighty inmates in the current batch, they said, fitted the classification of 'substantial or high-level professional'. It was a matter of some interest to note that the same three people were named at a later stage in the visit, in the course of private discussion with a prisoner.

Breda apart, the impression one got from the experience of the other Netherlands penitentiaries and therapeutic institutions, as interpreted by the staff and the inmates, was that it tended to support the opinion expressed by Professor Baan in a recently published article (Baan, 1969, pp. 76-7). Professor Baan's finding about the 'professional' criminal, based on extensive therapeutic contact with offenders, is clear, concise and original: it is that there is no such animal – the 'professional' criminal is a myth. Professor Baan does not go very closely into the origin and function of the alleged myth, but it might be inferred from the general drift of his observations that it could have been invented by the police to make themselves more important. It must be said that the police authorities and other law enforcement officials consulted firmly rejected this point of view. One regrets that this is not the place to pursue this conflict at length. One can offer, very briefly, some possible reasons for the differing evaluations. One probably decisive factor is that the parties concerned bring very different backgrounds and experiences to the task of selecting and defining the salient aspects of a highly complex subject. The police study the criminals in terms of their behaviour in open society, and they include in their conspectus a large proportion of offenders or suspected offenders whom they find it difficult to transform into officially labelled offenders. The therapists generally study only those who are detected, convicted and incarcerated, including the small number of so-called 'professionals' in the prison population. The conflict of opinion arises also from profound differences in methods of approach and levels of considerations: the police look at observed behaviour and the patterns of criminal development, while the therapists are mainly concerned with the clinical aspect of personality development and with criminal modes of behaviour regarded as attempted solutions of problems of personal stress. Very broadly considered, there is no necessary contradiction in specific cases between the two statements (a) 'The offender is a successful "professional"' and (b) 'The offender is a neurotically disturbed person'. Practically considered, as one knows from a number of investigations, the offender, and particularly the socially skilled offender, is capable of adapting his behaviour, attitude and conversation to the expectations of the investigator.

There are proportionately more long-sentence prisoners to be found in the Federal Republic of Germany. (The statistics suggest that the same applies to Belgium, France, Denmark, Great Britain and Italy.) But even in Germany, and in other countries, the authorities are very reserved in the views they express regarding successful 'professionals'. They quote many cases of 'classical professionals', examples are the offender who operates on his own; also the small groups of safe-breakers who are actually arrested, sentenced and imprisoned fairly regularly. They also refer to the more modern types of operator whose enterprises are highly organised: prison officers and inmates are agreed that these modern professionals are

Table 13.1
International prisoner quota
comparison[a]

| Country | Population in millions | Total prisoners | | From these: | | | |
| | | | | Sentenced prisoners and preventive detainees | | Detainees under remand | |
		No.	Per 100,000 of the population	No.	Per 100,000 of the population	No.	Per 100,000 of the population
Germany (FR)	61.0[b]	46,400[b]	76[c]	35,300	58	11,100	18
France	50.0	35,000	70	22,500	45	12,500	25
England[d]	45.5	33,000	73	28,500	63	4,500	10
Netherlands	13.0	3,300	25	1,900	14	1,400	11
Belgium	9.5	6,000	63	4,700	50	1,300	13
Denmark	4.5	3,300	72	2,500	55	800	17

[a]Date of survey, November 1969 (Federal Republic of Germany, 31 December 1969).
[b]Population rounded off to a full million or 500,000 prisoners rounded off to a full 100.
[c]Proportional figures, also rounded off. Only comparable in the order of magnitude because 'population' as reckoning basis cannot be defined in the same manner in each case.
[d]Scotland and Ireland excluded.

only infrequently to be found in prison. Such estimates as exist suggest that as regards the maximum- or medium-security prisons and the institutions of preventive detention 20 per cent of the institutional population are 'good' habituals, but hardly more than 5 per cent are substantial 'professionals' in terms of the definition given earlier in this report.

Judging from the material one has to go on — and there is very little of this, as we have seen — one's general impression is that 'professional'-type offenders are almost indistinguishable from experienced habitual criminals in their actual prison behaviour. The experienced habitual criminal fits in as a matter of habit. The 'professional' likewise fits in, but here it is a matter of deliberate volition: he looks upon his sentence and the ensuing imprisonment in the light of a business risk — one has suffered a sort of accident at work and one has to make the best of the situation until it is possible to take up regular work again. As a result of this they show little emotional disturbance, and also little in the way of positive emotional reaction towards the prison officers and the prison environment.

Both types of offender have a clear grasp of their rights. The professional type is perhaps quicker and more flexible in his reactions. They know also the rights and responsibilities of the officials, and they are capable of taking advantage of any possible deviation by prison officers. Basic attitudes often quoted to us were: 'Leave me in peace and I'll leave you in peace', also 'If you make a confession to me then I will show you my gratitude'. Welfare workers, psychologists, and clergymen report that the 'professional' type of offender hardly ever comes to them with real problems; he responds only when he has a particular request to be met or when he believes that the visitor can help him in some specific way. In brief the profit-oriented and business-like mode of behaviour which is characteristic of these offenders in open society appears to be carried on just as strongly during imprisonment. This way of behaving is not without benefit to the official side: these offenders don't go in for rebellious behaviour, they don't trouble the officials with their problems or their sorrows, and as a result they don't take up much of their time. In other prisoner groups, especially in the case of violent or sex offenders, the rate of mentally weak and emotionally disturbed offenders is considerably higher than in the ordinary population. This is conspicuously not the case with the 'professional' type of criminal to judge by commonsense observation.

These rough generalisations have not so far been supported by systematic investigations comparing groups of randomly selected individuals. In one field, that of recidivists and preventive detainees in some Netherlands prisons, good work has been done (see Van Den Aardweg and Dorpmans, 1966). The prisons apart, a vivid picture of the relationship between the law enforcement system in general and the 'professional'-type criminal was given in interviews with the police. Here there is room for only a brief sketch. Regardless of the particular specialism of the individual offender the 'professional'-type criminal keeps a strong guard over his feelings in his contacts with the police; correspondingly the writer has noted again and again in the descriptions given to him by police officials that they too regard their opponents without emotion, with a kind of matter-of-fact calculation, often even with a certain amount of respect. This provides some extremely interesting leads for a study in organisational theory and social communication which could be based on the premise that the police and the rational-economic criminals are both in a number of respects parts of the same social system, understanding each other quite well, and opposed only in their attitudes to the values embodied in social institutions and enforced by the law.

In the majority of cases the two groups are radically opposed, but not irreconcilably hostile to each other. The police are regarded by many 'professionals' as a 'necessary institution', but the fact remains that one has business to do which requires taking the law into one's own hands and which is unhappily impeded by the police. The criminals planning an offence take into account the obstructive activities of the police in their calculations of the risk factors involved. If the risk is imprecisely estimated then one gets caught — this is bad luck and must be paid for; it is to be hoped that the next time the opponent will be outwitted.

In many cases, and as a result of long competitive experience, the

138

opponents are known to each other personally; some police officials have a long list of 'old acquaintances' whose methods of operation they know very well. Correspondingly, some 'professional' offenders desire to be dealt with by 'their' police commissioner when they are arrested. The criminals usually take any advantage presented by the stress situation they are in, but when positive defeat is imminent they tend to confess immediately and give up further resistance.

A subject still to be studied in Europe is the so-called 'fix'. There does appear to be a mild European version of this primarily American phenomenon, but it is much more a matter of gentleman's agreement between the two groups of adversaries than one mediated by the lawyers. In general the police hold that they never go along with the offender's proposal for such an agreement. It is however hard to decide whether or not there may be occasionally − indeed more than occasionally − a tendency towards accommodation. In all events it is certain that the practices described in the relevant US Task Force Report are absent on this side of the Atlantic; European laws and modes of court procedure are much less flexible and much more restrictive.

Here are some concluding observations. First: practically all the police officials agreed that they need normally have no fear of violence by the 'professional' offender in the course of their duties, nor need they fear that firearms will be used against them. Violence is generally confined to youths who are attempting to begin their criminal career, or rather to break into the big time; youthful operators who after several small-scale operations are attempting a large *coup* and who when caught in the act fight their way through by every means. There is one exception to this rule of the comparative non-violence of the professional offender; the police are at risk in the case of the growing number of hold-ups and armed robberies carried through by major and experienced operators.

Second: there is some evidence that the top-level criminal is protected from arrest, and even more from imprisonment, by other lesser criminals. It is said that groups of criminals maintain a kind of insurance fund for the maintenance of the lesser criminals, where the latter take responsibility for the crime and divert suspicion upon themselves. It would of course require a much more intensive survey before one could decide what is rumour and what is truth in this very interesting information.

Lastly, an observation about the prisons. According to recent reports the number of business-type criminals to be found in prison is gradually increasing. A number of these, especially those with a middle-class background, find it hard to reconcile themselves to the life of the prison and are continually looking out for special benefits. A larger proportion are not only conformist but positively co-operative; they can be used in confidential matters and are willing to undertake special tasks. Here again little has so far been done in the way of investigation of these matters, so that these observations must be classed as impressionistic.

Note

1   This brief sketch is based on observations made in the Netherlands and Germany. Ten institutions were included in the survey: these were selected so as to provide a variety of prison environments and methods. The institutions ranged from Zandwijk Institute for wayward and/or endangered youths in Amersfort with only 20 inmates – this institute is concerned with potential criminal beginners – through a variety of therapeutic institutions and prisons in Breda, The Hague (Scheveningen), Utrecht, Venhuizen, Winschoten, Freiburg and Ulm – to the maximum-security prison in Bruchsal which has over 500 inmates, and which represents the potential 'last stage' in the criminal's career.

Interviews were held with about 30 individuals; these included leading officials, guards, and therapeutic workers, especially psychologists. Discussions also took place with different types of prisoner including those classified as 'professionals' (but not necessarily 'high-level professionals'). Questions concerning the associations and network connections maintained by criminals and prisoners were gone into in some detail at each police department visited.

PART IV

Criminal Organisation Research

14 Review of Current Research

The general drift of criminological theory today is two-way. Knowledge of crime is advancing, or to be more precise facing, in opposite directions. The first is towards a greater generality. Carson puts it well.

> Although types of criminal behaviour differ widely and may be expected, therefore, to have aetiologies differing in some respects, they all none the less possess the common denominators of proscription under the criminal law and the at least hypothetical possibility of a punitive reaction by the state . . . In recent years a substantial body of literature has gradually accumulated around the related problems of how society selects certain forms of behaviour and subsequently some but not all of the individuals engaging in those forms of behaviour to be 'labelled' as deviant or criminal (Carson, 1970, pp. 385-6).

The argument of this book points in the opposite direction, towards greater specificity or doing one thing at a time. It will already be apparent from the preceding chapters that the two lines of attack are complementary. One hopes they will meet at or near the mid-way point in their around-the-world journeys. But the promise of mutual benefit is unlikely to be fulfilled unless there is a considerable redistribution of the world's scarce criminological resources. It could be estimated as late as 1970 that the ratio of criminologists (taking North America as a sample area) who apply themselves to the serious[1] study of juvenile delinquency to those devoting themselves to the crime industry was in the region of a hundred to one (p. 191 below). The ratio is now altering very slightly in favour of the minority group, but the big shift is from juvenile delinquency to deviance theory. This is also a shift, as we have noted, away from specificity and concern with fact. Nevertheless it is a small step in the right direction. Deviance theory is in principle concerned with all varieties of proscribed behaviour, and even more with differential selection of individuals (and whole social groups) for punishment in respect of like systems of behaviour. It follows that deviance theorists are especially interested in the contrasting definitions and treatments of traditional and non-traditional predatory crime we discussed in chapter 2. But this interest is still very general, and will make little headway in theory or practice until a more systematic attempt is made to get at the facts about the many different types of criminal and near-criminal behaviour (or more precisely, *pace* Carson, the diversity of heterogeneous phenomena forced into a formal collectivity by the criminal law). Particularly desirable for the clarification of deviance theory,[2] as of criminological theory, is that empirical study of criminal organisations, and criminal organisation, which is only now beginning to be attempted in a systematic manner.

Review of current research

This new beginning is fairly evenly distributed between America and Western Europe.[3] It consists of those studies which, guided by generalisations derived from observations made in earlier periods (e.g. by Sutherland and Maurer in the USA, and by Bonger and others in Europe), attempts to test these and other generalisations by systematic empirical and historical research.

The work now to be reviewed covers a wider region of discourse. In this as in other fields the majority of those interested confine themselves in the main to accounts and analyses of previous and current work, with or without further illustrations of the theses put forward. These general summations serve at their best to suggest topics for further enquiry. A smaller group have applied themselves to original studies of selected types of crime and criminal, based on sample derived from police and prison records or on studies from the life drawn from prison populations. Both of these modes of study are in the classical tradition, interested in the criminal rather than in the organisation, and tending to accept official classifications as sociologically valid.

Nearer the centre of our target are some typological studies. All of these are explicitly focused on criminal organisation and all date from 1970 on. Finally we are able to include a few pieces of first-hand observation of criminals in open society. Two of these, published in 1971 and 1972 respectively, are studies in criminal organisation, and specifically in the organisation of US syndicated crime.

General summations — USA

These are fairly numerous. The reader is referred to the accounts given in the relevant sections of those text-books which consist of selections from more or less recent published work; and in particular to the introductory summaries and reviews provided by the editors of these text-books. Clinard and Quinney, 1967, may be selected as a particularly well-organised example of this *genre*: the relevant sections are those on

144

'Professional Crime', 'Organised Crime' and 'Occupational Crime'. This last includes our business-type crime, white-collar variety.

General summations — Europe

These belong to the null category of 'Snakes in Iceland' (see p. 97 above). There is so far little or nothing in the way of European research studies, prior to 1970, to sum up. There are however some short reviews which are worth consulting. A useful discussion of Bonger is that by Radzinowicz in Radzinowicz and Wolfgang, 1971, pp. 420-8. The only relevant item we have come across in the French literature is Pinatel's interesting paper on 'The Professional Criminal' (1957), a moderate essay in the constitutional or pathological tradition of which Baan's paper is an extreme example (see p. 136 above).

The German literature consists in the main of reflective and scholarly writing, as the following summary shows:

> Discussion of the problems of the so-called 'habitual' or 'incorrigible' criminal has been sustained since the beginning of the century; e.g. Franz von Liszt made several attempts at 'abstract' scientific definition and at descriptions of types of criminal. After the First World War a strong interest developed in crime and criminal legislation. Robert Heindl's *Der Berufsverbrecher* (The Professional Criminal) (1926) is the first solid stocktaking of this sector of crime. Heindl drew attention, in a manner highly original for his period, to the following characteristics of professional crime: organisation in groups; rational and business-like planning; division of labour; stealing to order; and similar items. Also in 1926 Palitzsch published *Die Bekämpfung des internationalen Verbrechertums* (The Fight against International Crime). He described various types of itinerant international criminal: pickpockets, hotel thieves, card-sharpers and gamblers, confidence men, and banknote forgers. His book includes also a history of the first attempts at international police co-operation. In the following decade Franz Exner and his pupils gave an account of the characteristics of different kinds of multiple recidivist. A succession of studies was made of single categories of offender — thieves, burglars, fences, and fraudsters (John, Müller, Schurich and Wend). This work is concerned mainly with Mack's category of 'habitual prisoner' and not with typical professional criminals.

> In the following period between 1935 and 1960 there is little

worthy of note; the work of von Hentig should be consulted (e.g. von Hentig, 1947).

Hellmer, 1961, reports on the first twelve years of the administration of the 1933 law 'against dangerous habitual criminals'. His general conclusion is that very few real professionals had been dealt with under this law; it had been used mainly for not very dangerous habitual criminals. Goedecke, 1962, describes those criminals already officially labelled as dangerous habitual criminals; this study also misses most of the real professionals. Weidermann, 1969, attempts job descriptions for several types of criminality, including professional criminality; his work is based partly on court records, and partly on general literature.

In all of the above little is reported in the way of systematic empirical research. As the century goes on the work includes a considerable element of detailed phenomenological analysis.

As far as the Netherlands are concerned, van Bemmelen, 1952, gives a general review of traditional professional crime. As in the case of the German work there is little empirical content.

There appear to be no plans at present in the research institutes of the Netherlands or of Germany for large-scale systematic enquiries in the field of substantial and well-organised property crime.

Studies by single category or type of criminal

Most of the American studies of single types of criminal are broadly in the Sutherland tradition, if often by way of reaction against it. We select here for special attention three type studies which not only do *not* take up and develop the clues given by Sutherland to the organisation behind the criminals; they make a point of drawing attention to those categories of criminal characterised by *minimal* organisation. The well-known Lemert study of systematic cheque forgery (Lemert, 1958), also Einstadter on armed robbery (Einstadter, 1969) find that criminals who specialise in these fields operate more independently than did Sutherland's professional thieves. Bruce Jackson's *Thief's Primer* (1969) is directly in the Sutherland tradition in a formal way, since it gives the story of Sam, safe-cracker and check-passer, in his own words. But Sam is not a professional in the sense indicated by the phrase 'organised at the professional level'; he is a 'career criminal', a 'character'. Working criminals such as Sam, says Jackson, 'do not form a society or even a group; they do form a category . . . Even though thieves like Sam sometimes work in small firms of two or three, they are essentially loners.

There is no love of craft, no allegiance to guild . . . Social relationships are highly transitory' (pp. 30-1).

These and similar studies are particularly deserving of attention since they serve to qualify considerably the general thesis of this book. They not only draw attention to the existence of full-time criminals of some substance who operate as individuals or in small transient groupings (although in their often quite prolonged resting and recreational periods they take advantage of the social opportunities provided by various *milieux*);[4] these studies also underline the warning we gave earlier that criminal organisation is much more informal and rudimentary than that of the average law-abiding occupation. It is also of course less accessible to observation, which suggests that one should be cautious in one's generalising.

The only current European single-type studies we have come across are those of Sveri and Werner, 1963 and Spencer (in Grygier *et al.* 1965). The first is of safecrackers, the second of minor white-collar criminals. Both are based on samples drawn from prison populations. (So is Lemert's investigation.) The general finding of the Sveri and Werner study, as mentioned earlier, is that the safebreakers in question are neither substantial nor very successful. This is possibly a result of the nature of the sample; on the other hand, general Swedish experience is that the typical Swedish full-time criminal spends a considerable proportion of his active life in prison.

A second unpublished study by Sveri is of considerable methodological interest.[5] Sveri insists that sociologists should not accept a police list of professional criminals as their datum. They should instead work out their own definition of the professional criminal and go on to verify from the available statistics and records the volume and incidence of the category of professional crime as specially defined for the purpose of the investigation by the investigator himself. Sveri had made his definition in terms of four criteria: the criminal should have been at least five years on the job; he must have no other visible means of support; he must be 21 or over; he must have shown the capacity to commit a professional type of crime, for example safebreaking. The general opinion, police and criminal, was that the safebreakers were the top criminals, the elite. Out of 44 incarcerated safebreakers Sveri selected 25 as satisfying his criteria. It is to be hoped that the findings of this interesting study will be published. As it stands it affords an example, as we see it, of misplaced or excessive academic and scientific rigour.

The same comment does not apply to the Spencer study. It is difficult to conceive any other way of studying white-collar criminals in the stricter sense of the word — i.e. businessmen of good repute who have exploited that repute in a manner prohibited by the criminal law – except in terms of detected, and as a matter of research convenience incarcerated offenders; for the simple reason that white-collar criminality is at once defined and terminated by its being detected and made public.[6]

Finally, there is a very interesting current American study by Shover (1971) based on the writer's doctoral dissertation on 'Burglary as an Occupation'. The sample of 141 burglars who were interviewed or who filled up questionnaires is based mainly on incarcerated burglars but it included a very few 'free world interviews' (Shover's phrase); and the writer consulted also a good deal of general crime literature, including 32 autobiographies of thieves. Shover's main achievement is that he has to some extent overcome the disadvantages inherent in the selection of single-category criminals for investigation. To study one category of criminal, as officially defined, is to expose oneself to the danger of what Whitehead called the fallacy of misplaced concreteness (Whitehead, 1926, pp. 64-70). It is liable to divert research attention from such organisational data as may be lurking in the background. Shover observes and follows up a number of clues to background organisation. His short paper says enough to show that he has made a quite thorough study of the role of the criminal receiver or fence; he includes also some original observations on the role of the 'tipster', 'spotter' or 'finger-man' – the person who conveys information to a burglar about likely jobs. These observations include a useful account of that class of tipster which is composed of ostensibly law-abiding persons. This is a point already familiar from popular crime literature; it is useful to have it confirmed by systematic research. That it is far from being all of the 'tipster' story is suggested by further research reported below.

Typological studies

Most of the criminal typologies extant have two defects. They are typologies of offenders, almost invariably incarcerated offenders, and they usually over-emphasise the part played by pathological criminals, a group which largely overlaps with pathological non-criminals. The second and much greater defect is inherent in the historical drive to make criminology a science of the kind in which the phenomena under study can be systematically classified *without remainder*. This leads to the belief, hinted at by Carson, that because all crimes are socially and juristically defined as such, all criminals have something in common as a matter sociological fact. It also explains those frequent attempts, like that of Clinard and Quinney, to produce a *complete* classification of types of crime. The typologies discussed here work very differently. They separate out, from the enormous diversity of situations and types of activity which involve the liability of incarceration for certain of the persons concerned, this or that limited sector which gives evidence of a high degree of homogeneity. The general assumption is that the behaviour collected under the legal definition contains a fairly small number of homogeneous sectors and a comparatively large residue of heterogeneous items of behaviour, items which do not fit into a comprehensive criminological typology, items which are essentially allergic to any such typology.

The essay by Gibbons and Garrity (1962; conveniently reproduced in Radzinowicz and Wolfgang, 1971) escapes from the pipe-dream of a complete typology of offenders since it is restricted to property criminals. But it is too wide, since it includes all property offenders. A second drawback is that it is a typology of offenders, and so tends to overlook the factors making for cohesion and organisation within certain areas of property crime.

Two papers by Mack — on 'Full-time Miscreants etc.', 1964 and 'The Able Criminal', 1972 (pp. 185-94 below) — report a continuing research project centred on substantial practitioners of rational-economic crime, a distinctive set of criminals which constitutes not a category but a group.[7] It is to be noted that the substantial criminals being studied are not in themselves an exclusive group; they are leading and representative figures giving structure and continuity to a much larger population which contains lesser full-time miscreants. The main point tentatively established by this research, the importance of the background operators, is noted on pp. 10-12 above. This finding has directed research attention to the internal organisation of the group, and also to systems of communication and economic exchange which connect it, through an intermediate area of shady business dealings, with the wider society. A third point is methodological. The groups selected for study are chosen in consultation with the police. This deliberate research policy contrasts with that pursued by Sveri. The basic idea is to select for study in any given area all or most of those in whom the detective forces of the area are specially interested. The emphasis in the gathering of data is quite as much on detective 'know-how' as on documentation. Some of the difficulties involved in this approach are sketched below (pp. 179-80). The work done so far has tended to confirm the initial assumption that the police know more about crime *as a major behaviour system* than any criminologist can get to know *without their help*. A minor point of present relevance is that the system of criminal roles in the Mack study includes that of provider of services, one of the services in question being the gathering and passing of information. The 'tipster' function described by Shover may be partly a matter of getting information from casual non-criminal acquaintances; it is also and mainly discharged by full-time criminal operators as one of a number of their activities.

The most clearly worked-out enquiries into the organisational aspect of gainful crime are those of Cressey. His 1972 study of 'Criminal Organisation' has the incidental merit of bringing together, for the first time, Sutherland's rather scattered remarks on organisation. It also discusses the fact that the criminal law is limited to the prohibition of overt criminal acts, since no way has yet been found to prohibit the taking part in the organisation and preparation of criminal acts. Another theme of the book is an attempt at a schema of six varieties of criminal organisations, ranged as to scale and degree of rationality in a comprehensive and unilinear hierarchy, with syndicated crime, General Motors model (see p. 43 above) at the top, and 'professional' or 'task force' crime lower down. This is of course a highly formal exercise, given the absence of factual organisation studies, and the assumption that there is in fact a General Motors model of syndicated crime in the USA is a heavy load for any schema to carry. On the other hand criminology will get nowhere if it neglects theory, and this particular attempt at a 'limited sector' schema has distinct potential. If its criteria could be amplified to include, besides rationality and scale of operation, the factor of degree of involvement with and interpenetration of the legitimate economic system, it might open up fields of enquiry more rewarding than any attempted in the past.

Two current studies using historical material may be taken as examples of what should develop into a highly fruitful line of research. Mary McIntosh, whose work is justly described by Cressey as 'among the most perceptive and fruitful of all such explorations', writes in the tradition of contemporary Marxist historical scholarship in which Eric Hobsbawm is a leading figure (McIntosh, 1971*a, b*, 1973). This enables her to relate developments in criminal technology and organisation to general social and economic factors in a most illuminating manner. Her twofold typology of 'craft' and 'project' crime[8] (a well-judged cut-down from an earlier fourfold classification: 'picaresque', 'craft', 'project' and 'business') is a useful articulation of the industrial analogy and serves to emphasise the fact that the organisation *of the actual criminal operation* is complex enough as far as the crime industry is concerned but low down in the complexity scale in comparison with legitimate enterprise. McIntosh describes her work as based on a wide but far from complete range of empirical material. She makes good use, as Shover does, of books by criminal practitioners. These emphasise, as indeed most of the scholarly work emphasises, the persistence through time of the criminal 'underworld'. This is of course a salient feature of well-organised crime in all periods. But a distinguishing mark of contemporary crime is the large part played by what we have called 'substantial incomers' (cf. pp. 54-5 above), very many of whom may have by-passed the traditional initiation. It is also the case nowadays that the top-ranking criminals, 'incomer' *and* network-connected, no longer frequent the older type of criminal *milieu*. A reliance on information from 'inside the underworld' (cf. Fordham, 1972) may yield a rather old-fashioned picture.[9]

The second example of the historical method of research is a 1972 paper by Chappell and Walsh on receiving in eighteenth-century England, with particular reference to the notorious Jonathan Wild. The function of the fence, a topic of first importance to the realistic study of criminal organisation, has so far been untouched by criminological research.[10] It is good news therefore that the same writers have a series of papers in mind which apply the methods of operations research to the contemporary thief—fence relationship (Walsh and Chappell, 1973, and references), and that Professor Clockars of Philadelphia has in the press a study, in the tradition of Sutherland's *Professional Thief,* of the life history of 'a particularly successful fence' (Clockars, 1972; also 1974).

Direct-access studies of criminal organisation

We have already mentioned Bruce Jackson's essay in the manner of Sutherland's *The Professional Thief.* This throws considerable light on the changing criminal culture in the USA as seen from the standpoint of a comparative isolate.[11]

To Ned Polsky falls a special distinction. A paper of his in *Hustlers, Beats, and Others* (1967) signalises a new start in criminological method. There are many reasons why criminologists should have neglected the study of what common opinion holds to be 'real' crime; the most obvious of these is the scarcity of available data and the difficulties of adding to what data there are. What cannot be justified is the failure of criminologists to think hard about how to overcome these difficulties. There has been since Sutherland no discussion of how to get to know about successful criminals, who are not usually to be found in prison except in small numbers and unrepresentative samples. There has instead been a general disposition to rest content with the view expressed in the principal text-book, that of Sutherland and Cressey, which is that one cannot mix with criminals on their own ground, in open society, without becoming involved with them to the point of identification, of accepting their values and even joining in their operations — (Sutherland and Cressey, 1960, p. 69). There is a suggestion here that subterfuge — disguised or concealed 'participant observation' — would be necessary. Polsky asserted on the contrary (*ibid.* p. 24) that research can proceed without these complications *if one explains oneself properly*. More important, he gave several demonstrations of how this had been done by himself and could be done by others.

It can be argued that any such direct approach is likely to be successful only with fringe groups of small fry, full-time miscreants rather than full-time criminals. This is the gravamen of Mack's argument that the study of *major* systems of criminal behaviour must *in the first instance* attempt an exhaustive study of police information and 'know-how', and might well have to make do even in the long run with only a small quota of directly acquired information about the big fish and their organisations. To put the point in a nutshell, successful substantial criminals are by definition inaccessible. But the Polsky line of advance has been strengthened by two very recent pieces of work, those of Albini, 1971 and Ianni, 1972. It is true that these fall within the special field of US syndicated crime, and have been made possible, or so it can be argued, by a disposition on the part of the organisations concerned to accept and respond to the approaches of sociologists which is quite unprecedented and would have been impossible to conceive of even in the quite recent past. This last circumstance opens up vast areas of speculation and points for further enquiry; but it does not affect the main point, the success of the two researchers concerned in getting to know by direct access salient facts about major criminal organisations.

This is not the place to describe the full extent and achievement of the two researches; one might note in passing that their findings considerably reinforce those of Hess on the non-existence of the Mafia (or Cosa Nostra) in the sense of a national or continental or international organisation. What can be discussed here is the different methods by which the objective was achieved in the two cases. A recent review of the Ianni book (Mack, 1972) sums this up; the following excerpts begin with a discussion of why the syndicates in question relaxed their 'rule of silence'.[15]

'Why this readiness?' is a harder question to answer. It could be the passing of the old order, or the transition to comparative respectability, following distinguished precedents, or a combination of the two ... It is also probably no accident that both writers are Italian-American. The hordes of Goliath [the reviewer's term for those large bodies of US opinion, lay and learned, which accept the official Task Force Report thesis] will no doubt read them as attempting a public relations job for their entire group — indeed this charge has already been laid. But the Goliath armies are notoriously poor readers. The point here is that Italian-American scholars have a head start in this field.

Professor Albini tells me that he made progress in his field work by a happy accident. Most happy accidents in research are of course a result of first-class unconscious planning and preparation. It appears that his lectures in Detroit earned the commendation of a mature student of his. The subject was organised crime (later he renamed it syndicated crime) and the student, who had special authority in this field, told him he seemed to know what he was talking about — in contrast to many teachers of the subject — and he ought to meet so-and-so. This was arranged, and led to further meetings, including discussions with persons of consequence which involved long journeys. It seems that Albini found his way from point to point of a network, as distinct from being accepted into a closed group, which was the equally good fortune of Ianni.[12]

A distinctive feature of Albini's work is that he was and is interested in syndicated *crime*. This is doubtless why, if one may guess, he found his way into a network of people who did not necessarily know each other. That is probably the way it is in syndicated crime. The distinctive feature of Ianni's work is that he is interested in *syndicates* . . . as distinct from syndicated *crime*. His approach is that of the anthropologist. He had no connection with any law-enforcement agency. The same is true of Albini. Ianni's position is strongly grounded in methodological theory. He points out (p. 8) that . . . practically all recent research into syndicated crime has been based on agency files, and that the focus of these agency studies as he calls them, 'has been on criminal activity rather than on the nature of the organisation through which the activity occurs'.

Ianni therefore secured — we are paraphrasing the rest of the review — the agreement of all the members, including the senior members, of one of the New York 'Families' — generally alleged to be five in number. The 'Lupollo' family as he calls it may be typical of the fairly large Italian-American syndicates. If so it is on the way out (and, it could be said, up). A large and growing proportion of its highly lucrative enterprises are in the legitimate business class. Many of the younger generation take no part in any of these enterprises, being professional people or in non-Family firms. It may be of course either that this particular Family is untypical, or that the people in it quite naturally conceal an unknown proportion of the criminal side of the enterprise, leading to a general

F*

underestimate of the Family's criminality. These matters do not lessen Ianni's achievement. He has managed to share in the life of the Lupollo extended family without identifying with it — a risk regarded as insuperable by earlier writers.

Ianni has gone on to further research innovations which are of great methodological interest. He recruited for his new study of syndicate activity among Blacks and Puerto Ricans (see p. 183 below, note 7) a group of eight newly released convicts who looked up their friends and acquaintances in Harlem and elsewhere and reported back to Ianni. This looks like being a most profitable variation on direct access research; its merits, and risks, will undoubtedly be closely examined by others working in the field (Ianni, 1974).

Other specific studies

Little has been said in this book about argot studies. The team came across very little of this phenomenon. Either argot is very well concealed, or it is a feature of those well-established criminal networks which do not present contemporary law-enforcement agencies with their biggest problems. Criminal vocabularies are probably more consistently used in convict or prison cultures than by criminals in open society. Even within these cultures, if one may hazard a guess, the terms in use may change fairly rapidly.[13] However, the classical work on the subject by Maurer and others is being carried on. A valuable brief treatment, including a glossary, is to be found in Jackson, 1969, pp. 48-61; also relevant to this point is Clemmer, 1959. An interesting European study is Bondeson, 1968: its title, 'Argot knowledge as an indicator of criminal socialisation', is self-explanatory.

The most celebrated animal in detective fiction is Sherlock Holmes' 'dog that barked in the night-time'. It will be recalled that the dog did not bark. One of the more notable non-events in current criminological studies is the lack of research into business and company fraud. The United Kingdom has produced in recent years some first-class journalistic writing, as we have noted above, but the only piece of systematic scholarship we have come across is the paper by Hadden on the control of company fraud (Hadden, 1968). There are of course many explanations of this particular gap. It is heavy going for even quite senior researchers, and first-hand material is not readily available.[14] Another consideration is the difficulty encountered by even the most expert students in keeping up with the incessantly changing complexity of the subject. Hadden gives a useful summary of United Kingdom official enquiries into company legislation over the last century and more. There is a never-ending race between the forces of company law amendment and the very vigorous processes which are regulated by company law. Between 1840 and 1940, very roughly speaking, company legislation and official enquiries into the subject were concerned to a considerable extent with the explicit task of controlling abuses. Some of the company law amendment committees (e.g. Davey 1895, Greene 1928, and Bodkin on share-pushing 1936) were intended among other things 'to provide an effective system of dealing with malpractice and fraud when they occurred'. In contrast the Cohen Committee, 1945 and the Jenkins Committee, 1962 were not interested in abuses to anything like the same degree. The latter committee 'considered that the existing law had been "found by experience to have worked reasonably well" ' (Hadden, 1968, p. 280). It is possible that the next committee to tackle the subject will be less sanguine. But even the best committee reports are a poor substitute for systematic research.

They order these things differently in France. As already noted, we have been unable to turn up very much in the way of French discussion of full-time criminals either in the form of general treatments or of empirical research. The taciturnity of the French police as regards these matters appears to be exceeded, if anything, by French criminologists. Nevertheless French criminology, in providing an exception to this rule, has been responsible for what appears to us to be the best single piece of original research in the field of business-type crime, as far as Europe is concerned. We refer to the pioneering work of Jean Cosson, 1971, already briefly sketched (p. 17 above). This is not, as it might appear on the surface, a single-category study drawn from police records. It is an original discovery of new types of criminal exploitation of business opportunities. It is likely to maintain its present pre-eminence for some years, and it may well survive as a classic study of what the author has called 'fiscal fraud'.

Computer abuse

The final item in this review enables us to make some kind of *amende honorable* to the research community. One main finding of this book is that criminologists since Sutherland have by and large neglected the study of major rational-economic crime, and have in particular left almost entirely unexplored the rapidly developing activities of business-type criminal operators. This finding is emphatically confirmed by the observation just made that the systematic study of criminal organisation is only now beginning. But there is one highly organised area of criminal opportunity in which the scholars are well ahead of the operators. *Computer Abuse,* the first of a series of reports being made by the Stanford Research Institute (Parker *et al.* 1973), is not so much a situation report as an anticipation of the rational-economic crime of the future. Computer abuse is defined as 'all types of acts distinctly associated with computers or data communications in which victims involuntarily suffer or could have suffered losses, injuries or damage or in which perpetrators receive or could have received gain'.

There are many forms of possible computer abuse notably those which threaten the privacy of the individual. The Stanford research project is primarily concerned with the criminal potential of the computer. It can and almost certainly will render obsolete the traditional type of *physical* large-scale robbery involving banks, bank messengers and security vans. 'Negotiable securities will be stored magnetically and electronically as data inside computers and transmitted over communication circuits from one computer to another. Perpetrators of security thefts will use the skills, knowledge, and access associated with computer and data communications technology . . .'

The report lists 148 cases of computer crime, all of them amateur and/or white-collar and most of them small in scale, occurring between 1964 and 1973. The record confirms the general impression noted earlier in this book that the criminal exploitation of large-scale technical innovations is invariably slow to develop. But the list includes at least two examples of what may well become a major criminal development in the foreseeable future.

> In New York City the head teller of a branch of the Union Dime Savings Bank is under indictment for embezzling over $1.5 million by manipulating accounts in a central computer through a teller terminal . . . In Los Angeles a $2,000 million fraud in the resale of 56,000 fake insurance policies and other financial manipulation by the management and some employees of the Equity Funding Insurance Company is alleged . . . External auditing of this company failed to detect any problems for three years, and indeed, in both cases, detection of the acts occurred independently of any protective actions of the victims.

Notes

1 'Serious' in this context means empirical, involving the systematic collection of new or hitherto uncollected data, and particularly of data obtained by direct observation. The ratio concerns of course only a small

156

segment of the criminological sphere of interest. It is based on a rough calculation of the incidence of published work within that segment over a period.

2 Deviance theory is of course far wider than its 'labelling' corollary. One weakness of labelling theory, in so far as it equates criminality with overt social stigmatisation, is that it is obliged to ignore the existence of those criminal organisations which are sustained by largely successful and inaccessible criminals.

3 The Council of Europe Report was restricted to work done in these two areas.

4 True of Sam; *not* true of Lemert's cheque forgers.

5 This account is based on a discussion with Professor Sveri in 1970.

6 A *successful* white-collar criminal is in the nature of the case an undetected white-collar criminal. When detected he is given the appropriate label; simultaneously he loses the repute, the exploitation of which constituted his white-collar criminality. He may go on to further crime, traditional or more probably business-type, but this will be outside the white-collar enclosure.

7 For a useful account of the distinction see Goffmann, 1963, pp. 23-4: it is aptly quoted by Jackson, 1969, pp. 30-1.

8 The distinguishing features of craft theft 'serve to reduce the risk of criminals being caught and brought to justice, even at the expense, to the criminal, of restricting the profits that he makes from crime . . . The routinized patterns of behaviour make it a relatively safe way of earning a steady but rather low income.

When large amounts of valuables are being stolen, and owners improve their ways of protecting them, each theft becomes a more complicated job . . . nearly always involving special advanced planning and the taking of greater risks. Each theft then becomes a project in itself. Project thieving, in contrast to craft thieving, is a high-risk operation for high stakes' (in Cohen, ed., 1971, p. 105).

9 A similarly limited and old-fashioned picture is drawn by Inciardi (1972) — 'The natural area of the professional criminals are the "bad lands", the submerged regions of disorganisation and their underworlds of crime and vice. It is within the crime and vice areas that the professionals segregate themselves . . .' (p. 229).

This is roughly true of various metropolitan areas in the first half of this century and earlier; for a more up-to-date picture of top-ranking full-time predators and mobsters see pp. 88-90 above.

10 There are some useful accounts by practitioners. See for example Gregory, 1932.

11 Although Sam *works* mainly on his own, he *thinks* of himself as

part of the criminal culture, as far as his thieving is concerned. 'Sam wants to make it in the society of thieves (however amorphous an entity that may be), which require a certain style and the establishment of certain skills . . . ' (Jackson, 1969, p. 25).

12   Professor Albini has read this note and adds: 'The techniques I used to gain entry into the network were varied. I came across the student mentioned above entirely in his role of student. It came out later that he was a professional gambler, but this was only after the end of the course. He had offered his help and I had accepted it some time before this. I was simultaneously getting access through relatives of syndicated criminals and through other contacts in the Italian-American community' (personal communication).

13   Probably for the same reasons as in the US black culture. The object here is to exclude the so-called 'liberals' who use the black argot to show how 'in' they are. 'When those words are picked up and used by whites, the black community will find others . . .' (Jackson, 1969, p. 50).

14   'Research in this area is of course particularly tricky and except for the most able and mature young man, is unlikely to be recommended to doctoral candidates. What is perhaps even more important is that research students are unlikely to be accepted by those responsible for granting access to files, documents, etc. A few people are, however, now engaged in research work on this topic' (Professor F. H. McClintock — personal communication).

15   Quoted by courtesy of *New Society*, London — The weekly review of the Social Sciences.

15 Areas of Future Research

This section provides not so much a programme as a sketch for a programme for future work. The team's precise remit from the council was to provide guidance for further study of an intensive kind (p. 168 below). There follow here three sets of recommendations under the headings of topics, points of method and points of organisation.

Topics for research

The following suggestions are offered with two major reservations. The first is that since all fruitful research is essentially creative, and since creative thinking involves original ideas worked out by the people directly concerned, the topics which will finally emerge and strike oil can only be barely anticipated in an account like this. The second reservation is that since the field of possibilities is so wide and the resources so few, the propositions offered could easily become a purely theoretical or academic exercise in the pejorative sense of these much-abused terms.

The research community will draw their own conclusions and make their own choices from the foregoing pages. In the following selection by the writers the first two propositions have a slight priority:

(1)   *The scale of the problem*

How important is major rational-economic crime, as compared with established and other emerging fields of research? The question of its *economic* importance is touched on in pages 10 and 24 above, which suggest that the economic cost of this type of crime might be measured against the scale of economic growth. Attention should also be paid to the moral, and morale, effects of this type of crime. Successful large-scale criminal operations have a profound effect on the morale of the vast population of lesser criminals, and an equally profound effect on the morale of the police; in the latter case it can be stimulating and not merely depressing. A special aspect of the moral effect is perceptible in the way in which the communications media tend to romanticise the big criminal operators. Another special aspect, the tendency of criminals and their café-society sympathisers to justify their depredations by reference to the comparative success and lack of public condemnation of certain forms of big-business type crime and near-crime, links this topic with (5) and (6) below.

(2) *International criminal networks*

This difficult theme includes major criminal operations involving three or more countries; also those large-scale operations which exploit the gaps between the national law-enforcement systems. These and other connected topics are referred to in chapters 3 and 10 above.

(3) *The background operators* (pp. 10-12 above)

This and the following topic constitute the most outstanding features in the development of the more traditional sectors of rational-economic crime in recent decades. It is suggested that there are at least three types of background operator: organisers, planners etc.; big receivers; and an x category. The first two of these have usually a respectable cover or 'front' occupation and usually conduct a considerable amount of legitimate business, the cover is seldom a mere cover. The x category are a special case; they operate internationally, and their criminal role and performance are unknown to all but a small group of knowledgeable policemen and governmental figures.

One hypothesis underlying this proposition is that the traditional criminal 'underground' is no longer to be regarded as a counter-culture on the Beggars' Opera model but has many connections with the law-abiding economic sphere. In the present absence of empirical knowledge this is a largely speculative suggestion. There are however important factual sources accessible to researchers, some of which are mentioned in the next section on 'points of method'.

It is suggested that the difficult research operations opened up by this prospect should include a study of receiving on an international scale, comparing the phenomenon in different countries. It is a matter of acute interest to the team that the only topic on which their findings diverge from those of Interpol is that of the scale of operation of receivers in Europe (see pp. 110 and 111 above).

(4) *The substantial incomers*

For an example of these see the comparatively 'anonymous' group referred to in chapter 4 above, pp. 53-4. The 'incomers' are of first-class theoretical importance, since they call attention to the relative accessibility, from the point of view of police control, of those full-time criminals, members of the established criminal networks, who are by definition better known to the police. The much less accessible activities of the substantial incomers are not characterised, so far as one can see, by any considerable *economic* 'organisation in depth'; on the other hand they contribute to and are sustained by the criminal sub-culture as a whole. Two important practical considerations are that the economic cost to society of commando-type armed robbery is rising quickly; and the exponents of this type of crime contribute, out of all proportion to their numbers, to the romanticising of crime.

(5)   *Business-type crime*

This refers to those business-type activities which are unquestionably in contravention of the criminal law. This is a highly topical subject in view of the continuing prevalence of company fraud and other types of fraud on a large scale, conducted not only by crooks and shady businessmen but also by people in good standing in business and political circles. The European tradition of linking legal and criminological study, with criminology very much the junior partner, helps to explain why this field is for all practical purposes unresearched. But the situation is changing with the growing independence of criminology and the growing interest among lawyers in the sociology of law. It would in any case be in the worst tradition of classical criminology if the newly beginning study of criminal organisation were to confine itself to the field of physical predatory crime. (See topic (1) and pp. 24-5 above).

(6)   *Business-type crime question-mark*

This is the continuum ranging from specifically fraudulent practices, through dubious exploitations of business opportunities, to praiseworthy business innovations. Too much discussion has been concerned in the past with whether criminologists should concern themselves with operations about which the question can be asked — is business-type crime really crime? The suggestion here is that while this may or may not be a proper topic for criminological enquiry, it is certainly a first-class topic for general sociological enquiry. One need not labour its implications for political theory and political practice alike. No topic raised in this book is more in need of clarification, or more difficult. See pp. 13-15 above.

Points of method

These topics for research at once raise a prior question. It cannot be over-emphasised that an essential preliminary condition of doing research into topics of this kind is the spending of a lot of time on devising means of access to information. This has so far been a matter of the initiative and good luck of a scatter of individual investigators. The interests of the Council of Europe in this field of enquiry manifested in their remit opens up the possibility of a more organised attack on the problem, as far as official and police sources are concerned. While knowledge gained from police sources must be checked and tested by knowledge gained from direct access to criminals and to criminal organisations, the converse is equally valid. We suggest moreover that a comprehensive or all-round picture of major criminal systems of behaviour can best be gained by *beginning* on the police side, while guarding against the danger of confusing police methods of organising their material with actual forms of criminal organisation. Another essential consideration is that the criminal sub-culture, and the general sphere of criminal operations on a major scale, is structured to a considerable extent by the agencies of social control and particularly by the police.

The two principal sources of data on the police side are statistics and 'know-how'.

(1) *Statistics*

The published criminal statistics of any country do not differentiate between major, minor and petty criminal operations. On the other hand police have at their disposal the raw materials of a precise statistical and documentary register of crime which could enable researchers, police and non-police, to achieve a high degree of discrimination as to the proportionate prevalence of the different types of major crime as known to the police. This is no pipe-dream. One of the more remarkable research essays in the field of statistical control is that of McClintock and Gibson, 1961, whose classification of different types of robbery was adopted almost at once by Scotland Yard. Professor McClintock is in process of organising a wider range of statistical and other data in this field. This kind of work seems to us to be an indispensable indicator, to the considerable degree that this material allows, of changes in the different types of major crime. Statistical instruments and methods of a precision equal to those of the Metropolitan Police are being operated in the German National Police Research Centre in Wiesbaden.

This particular type of access work does not in our opinion call for a major reorganisation of the published criminal statistics. These matters are in hand in the United Kingdom and in other countries, but they will take all of twenty years to work out. We suggest instead two or three highly organised research operations in which researchers collaborate closely with specially designated police researchers, who are kept on the job for the period — it might be as much as two years — required to produce a comprehensive answer to specific questions. Such projects would be a necessary condition of the successful carrying through of topic (1) above (Scale of the Problem), which would require an accurate calculation of the estimated value of the items stolen in major organised criminal operations.

For many of the special topics which fall under topic (3) (Background Operators) there is an immense amount of accurate statistical material which is recorded not by the police but by large industrial and commercial organisations and by trade associations. An effective approach to the study of large-scale receiving, for example, might be through hijacking (ground operations) or long-firm fraud. There is a great deal of material on these subjects, already well organised, to be found outside police sources. Most of this material is ordinarily inaccessible, but there is a growing disposition, in the trade circles and particularly in security organisations, to co-operate in research. An important recent discussion on this subject is reported in Wiles and McClintock, 1972, pp. 91-100.

(2) *'Know-how'*

The informal knowledge acquired by active detectives over many years of experience on the ground is at once the most elusive and the most potentially valuable of the police sources. It is impossible to do it justice in a brief account such as this. Our experience in the survey and in other research projects suggests that with the authorisation and full support of the police authority, and of the police chiefs, a research operation combining non-police researchers with a team of detectives would produce first-class sociological work. The merit of the sociological or anthropological approach in this field is that it is interested in the nature of criminal organisation and culture and the way in which things are done rather than in facts about individuals and about particular historical episodes, much of which must remain confidential. The combined team would necessarily share much of this confidential information, for the simple reason that the informal knowledge possessed by the police is organised round individuals, but publication would normally take the form of sociological as distinct from historical propositions.

(3) *Direct access*

As will be seen from the preceding section, direct-access investigations have so far been a matter of luck and good judgement on the part of

163

G

individual researchers. The team have no ideas as to how this kind of investigation can be organised. It is a matter for creative research. On the other hand the experience of one project suggests that a team combining access to police information with direct-access studies should keep the two operationally distinct and separate. This is not primarily a matter of confidentiality. It is good research design to ensure that two methods of enquiry planned with a view to reciprocal verification should proceed independently.

Points of organisation

The following points concern primarily recommendations for action by the Council of Europe and its research consultants and correspondents.

1 The Council (through its European Committee on Crime Problems) might convene a series of meetings, combining research and police experts with others drawn from government departments of industry and trade. The form, duration and agenda of these consultations would be a matter for the Committee and its advisers.

2 Criminological and sociological research institutes in a number of countries already have post-graduate research courses of a year or more in duration, attended by police and other law-enforcement officers together with post-graduate students. The general practice, as in the Cambridge Institute of Criminology, is for the individual student to write a thesis on a subject of his own choice. It is suggested that joint or team studentships might be created combining students from law-enforcement agencies with post-graduate students in the preparation and publication of work in this field, with particular reference to the matters of method outlined above.

This recommendation might be accepted for study and discussion at one of the meetings of directors of research institutes convened annually by the Council of Europe.

Action point

A final action point is outwith the bounds of the remit given to the team, and indeed outside the jurisdiction of researchers. It is based on the recognition that research takes a long time, and only occasionally produces findings of operational significance. A number of matters referred to in these pages might in our opinion be regarded by the competent authorities as requiring special measures of co-operation

164

between the countries of Europe, and particularly between their law-enforcement agencies. One such matter is the need to close the gaps between police systems exploited by travelling criminals. A second such matter is the possibility of criminal exploitation of the opportunities provided by the adoption of countries of Europe of new forms of economic and commercial controls. It is suggested that these matters be discussed not only in terms of research but also in terms of intergovernmental executive action.

Appendix A

The Council of Europe remit

The remit given to the research team by the Secretary-General of the Council of Europe embodied the proposal of the Council's European Committee on Crime Problems that the theme of the Co-ordinated Criminological Research Workers' Fellowship for 1970 should be 'Certain Aspects of Organised and Professional Crime'.

The programme of Fellowships for criminological research began in 1968. The aim of the programme, which includes individual and co-ordinated Fellowships, is to secure the participation of research workers in criminological study and research of common European interest. The present study is the third in the series of co-ordinated Fellowships. The 1968 study had as its theme 'The Prison Community', and was directed by Professor Mathiesen of the Institute for Social Research in Oslo. The 1969 study, on 'The Role of the School in the Prevention of Juvenile Delinquency', was directed by M. Jacques Selosse, Head of the Research Department at the Vaucresson Centre for Research and Training (Ministry of Justice, France). In each case the Director has the collaboration of a team of three workers from different member States of the Council of Europe, who are enabled in terms of the Fellowships to undertake individually or jointly 25 days of enquiry abroad — i.e. outside their own country — on the basis of tasks assigned to them.

The director of the project was Mr John A. Mack, then Head of the School of Social Study in the University of Glasgow; now Senior Research Fellow in Criminology in that university. The remaining three members of the team, nominated by their respective governments, were as follows.

M. Jean Susini (France): Head of the Bureau of Criminology and of the Human Sciences of the National Police. M. Susini demitted this office in 1972. He is also lecturer in Criminology of the Institute of Legal Medicine (Faculty of Medicine), Paris; and visiting professor in Criminology in the University of Montreal.

Mr Hans-Jurgen Kerner (German Federal Republic): Assistant at the Institute of Criminology of the University of Tübingen; specialising for the Institute in the subject of the present study.

Mr Aldo Peronaci (Italy): President of the First Court of Assizes of

Appeal at Rome; a specialist student of criminal law. Mr Peronaci, having completed the main part of the field work allotted to him, retired from the team in early 1971 on taking up an important judicial appointment.

The director's task in these co-ordinated Fellowships is to arrange the plan of study. It is clearly understood by all concerned that given the limited means available, both in time and money, the team is not expected to undertake research properly speaking, but might be able to fix the starting points for more intensive study to be undertaken at a later stage. The team might in particular trace guiding lines from the methodological point of view.

The remit suggested that the following points might be examined: definition of organised and professional crime; size of the problem in member States, especially with regard to the social costs and damage involved; survey of research carried out or in hand; brief accounts of such studies; any discernible tendencies; structure of professional criminal organisation.

Plan and method of work

The plan and method of work was quickly decided. The operational limits of this enterprise are strictly defined and determined, not only by the comparatively small amount of time and other resources available, but also and mainly by the undeveloped state of the subject. Current European studies in this field are practically non-existent; indeed it may be said that they are only now beginning to emerge; and there is no continuity with the few enquiries into the subject made earlier in the century. The situation in the USA is more promising; but the few systematic studies made in recent years are small-scale and exploratory, and there are major differences in definitional approach which make even the best American work a confusing and indeed misleading guide to the European scene. The general conclusion arrived at by the team in the preliminary discusssion was that serious criminological investigation into organised and professional crime has made little or no progress in the last thirty years, and is in fact casting about for a new beginning. It followed, to quote from the preliminary statement agreed by the team, that 'we should aim at producing nothing more ambitious than a sketch-map, from such positions as can be speedily attained, of territories still to be explored'.

It was accordingly resolved to attempt a few brief field studies, working on the surface of events, and consulting knowledgeable individuals and organisations. Each member of the team undertook a series of visits, interviews and enquiries, in a country other than his own, and undertook also to compile information or additional information about his own country. It was further agreed to attempt some degree of functional as well as geographical specialisation, by studying for example criminals whose operations extend through a large number of countries and overseas to other continents; problems of law enforcement and of the gathering of evidence; and the interaction between the penal system, particularly the prisons, and the behaviour systems sustained by persistent criminal operators.

One major omission in this report is that of the criminal traffic in narcotics: the reader will find only a few scattered references here and there to this subject, which is at once too complex and too inaccessible to be dealt with here in any detail. It is also to be noted that various aspects of this problem are at present under study by different sections of the Council of Europe.

Trends and estimates

The main practical question set by the Committee − the size of the problem in member States, especially with regard to the social costs and damage involved − was closely considered. The proposition was broken up into a number of more detailed questions: e.g.

Is it possible to produce comparative estimates of national trends in serious crime (i.e. crime above a certain level of measurable social cost)?
Is serious crime increasing in total and as a fraction of all crime?
Is this increase in serious and large-scale crime the result of an increase in the number and range of activity of practitioners of organised and professional crime?

The preliminary discussions produced tentative answers which on the whole have been borne out in the event. The provisional answer to the first question is that international comparative estimates will be possible only when national criminal statistics are recorded and calculated on a uniform basis.[1] At present there is no such uniformity, either as between nations or as between local areas within any given nation. There is of course some progress towards uniformity in the latter field in certain countries.

As regards the second question, it was thought that a fairly definitive answer would be possible, at least as regards those countries in which special investigations had been or were being made.

The third question was thought to be strictly speaking unanswerable. Precise measurement depends on precise definition. No country records in its criminal statistics crimes committed by practitioners of organised and professional crime, for the simple reason that no country has any such official classification. Indeed, even if any system of statistical recording included a heading 'Practitioner of Organised Crime' or 'Professional Criminal' it would be difficult if not impossible to obtain general agreement on what crimes and offenders should be included under those headings. For the current situation is that the field of organised and professional crime has still to be delimited and analysed; the phrase has still to be precisely defined. This was one of the first tasks attempted; as a result the team came to the view that it would make for a clearer grasp of the phenomenon if the phrase were discarded. This finding emerged only gradually. In the early stages of the study it was natural and convenient to use the conventional wordings. 'Organised' and 'professional', inadequate as definitions, are highly effective as signals: people knew at once what one was getting at even if there turned out to be big differences in interpretation. It is for this reason that the matter of definition is dealt with on two levels: the definitions indicated by the remit and used in interviews; and the reformulations arrived at after working through the results of the interviews, and in the course of discussion with fellow-scholars in Europe and the USA.

Definitions[2]

The phrase 'organised and professional crime' is not a description but a label; it is moreover a label that fails to list properly the contents of the package. This is a common fault of criminological language, much of which is taken unaltered from the official wisdom. But there is a special ambiguity about this particular phrase. It means one thing in Europe, another in North America. In the European sense of the phrase the words 'organised' and 'professional' stand for two interacting aspects of the same complex process. In the North American usage as typified by the tasks set by the US President's Commission,[3] organised crime and professional crime are separate concepts denoting two different sectors of criminal activity, closely related in certain respects but essentially distinct in practice and theory. A further complication is provided by the fact that some of those now working on the comparatively unexplored subject of criminal organisation ('organisation' being used here in its general or dictionary sense) are themselves North Americans: D. R. Cressey is their leading figure (Cressey, 1972).

170

European usage has always remained faithful to the dictionary meaning of 'organised'. On this side of the Atlantic it covers all degrees and types of organisation. It is thus wider in extent than 'professional'. It takes in all criminal operations, however small-scale and inadequate, in which more than one person participates, and in which some rudimentary role-differentiation occurs. The most primitive degree of organisation might be placed at one extreme of a continuum from less to more structured. An alternative model is a hierarchy of degrees of organisation. The least structured continuum point, or the lowest level of the hierarchy, might be exemplified by a pair of small boys, one of whom diverts the attention of the short-sighted shopkeeper while the other removes some sweets. The organisation is informal; the element of calculation — rationality as Max Weber defines the word — is minimal. The same pair of small boys might move themselves along the continuum if they repeated the operation and persisted in it until such time as their organisation was broken up. (See also Cressey, 1972, p. 12.) Further along the continuum, or higher up the scale, organisation becomes more formal, more rational, less impermanent. At this point it begins to look more like other organisations in business or politics. At this point too the schematism becomes more crudely specu-lative, for sheer lack of empirical content. Theoretically speaking (says Cressey) . . . 'it should be possible to place these organisations on a continuum of rationality, perhaps according to characteristics such as the skills required of the participants, permanence, discipline, and immunity from arrest. But it is not possible to do so now, for the simple reason that the English-language literature, at least, contains very few descriptions of what the participants in criminal organisations actually *do*' (ibid. p. 18). There is, however, one partial exception to this poverty of empirical content. The literature in both Europe and North America over the past thirty or forty years does provide a small number of studies of criminal activities at what is generally termed the professional end of the con-tinuum. There is also a steady flow of practical exercises. A recent exemplar in the UK is the Great Train Robbery of 1963. This was described by a British criminologist as the most outstanding achievement in the entire history of organised crime. It would also be agreed by criminologists and police alike to be a thoroughly professional piece of work. Organisation and professionalism, says a French colleague, are two aspects of the same process according as one focuses on teamwork and systematic planning on the one hand or on the skill, flair, training, status and success of the individual operators on the other. It is this level or sector of criminal organisation which is indicated by the Council of Europe remit.

On this European interpretation the two terms are interchangeable. But there is an alternative version, current mainly in North America, in which the reference is to two distinct and separate categories of crime. Professional crime so distinguished is what we have just begun to outline, and what we shall find to be our main interest in this European study. But professional crime so understood is overshadowed in North America by the growth of what is now generally known there as organised crime. Since we need a special distinguishing label for this latter phenomenon, and since it is frequently associated with the idea of criminal syndicates, it will be useful for our present purposes to call it syndicated crime. In this we follow Albini (1971). The term is not entirely satisfactory – it does not, for example, translate into French – but it will have to do.

In spite of what has just been said, syndicated crime is not a purely North American thing. It is probable that systematic investigation will discover something like it in a world-wide variety of settings, mainly urban, and mainly in complex economies. It will therefore be part of our task to attempt to locate and identify what Europe has to show in the way of syndicated crime. This is a matter for a later section: meantime a sketch of the North American scene will be helpful.

In Europe, as in most parts of the world outside North America, the thing is inconspicuous. In North America, or more precisely in the USA,[4] it is and has been for most of the present century a major feature of the criminal and political landscape. The USA shows us the thing 'writ large', as Plato would say. This is not to assume that the USA today gives us a preview of European crime the day after tomorrow. It simply gives a hint as to what to look for, and what not to look for, in Europe.

We now go on to list what features the two types of crime and criminal have in common, and also what features distinguish them from each other. Here we are working on the conventional definitions, adding here and there such modifications as are being suggested by recent first-hand research.

Syndicated and professional crime – common elements

First the common features.

In the first place, both are in crime as a full-time occupation, just as other and law-abiding persons are in banking, or in medicine, or in wholesale stationery, or in the motor car industry. There are two reservations to the use of the word 'full-time'. The special nature of the crime industry requires it to work under cover, so that it is usual for its practitioners also to have a respectable occupational role as a 'front' — e.g. laundry proprietor, or demolition contractor, or shipyard labourer. The second reservation is that these 'front' roles are not necessarily spurious.

Secondly, both sets of criminals are in it for the money; their behaviour is in the main economically rational; to the same degree, that is, no more and no less, as the behaviour of people in the non-criminal trades and professions is economically rational.

Thirdly, both are on the whole moderately successful, in some cases exceedingly successful, judged in terms of money-getting, and of their ability to avoid the occupational risk of loss of liberty.

Fourthly, crime is for both not only a main source of income; it is also a way of life. Full-time criminals tend to organise their friendship and recreational patterns on the basis of their work relationships, just as medicals, or lawyers, or dockers do; they sustain a distinctive occupational sub-culture. The criminal sub-culture is more isolated than those of the law-abiding trades or professions. (Cf. Clinard and Quinney, 1967, p. 429.) It is also much more given to internecine violence and intimidation. But it is a distinctive occupational group for all that, with a long history. Its existence is to be traced in general literature, so far as Europe is concerned, from the fifteenth or sixteenth century on.[5]

Syndicated crime — distinguishing marks

Current descriptions of US syndicated crime (generally entitled 'organised crime' in that sub-continent and beyond) are a wellnigh inseparable mixture of observation and speculation, fact and fantasy. The following summary account attempts to keep as close to the ground as is possible in this lunar landscape.

First, the US syndicates are *primarily* commercial enterprises. They have some degree of *Gemeinschaft,* witnessed to by the Mafia legend, but they are also and mainly business undertakings of uncertain, allegedly vast magnitude. In their beginnings, before Prohibition opened up the highly profitable trade in bootleg alcohol, their activity was parasitical: that of extortion and 'protection' inflicted on more or less shady concerns and individuals, or confined to ethnic minorities. These rackets remain a steady source of income, ramifying in a variety of ways and covering a wider selection of victim groups. A prime example is labour racketeering; it consists of syndicate control of the supply of labour, usually unskilled or semi-skilled, in certain districts or restricted sectors of industry. But the main and distinguishing function of the syndicates in these latter days is that of the trader, the middleman. The core of organised crime activities, says the Task Force Report, is the supplying of goods and services which are prohibited or limited by law and for which there is a strong and lasting economic demand; examples are gaming, usury (loan-sharking), and (though there are reservations here) the importation and distribution of narcotics.

Protected as they are from the competition of the lawful market, the syndicates tend towards near-monopoly. The territorial extent of these near-monopolies, being a function of the size and persistence through time of the syndicates and syndicate-cartels, is a matter of acute controversy.

Second, they are commercial undertakings with a difference, the difference being a second consequence of their extra-legal status. Since they cannot call on the public law to maintain internal and inter-syndicate order, they promote these necessary functions partly by consensus, mainly by the systematic use of intimidation and violence ranging from roughing-up to homicide. Historically speaking, the violence came first; the economically profitable use of it came next; the final synthesis subordinated the violence to the business; the violence, including con-tinuing homicide on a large if diminishing scale, remains the cutting edge of the organisation.

Third, the syndicates appear by all but a few accounts to persist through time to an extent that strains European credulity. The varieties of syndicate-type organisation, and possibly the principal syndicate-combines regarded as continuing organisations, have survived close on a century of more or less vigorous attempts at suppression by the forces of law and order. Even in the last ten years of massive mobilisation of the nation's resources against organised crime it has proved difficult to get and keep the mobsters behind bars.[6] And even if they do get locked up the nature of the organisation is such that the rôle-system goes on though the rôle-bearers may change (here differing from the more idiosyncratic and person-centred 'task forces' of so-called 'professional' crime).

These are some of the basic features. We are still only at the beginning of an adequate description of the USA syndicates. The above statements, restricted as they are to what would be generally agreed by most observers, give rise to numerous questions about other and essential matters about which no agreement exists. What, for example, is it that enables the syndicate system to persist? A stock answer is 'corruption'. Some leading theorists, notably Cressey, make corruption the defining principle of the USA syndicates. By corruption is meant the illicit influencing of individuals and groups discharging public responsibilities. This line of explanation is usually conjoined with the Mafia or Cosa Nostra hypothesis, namely that the power and persistence of the syndi-cates is to be explained by their coming together in a continent-wide conspiracy, a confederation controlled by the Italian-American syndicates. This is the thesis of the Task Force Report of 1967, and may therefore be regarded as official doctrine. But it is far from being generally accepted by criminological and political scientists in the USA.[7]

There are two powerful counter-arguments to the corruption-cum-Mafia hypothesis. The first is that 'corruption' as defined above is not exclusive to the syndicates. It is not an activity which distinguishes the syndicates from other non-criminal bodies. US government at all levels is largely a matter of pressure-group politics. By far the majority of the innumerable lobbies which seek to influence public authorities and executive bodies in their favour are concerned to promote legal objectives, even if they are not too particular about the methods they use. The power and influence wielded by the syndicates might reasonably be regarded as simply an extension of the non-criminal pressure-group system.

The second argument is that what makes the syndicates influential is not so much intimidation or bribery as the recognition by the so-called corruptees of the fact that they are meeting a genuine and popular if formally illegal demand. Admittedly the syndicates are an insanely expensive and damaging supply device; but they will persist and indeed flourish so long as US governments, and particularly state governments, maintain their habit of passing exemplary laws, laws which they are unable or unwilling to enforce.

These are vast questions, or possibly pseudo-questions; for a further discussion, with particular reference to the topic of syndicated crime in Europe, see chapter three above.

Professional crime — distinguishing marks

We turn now to our main topic of professional crime. The term has been used somewhat indiscriminately in recent years.[8] But most of the text-books restrict themselves to variations of the themes initiated by E. H. Sutherland's celebrated study of *The Professional Thief* (1937). It is significant that the subject discussed is usually professional criminals, rather than professional crime.

The following propositions should be read along with those on pp. 172-3 above — 'Common elements'.

First, *professional criminals are traditional predatory criminals.* Their techniques can be original and unorthodox, but the crimes they commit are of the kind generally agreed to be crimes — the main examples being burglary, robbery, thieving and fraud.

Second, *they are property criminals.* Such crimes of violence against persons as they commit are generally in the furtherance of the acquisition of property.

Third, *they operate within the traditional criminal–victim relationships.* It is this that most sharply distinguishes the professional from the syndicated criminal. Professional criminals usually work on victims who dislike being made victims. Syndicates sell their illicit goods to willing buyers. Abolish burglary and no one will complain except the burglars. Abolish the syndicates and you will have powerful unsupplied demands cruising around looking for new sources of supply.[9]

Fourth, *professional criminals are an élite,* a minute and admired fraction of a larger group of full-time miscreants.[10] This point is made clearly by Sutherland. The élite status is derived from a period of tutelage and testing by seniors, the consequent acquirement of specialised skills, and an endowment of sufficient intelligence to profit by the tutelage and learn the skills.

A fifth and final point is that professional criminals appear to be by and large physically healthy and psychologically normal. This proposition claims no more than that the incidence of physical and mental illness in this small criminal group, and indeed in the larger group of full-time able[11] small-scale miscreants, is likely to be no higher than in the general population, and could well be lower.

Since this list of generally accepted criteria is based on current text-books it is worth noting that some recent commentators exclude 'heavy' operators (for example robbers with violence, users of explosives, etc.). Clinard and Quinney (1967, p. 429) would restrict the 'professional' caption to thieving. This may be because the only first-hand accounts so far extant are restricted to thieving and fraud (Sutherland, 1937; Maurer, 1955). Sutherland himself makes no such exclusion. He talks about the professional burglar and the professional stick-up man (man with a gun), though he does no more than mention them. Also general police opinion today gives the higher status to 'heavy' operations as compared with the clever manipulation of people practised by the pickpockets and confidence men described by Sutherland and Maurer.

The professional label criticised

The foregoing statement is a fair summing-up of the conventional wisdom on the subject. It has remained broadly unchanged since Sutherland's classical description in 1937 of one category of professional criminals operating over the previous twenty years. It calls for criticism on two grounds. In the first place some of it is out of date. The people and activities and situations referred to by the term have changed greatly in the last fifty years. This is simply to say that since Sutherland criminologists have on the whole been exploring in other parts of the forest, and no

176

thoroughgoing reappraisal has been attempted. It would be highly surprising if great changes hadn't taken place here as in every other field of activity.

The second and more fundamental criticism has already been indicated. It is that the conventional wisdom in this field is excessively inaccurate, and has been so since the beginnings of systematic exposition in Sutherland. The 'professional criminal' stereotype plays down the organisational factor. (This is not a criticism of Sutherland, who says very sensible things about criminal organisation; but his motion that these aspects be followed up has been lost in subsequent discussion.) It gives too simple a picture of the complex undercover activities and relationships sustained by full-time miscreants; it is like a primitive painting, all foreground: it puts the spotlight on one particular group, and brings it out larger than life. Its most misleading feature is that it insists over-much on the uniquely élite status of this particular group. The crime industry may be a small-scale affair compared with the major legitimate undertakings, but it has numerous varieties and grades of operator. In fine the concept treats a fairly complicated system of relationships as though it were a primitively structured aggregate of individuals, a mass of petty criminality dominated by a high table of criminal eminences.

It is therefore, we suggest, desirable to get rid of the 'professional' terminology. But not because the group itself has disappeared, as Cressey suggests. Cressey is discussing the disappearance of Sutherland's professional thief. The title, he argues, 'should disappear with him, rather than lingering on to be . . . applied indiscriminately to criminals who would have been the subject of ridicule and derision by the professional criminals of the good old days . . .' (Cressey, 1972, p. 45). This is possibly sound doctrine as regards the Chic Conwell type of professional, but it is quite unsound in relation to the high-level 'heavy' operators of the present day, whose activities are quite as varied and at least as highly organised as those described in the classical texts.

Our general conclusion is that the conventional wisdom is by no means all fantasy and folklore. The things referred to with more or less precision under the rubric of professional crime are real things which persist through the changes. There are individuals and groups recognisable as 'professional criminals'; people who satisfy, by and large, most of the criteria indicated above. What is needed for a more adequate criminology is, first, to establish their exact location and function within the contemporary systems operated by full-time miscreants; second and more important, to focus criminological attention on the nature of criminal organisation, and of criminal organisations, rather than on this or that grade or group of individual operators.

A clue to location is given by a recent paper in which a broad distinction is made between background and front-line operators (pp. 10-11 above). The figures in the background are organisers of criminal undertakings; they command effective intelligence networks, they set up jobs, they plan in advance for the disposal of the spoils, they sometimes operate an informal welfare and after-care system for lesser criminals and their dependants. In so far as they confine themselves to these functions — there is some mixing of roles — they seldom or never come into contact with the victim, or with the victim's property prior to the completion of the direct operation. The front-line operators are the housebreakers, or the van or bank robbers, or the hijackers or the fraudsters. There are intermediate categories. The traditional role of the receiver or 'fence' is by its nature a background one; the more heavyweight or important the receiver is, the more likely he is to combine his role with that of background organiser. Another intermediate role is that of the provider of services, the contact man, the carrier of intelligence, the transport organiser. These are usually but not always lesser functionaries, working some in the background, some in the foreground.

The professional stereotype has little or nothing to say about the background organisers. Most accounts of the professional criminal make reference to fences, but are rather hazy about their role in relation to professional crime, and usually imply that the fence is an ancillary rather than a professional. Likewise the 'providers of services', so far as they are considered at all, are thought of as ancillary specialists of a lower status than that of the professional criminal. Indeed, the only role adequately covered by the 'professional' concept is that of the high-status front-line operator. Since these people exist, and in individual cases enjoy very high status indeed, the traditional concept certainly applies. But it applies to a rather limited extent, and it fails completely to cover the fact that category for category, and setting aside questions of the prestige of this or that individual or the way in which some individuals combine the background and front-line roles, the background operator enjoys a higher status than the direct predator. A series of discussions with a group of high-ranking British detectives brought out clearly the conviction on their part that any individual operating in the front line, in direct contact with the victim and the property, was by definition in the second rank of criminal operators. The research team in question had some reservations about this, but the point was emphatically asserted by these experienced policemen.

It follows that it may not be too difficult to establish the place and role of the professional in the high-level criminal system. He is a front-line operator, and as such a secondary figure, in a system which is predominantly and increasingly characterised by organisation in depth. Further than this it is not now possible to go. The report includes some material on criminal organisation (and criminal organisations) at the level hitherto indicated by the term 'professional' — the organisation behind the front-liners, to use the language here suggested. But an adequate characterisation of this comparatively unknown territory is very much a matter for future first-hand research.

Organisation and field visits

The field visits and interviews were carried out by Mr Kerner as regards the Netherlands and the German Federal Republic, by Mr Susini and Mr Peronaci as regards Italy and France (this was a combined operation, although Mr Susini had the main responsibility for the Italian interviews and Mr Peronaci for the French interviews), and by the team director as regards the United Kingdom and Denmark and Sweden. This division of labour was adopted in preference to the method of collective team visitation practised in the previous Co-ordinated Research Fellowship projects. This was a pity, in so far as it deprived the team of the frequent opportunities for discussion and comparing notes which would have been afforded by going round together. But there were two decisive drawbacks to the collective model of enquiry. For the student of the criminal 'underworld' (we began by thinking in these popular terms) there is nothing to see above ground — no prisons, no schools, no clinics, no probation hostels. Moreover, neither the criminals themselves nor the police would be likely to expand on the more informal and realistic aspects of the subject in the presence of a deputation. As it turned out no member of the team made much of an attempt to gain direct information from criminal practitioners. That this is not impossible, even in the space of a short survey, is shown by the work of our American predecessors in the US President's Working Party. They interviewed quite a cross-section of criminals in the space of two or three months. But the results were not (as we judged them) entirely relevant to our subject, which we had broadly defined as criminal activity at the 'professional' or highest level of the criminal organisation continuum.[12] The individuals described and quoted in 'The Professional Criminal'[13] are comparatively small fry (cf. Cressey, 1972, p. 47). So we confined ourselves by and large to discussion with knowledgeable policemen, prosecutors, and others in the law-enforcement process.

The team were under no illusions about the extent or value of the information likely to be yielded by police informants to strangers,

H

however well authenticated, in such a short period of time as a month or usually less. The same reservation would apply to an enquiry sustained over a much longer period. This is of course the elementary grammar of this kind of investigation. The first problem to be tackled by researchers into major crime — the first in time if not in importance — is that of access to information. This topic belongs to another section of this report. Here we need mention only one characteristic of the good police detective. He is apt to be almost as uncommunicative as the able criminal. This is the mark of the top-ranking detectives of the old school. They had their own special sources of information, their own contacts, and they shared the fruits of these only very sparingly with those few colleagues whom they had come to trust in the course of a long period of working together. It is also perhaps part of the nature of police work in relation to the more highly skilled criminals. The new systems of criminal intelligence whereby information (and more important inspired guesses) are recorded and shared, has made great advances in a number of countries;[14] but it has to contend with certain lessons burned into the minds of experienced detectives. There are few senior policemen who cannot quote with great regret the way in which some very promising thief-catching enterprises, based on first-class information and insight, came to nothing. As it happened, the actual thief-catching operation had had for a variety of reasons to be entrusted to some neighbouring police force or police division, or even to some other branch in the same force. The modern detective is now being trained to share his knowledge and insights, and also to co-operate effectively in the increasingly elaborate task-force operations which are nowadays required to counter successfully the highly organised operations conducted by organised criminals. But this sharing of information within the police tends to carry with it a strong disposition to communicate with outsiders only in the most general terms.

We were the more pleasantly surprised to find quite a number of our contacts ready and willing to come more than half-way to meet us in our discussions. We argue elsewhere in these pages that the first requirement for research in this field is the development of informed co-operation between the knowledgeable policemen and the social researcher. Our experience in our short visits renders this a not unhopeful prospect. This is in part the result of a widening of police horizons in matters of research. We encountered, in more than one country, police research departments which do not confine themselves to matters of forensic science and criminalistics (activities conducted at a high technological level in most major police forces) but are also beginning to develop research interests in the broad field of the sociology of organisation. We were also privileged to meet here and there the kind of policeman who combines a capacity for

180

reflective analysis with a strong interest in the complexities of criminal organisation. The opportunities thus provided varied somewhat from force to force, and from time to time within the same force. A certain 'caginess' is still the predominant feature of such discussions as we tried to conduct; one team member commented rather caustically on this. But the net result of our enquiries has been distinctly positive; it was possible in a number of cases to combine the information provided in these discussions with documentary study and further reading in such a way as to produce reports rather more substantial than we had expected to achieve when we started off.

The team began by preparing a questionnaire for use in the interviews. This questionnaire is not reproduced here, since it was abandoned early by some members of the team and since it turned out in all cases to be useful only in part. This in itself was an important negative finding. The questionnaire was two-pronged. One prong followed out in detail the characteristics, and prevalence in Europe, of professional crime as the term is generally understood. The second prong undertook as a separate exercise to obtain parallel data on the *American model* of organised crime. The questionnaire was not accepted by the team without considerable and vigorous discussion. It was however finally agreed that there would be no harm in finding out by direct attack what evidence our expert police adviser would be able to provide about the nature and scope of American-model organised crime (or syndicated crime, as we came to call it later) in Europe.

As it turned out, the second prong failed to connect. Our consultants accepted the 'European' version of the 'professional/organised' distinction (see chapter 1 above), and tended accordingly to give identical answers to both sets of questions. In the course of further discussion they produced specimens of syndicated crime, European model. They were emphatic that while there could be occasional and short-lived outbursts in this or that city, this kind of crime was inconsiderable.

Finally there is a matter of presentation. The points raised in these interviews and discussions are set out country by country. No attempt at comparative assessment is implied. It would be a quite impossible task to decide either which country has the most able criminals, or which country has best managed to get its able criminals under control. In any case this kind of question is out of date. It is becoming increasingly apparent that the really able criminals, whether they operate in the realm of big business crime, or in the more familiar territories of traditional property crime, are finding their more profitable fields of enterprise in the international sphere and in the gaps between the national law-enforcement systems.

Notes

1 Nevertheless several students of the subject have attempted detailed comparisons: see, notably, Wolf, 1968.

2 This section is an expanded version of some of the points made in chapter 1 above.

3 The US President's Commission on Law Enforcement and Administration of Justice set one Task Force to work on organised crime and a second group to study the professional criminal. The Task Force Report on organised crime was published in 1967. The second report was not published, but has been made available to the team by courtesy of the editor, Mr Leroy Gould. The two working parties discussed their topics as separate and distinct criminal and criminological entities.

4 It is not entirely clear how well organised the thing is in Canada – whether, for example, the Canadian syndicates are part and parcel of the putative 'nation-wide confederation' of the USA, or whether indeed syndicated crime has developed in the Canadian metropolitan area on any scale of magnitude comparable to the major USA centres. See 'La Société face au crime', Commission d'Enquête sur l'Administration de la Justice en Matière Criminelle et Pénale au Québec (Quebec, 1969).

5 Possibly earlier. Cf. Judges, 1930 and 1965, p. xxvii. '. . . At some point since the beginning of vagrancy legislation in the fourteenth century . . . the picaro became a professional . . .' It is interesting that the term 'professional' has here a meaning quite distinct from that of our own time, and more relevant to its continuing criminal theme. The quotation goes on: '. . . The picaro became a professional, a professor of one of the crafts or mysteries odious to all right thinking of the commonwealth.'

See also Inciardi (1972), pp. 218-22 for a brief historical note. We understand Dr Inciardi has a book in the press on the history of professional crime to be entitled *Careers in Crime*. (See Inciardi, 1974.)

6 'The New York Joint Legislative Committee on Crime . . . found that of 536 Mafia leaders arrested on felony charges in the New York City area during the last 10 years, only 37 were imprisoned.' Harlow Unger: 'US criminals have best ever year', in *Sunday Times* (London), 23 May 1971.

See also Jack Newfield in the New York *Village Voice* vol. XIX, no. 16, Thursday 18 April, 1974: 'A survey of 1,800 organised crime cases conducted by the Senate Select Commitee revealed that Mafia members receive five times more dismissals in State Supreme Court than all other types of defendants' (p. 44). The article from which this is quoted is entitled 'Judging the Judges: a remedy for arrogance'. The reference is to the State of New York.

7 For example the whole notion of an Italo-American-dominated

syndicate system, questioned by Bell and many others (e.g. Bell, 1960), has been criticised more recently by Albini (1972) and Ianni (1972). Ianni has now followed up (1974) his case-study finding that the Italo-Americans are on the way out by an analysis of the growing power of Black and Puerto Rican syndicates. It is unfortunate that Ianni has chosen to perpetuate part of the myth he is criticising by calling his new book *The Black Mafia*. Is this a further instance of the (academically) malign influence of publishers?

8   Cf. Cressey's remark — the reference is probably to the US police — '... the "professional" adjective tends to be applied to almost all criminals believed by the police (but not necessarily by other criminals) to have intelligence levels something above those of idiots' (Cressey, 1972, pp. 45-6).

9   The last four sentences are a free paraphrase of Cressey, 1969, p. 72. The reference is of course to US syndicated crime.

10   See Mack, 1964, for this term. In this 1964 paper full-time miscreants are divided into full-time criminals (i.e. successful miscreants) and full-time prisoners (i.e. unsuccessful miscreants). The distinction implied above is between higher and lower-status groups.

11   The key word here is 'able'. The picture is quite different when one regards the mass of full-time unsuccessful miscreants — the stage army of the local prisons.

12   Our grading. For a different grading by Cressey see p. 150 above.

13   This useful paper exists so far only in mimeograph (Gould, 1967).

14   See for example the account of the setting up of the Intelligence Section in Scotland Yard in Jackson, 1969, pp. 131-3.

Appendix B

'THE ABLE CRIMINAL'[1]

J. A. Mack (Glasgow)

The inquiry sketched in this paper makes no attempt to elucidate the 'causes' of crime. It is primarily descriptive, classificatory and typological, directed towards one and one only of the many and heterogeneous phenomena lumped under the general title of crime. We are concerned with those criminals who make a full time job of crime, and who establish relationships, including networks, in the pursuance of their common occupational interests. This is a distinctive criminal group, and its existence is to be traced in general literature, so far as the United Kingdom is concerned, from Elizabethan times on.

How important are these full-time criminals? Statistically, not very important. They account for only a small part of the crime totals. The main burden of police work in the field of crime control is the great mass of criminal and near-criminal offences committed by offenders mostly not known to the police, including not only myriads of casual minor offenders but also quite high-level operators, 'substantial incomers' not hitherto known to the police. But the full-time criminal system operates at a very high *pro rata* economic cost to the community. It is also the case that when these operations are successful, not only in avoiding conviction or imprisonment, but also in getting away with large hauls, the effect on the morale of the vast lesser-criminal population, and for that matter the effect on the morale of the police, is profound. Moreover these full-time criminals carry on a distinctive occupational tradition. For the group we are studying crime is a way of life as well as a trade: the popular expression is a 'profession'. It is composed of those full-time criminals who are of more than average competence, and who carry considerable weight in their own circles. They will have other occupations or descriptions, but their interests are bound up with and their income derived from criminal pursuits. They are not all 'top criminals', although they include the few top criminals who are going about. They are simply a group of individuals of some substance whose lives are organised round a criminal way of behaving. There are a large number of others, equally involved as regards interest and use of their time, but smaller fry; these might number about twenty or thirty times the total of heavyweight or middleweight full-time operators.

A pilot study carried out some years ago, the Worktown study, was made possible by full information from two police forces (Mack, 1964). The question put to them was — 'What, in this urban area of somewhere between 80,000 and 90,000 people, is the strength, the establishment so to speak, of full-time, comparatively heavyweight, travelling criminals?' An initial list of about twenty was scrutinised and fined down to twelve; after further discussion it was agreed that four could be discarded as not heavyweight enough. The residue of eight could be regarded as the full-time criminal output of this area. This gives a rough and ready ratio of one fairly considerable full-time operator for every 10,000 inhabitants.

The pilot study at once produced a distinctive feature which has shaped our inquiries ever since. The small group of eight full-time operators divided itself neatly into two equal and opposite parts. Four of the eight corresponded with fair accuracy to the criminal as found in many textbooks. They came from a deprived neighbourhood. They had bad home circumstances in early life, and suffered from a lack of parental care and affection. Their behaviour showed some emotional disturbance, sometimes considerable. They were of low intelligence. They had juvenile records.

The other four were different in all respects but one, namely that they came from much the same social background as the previous four. But three had no juvenile records, and one was recorded as having only one minor juvenile offence. Their early home circumstances were either not known or not notably bad. They gave every appearance of being psychologically well-balanced, and were quite well thought of by the police as individuals; 'you can pass the time of day with them'. Their behaviour, particularly their criminal performance as known to the police, gave strong ground for supposing that they were above average in intelligence.

A further striking difference between the two groups came out when their full criminal records were compared. They divided neatly again into the same two groups of four. The first group, the textbook criminals, had spent on the average over 60 per cent of their adult life in prison, not allowing for remission. They were of the type which might fail to earn remission. The other four had very little prison record. They averaged 12½ per cent of their adult life from the age of 17, not counting remission (which they would probably earn).

The present study is on a larger scale, and is centred on an industrial city of about 1 million population. Among other things a sample of between 100 and 150 specified full-time miscreants is being documented and analysed. This group comprises all or most of those in whom the detective forces of the area are specially interested. The present paper is concerned with a group of 102 drawn from this larger total, consisting of those

186

operators considered by the research team, in consultation with the police, to be continuously active.

So far the results are in line with those of the pilot study. For example the present study tends to confirm that the ratio of major full-time criminal operators in the general population is in the region of one in 10,000. This is of course a highly speculative figure. A 'major full-time operator' in Worktown, with 80,000 population, would rank comparatively low in a city of 1 million population; similarly a 'major operator' in such a city might rate fairly low on the standards of the Metropolitan Police District; standards ratified not only by the police, but also by the criminal occupational sub-culture.

The second pilot study finding is also confirmed, namely that a large proportion of major full-time criminals are both able and successful in their criminal occupation. Success in this field is not easy to estimate by the usual criteria of profit and loss. A successful criminal generally makes a lot more money than he would make in such law-abiding occupations as are open to him. But how much, and how often, and how continuous, is very difficult to determine. It seems also that his expenses and expenditures are very high by ordinary standards. But the group we are studying is notably successful in another sense. While it is known to the police that they are persistently engaged in fairly large-scale criminal enterprises, they contrive to avoid imprisonment or conviction or even, at the top of the scale, appearance in court.

There is one notable difference between the two studies in respect of imprisonment. Whereas the very small pilot study population divided into two polarised groups, 'habitual or full-time criminals' at one end of the spectrum and 'habitual or full-time prisoners' at the other, the population now under review form a continuum, a continuum crowded towards the 'successful' end, so that the proportion of those who manage to keep out of prison most of the time is higher than in the pilot study.[2] In the following calculation five of the group of 102 are excluded as having had less than ten 'years at risk' of imprisonment – that is, they are under 27 years of age. The average age of the 97 remaining subjects is 38, the scatter is as follows:

N	Age at mid-1969	Years at risk
7	27-30	10-13
27	31-35	14-18
34	36-40	19-23
14	41-45	24-28
7	46-50	29-33
6	51-55	34-38
2	56-60	39-43
—		
97		

In Table B.1 the subjects are classified, very roughly, according to their *main* type of criminal activity, into six groups.

1 Organisers (O) or background types, who also tend to enjoy especially high status.
2 Resetters (R); this, like the others, is a versatile group, and includes a number who combine resetting and other activities, specially fraud, sometimes of the 'long firm' variety.
3 Thieves (T); including sneak-in merchants, shoplifters, and a number of thief fraudsters who sell commodities like non-existent advertising space and invisible whisky.
4 'Heavies' (H); i.e. housebreakers, safebreakers, bank robbers, wage-snatch operators, explosives experts, tie-up merchants, and so on.
5 Violents (V); the few in this category, while showing some degree of pathology, are included because their violence is employed for acquisitive purposes.
6 Providers (P); providers of services of different kinds.

The data as regards juvenile crime bear some resemblance to those of the pilot study. More than one-third, to be precise 36 out of 102, have no juvenile record, and a further twelve have one juvenile entry only. All of the seven who have no prison record have no juvenile record. Although a fair proportion may not have taken up crime until they passed 17 or 21, or even much later, it may be safer to infer, in some cases at least, that the essential skill exhibited in the avoidance of detection was developed early in life.

It will be seen from the table that resetting is a safer criminal activity than that pursued by the 'heavies'. But the main finding is that almost half of this group of persistent major criminal operators can well accept the occupational risk of incarceration since they have in fact kept out of prison for four-fifths and more of their time at risk; while no less than 78 per cent have been able to move freely about their avocations for at least three-fifths of their adult life. Of particular interest is the select group of the seven non-incarcerated. If one adds those who kept clear of prison in the ten years ending mid-1969 the seven become thirteen: three 'organisers', six 'resetters', one 'thief' and three 'general providers'.

These figures are not quite so alarming as they may sound at first hearing. While it is true that a sizeable proportion of persistent criminals, including a fair number of direct predators — thieves, robbers and housebreakers, as distinct from the back-room operators — are remarkably skilful in avoiding arrest and conviction, it also appears to be the case that their freedom of action is fairly drastically controlled. All of these major

Table B.1

Proportion of 'years at risk' i.e. since age 17, spent in prison, remission deducted, in period ending mid-1969

Proportion	O	R	T	H	V	P	Total
0%	1	3	1	—	—	2	7
0.1- 5%	—	5	5	4	—	—	14
5.1-10%	1	3	3	—	1	1	9
10.1-15%	—	1	3	4	—	—	8
15.1-20%	1	1	4	1	1	—	8
20.1-25%	—	1	2	1	—	3	7
25.1-30%	1	1	2	3	1	—	8
30.1-35%	—	—	1	6	—	—	7
35.1-40%	1	—	3	4	—	—	8
40.1-45%	—	—	1	4	—	1	6
45.1-50%	—	—	1	2	—	—	3
50.1-55%	1	—	—	4	—	—	5
55.1-60%	—	—	—	5	1	—	6
Over 60%	—	—	—	1	—	—	1
	6	15	26	39	4	7	97

operators have a strong distaste for the consequences of being caught, and the majority of them take very badly to imprisonment. Moreover the continuous vigilance maintained by the police limits considerably the risks they are prepared to take. A closer scrutiny of this aspect of crime control will be made at a later stage in the research. In the meantime it can be said that this fact of immunity from police and legal process provides a main focus for the present inquiry. The emphasis of the research has shifted to the study of the able or successful criminal He is of course a highly elusive figure, for criminologists as well as for detectives. Some have even argued that the 'successful' or 'able' or 'professional' criminal is a myth invented by the police to enhance their 'image' in the eyes of the public. But no one who has broken through the barrier of police reserve in these matters can maintain this proposition for long in the face of the evidence which the CID can provide in any large conurbation. It is not of course the kind of evidence that will immediately convince a court. But this is the very heart of the problem of the study of successful full-time crime. The first condition of such a study is the abandonment of the proposition that a conviction, or finding of guilty, is an essential element in the definition of criminality. The principle that these full-time operators should not be considered to be criminals until they are proved to be such in a court of law is good law and will remain so for as long as the present general ignorance on the subject of full-time criminals and criminal networks continues to be unrelieved by systematic research. It may even be good practical civics, though this is arguable. But it is indubitably bad sociology.

There is of course no direct conflict between lawyer and sociologist on this issue. The courts are concerned entirely with establishing, on the basis of their very strict and technical rules of evidence, whether or not this individual, or group of individuals, did actually commit a specified crime at a particular place and time. The interest of the social scientist is wider. He is not concerned with establishing the actual historical facts of specific situations: his object is to provide a systematic account of the criminal occupational sub-culture and with this in view to establish as precisely as he can the features and factors which distinguish that sub-culture from other groups in society. For this purpose the evidence of his own eyes and ears, provided he can get in touch with the criminals themselves and get them to speak the truth, is adequate, though it would normally be denied by his informants in a court of law. But direct information of this kind is extraordinarily hard to get. There is another possibility, another primary source of evidence, the experience and know-how of the police as well as their recorded information. Much of this evidence again is not normally reproducible in courts of law, but it is of great factual and analytical value for all that.

The main methodological assumption of this research is that essential facts about able criminals can be established with the help of the police, and cannot be established without that help. This raises the question of the acceptance of the researcher by the police, which is not altogether a simple matter. But the difficulties facing the researcher in this field are not unique. The problem of researching into the crime industry is no more and no less formidable than that of giving a systematic typological account of any other of the many semi-secret occupational sub-cultures in contemporary society. It is probably quite as difficult to find out what really goes on in the corridors of power.

This question of access to information is crucial. Successful criminals are by definition inaccessible. The major skill they have in common, over and above their special expertise, is that of keeping out of sight. They show this skill in not talking to people they do not trust; alternatively, what talk they do indulge in is designed to deceive. This fact, which seems so obvious as hardly to merit discussion, explains almost entirely one cardinal weakness of scientific criminology up to the present. That weakness is spotlighted by Gibbons (1970). The index to his book lists more than 300 behavioural and social scientists who have contributed to the serious study of youthful misbehaviour. 'Serious' in this context means empirical, involving data obtained by direct observation. Practically all of the studies cited are North American. It would be difficult to list thirty or even twenty behavioural and social scientists who are currently engaged in North America in the empirical and first-hand study of the able criminal. The number so engaged outside America is of course very much smaller.

This suggests a certain distortion of criminological perspective, a continuing and persistent failure to score on or near the centre of the target. It is at first sight remarkable that the majority of criminologists should be unconcerned with what common opinion holds to be 'real' crime. But the apparent paradox is at once explained by the scarcity of available material on the subject and the obstacles in the way of acquiring more. It is the most natural thing in the world that social and forensic scientists should study those topics on which evidence is readily available, and should ignore those other topics on which evidence is not readily available.

But to explain this neglect is not to excuse it. It is on any count deplorable that criminologists should be so very little interested in the problems set by the successful and inaccessible criminal. The literature contains very few discussions of the problem of access to successful crime. The orthodox viewpoint is expressed by Sutherland and Cressey (1960, p. 69), who make the valid point that it is difficult if not impossible to mix with criminals on their own ground, in open society, without becoming involved with them to the point of identification. The suggestion here is that subterfuge or masquerade would be necessary. Secondly there is the interesting claim made by Polsky (1967, p. 124), that research can proceed without any such complication *if one explains oneself properly.* This is probably true, as indeed Polsky has demonstrated as far as this or that marginal criminal group is concerned. But how does one study *major* criminal systems? Are the central figures likely to talk to the inquiring social scientist? And if not, should one just give up the idea? The assumption common to the two positions would appear to be that the empirical study of able criminals must be direct and unmediated, that one must go straight to the criminals themselves. But there are alternative possibilities. Why should not the researcher ally himself with the relevant police agencies, at least in the first instance, and work on their information? This is what Cressey has done in the last few years (1967, 1969).

He is the only one of a number of eminent criminological figures involved in the work of US government agencies in this field to have published his findings at length. It is possible to disagree with Cressey's main thesis — that there exists a highly integrated and nationwide Cosa Nostra[3] — and still to hold that this recent work of his exemplifies the only effective *preliminary* approach to the study of this or any other field of large-scale successful crime — the approach through *what the police know.*[4]

It is true that what the police know is patchy and largely inferential. It is also true that the police know a great deal more about crime as a major behaviour system than any criminologist can get to know without their help. But here again there are obstacles. The successful police detective is apt to be almost as uncommunicative as the able criminal. How can he be got to share his knowledge? What, for example, can the social scientist offer by way of *quid pro quo*?

This seems to us to be a major methodological issue, and will be dealt with in a later paper. Meanwhile a more basic question still confronts us. It is clear that bridging the communication gap between police detectives and criminologists is going to be a lot of trouble. Will it be worth while? How much attention should social scientists devote to developing closer relations with this side of police work?

The answer to this depends on how much importance one attaches to the phenomenon of the able criminal. At the very least it can be said that he is there, like Mount Everest, and should be tackled. Or, to use another simile, this is one of the few unexplored territories on the crime map. Here be criminals, able criminals: a group, not simply a category: a group about which a great deal is said but little known. The blank space on the map is not very big but it should be filled; otherwise our criminal geography is deficient.

That is the minimal case. Other and stronger arguments have been mentioned above. The maximal case for the study of successful crime is that a criminology which ignores it is *radically* deficient. It can be said, using a familiar analogy, that criminology has still to undergo its Copernican Revolution. But Copernicus is hardly the apt symbol here: a more accurate analogy is provided by van Leeuwenhoek who developed the microscope. Where would physiology, or virology, be without the microscope and its electronic successors? The formerly inaccessible data are now the only relevant data.

At present criminologists are generalising from the more to the less easily caught specimens. This principle of methodology is admirably stated by Trasler (1962, p. 11) — the principle of continuity of characteristics between the law-breakers to whom there is access and those to whom there is little or no access. He suggests that the presumption of continuity may be unfounded. 'The criminologist is usually obliged to make the working assumption that those who are caught are in all material respects representative of those who escape detection – probably an erroneous supposition.' If it is, then much of criminology as we know it rests on a mistake. This is precisely the conclusion suggested by the data being turned up by the present research. The persistent able criminal appears to have little in common with the persistent criminal failure. There would appear to be a fundamental flaw in much of current criminal psychology, in the criminal biology of Eysenck and others, and in criminal psychiatry. These disciplines have one thing in common: they are founded on a study of those characteristics which mark not the criminal, but the caught criminal. It follows that the bulk of contemporary criminological investigation is concerned not with why persistent offenders persist in offending, but why those persistent offenders who persist in being caught *are caught.* It is a study not of criminality but of catchability.

The resulting distortion goes far to explain the basic weakness of the classical criminological tradition. The 'typical criminal' of the older European texts is clearly a product of the continuity principle. From Lombroso onward it has been held that the 'typical criminal' is to be explained in terms of some detectable deficiency which marks him off from the bulk of non-criminal mankind. It is a fact that Lombroso and his major successors, notably Ferri, studied almost exclusively those criminals to whom they had easy access, that is to say, criminals in custody (Sellin, Wolfgang, in Mannheim, 1960). And this is still the general practice.

It is of course a matter of continuing controversy whether those persistent criminals who are usually to be round in prison are in fact marked off from the rest of mankind in the way required of them by the Lombrosian tradition. Lombroso himself was of the opinion that the differentiating factor was physically observable and genetically determined. But his evidence for the first of these propositions was shot to pieces by Goring (1913), who demonstrated that the incidence of Lombroso's 'criminal' stigmata was the same outside as inside prison. A similar comprehensive refutation persued and finally overcame the next formulation of the 'criminal-type' tradition – the view that the typical criminal, or typical delinquent, was distinguished from the non-criminal and non-delinquent majority by a measurable degree of intellectual backwardness. The current version of the tradition – the assertion that there is a differentiating factor and that it is to be defined in psychiatric terms – appears to be holding its own: it would certainly seem that the incidence of psychiatric disorder is higher in the prison population than in the world at large.[5] And moreover Professor Eysenck (1964) appears to be in process of reviving the original view that the differentiation factor is hereditary.

It could indeed be argued — though I would not subscribe to it — that opinion is currently swinging behind the Lombrosian type of theory. But the Lombrosian type of theory, in 1972 as in 1876, is limited to the demonstration of differences between habitual prisoners and habitual non-prisoners. It is still somewhat off-centre to those who are concerned with the study of crime and criminals.

The established mode of criminological study is of course highly useful for penological purposes, and will remain so. But the study of penology (which on the argument here put forward includes most of what is presently called criminology) will undoubtedly be clarified and strengthened by a clearer grasp of the distinction between the full-time criminal, to be seen at his most effective in the able operator, and the full-time prisoner, the archetype of the unsuccessful operator.

Notes

1   This paper, reprinted from the *British Journal of Criminology,* vol. XII (1964), pp. 45-55, is based on a report made to the Current Research Seminar of the Sixth World Criminological Congress (Madrid, 1970). The research it describes is mainly financed by the Scottish Home and Health Department, to whom grateful acknowledgement is made. The 1964 pilot study referred to (the Worktown study) was done by Miss M. Ritchie, M.A., and the writer. The team engaged on the present and more large-scale study also includes, or has included, J. A. D. Macmillan, B.A., M.Phil., Mrs S. T. Miller, M.A. and Mrs E. Woldman, M.A.

2   For a highly intelligent anticipation of this continuum see Chapman (1968), p. 194.

3   Mack, 1970*a*.

4   Mack, 1970*b*.

5   A useful review of this sequence of 'criminal type' theories is given in Vold (1958).

References

English, French, etc.

Albini J. L. (1971), *The American Mafia: Genesis of a legend,* Appleton-Century-Crofts, New York.

Aube L., 'Malfaiteurs "internationaux" ': *Revue Internationale de Criminologie et de Police Technique* (1954), pp. 309-17.

Avison N. H. and McClintock F. H. (1970), *Crime problems in Great Britain today,* Paper presented at sixth international congress on criminology, Madrid 1970.

Bejerot N. (1970), *Addiction and society,* Springfield, Ill.

Bell D. (1960), *The end of ideology,* Collier-Macmillan, London.

Besançon J. (1970), 'Guerini? Connais pas!', *Le Nouvel Observateur,* Paris (12 January 1970).

Biilmann J. and Buchardt K. (1970), *Alt hoad der er Stort. Bogen om Boss* [All That is Big. The Book About Boss], Chr. Erichsens Forlag, Copenhagen.

Blok A. (1969), 'Peasants, Patrons and Brokers in Western Sicily', *Anthropological Quarterly* XLIII, 159-70.

Bondeson U. (1968), 'Argot knowledge as an indicator of criminal socialisation', in Nils Christie (ed.), *Scandinavian Studies in Criminology,* vol. II, pp. 73-107, Universitets Forlaget, Oslo.

Bonger W. A. (1916), *Criminality and Economic Conditions,* Little, Brown, Boston.

Bertolt Brecht (1970), 'The Threepenny Opera' in *Collected Plays,* ed. Willett and Manheim, vol. II. Methuen, London.

Carson W. G. (1970), 'White-collar crime and the enforcement of factory legislation', *The British Journal of Criminology,* vol. 10, pp. 383-98, London.

Chapman D. (1968), *Sociology and the Stereotype of the Criminal,* Tavistock Publications, London.

Chappell D. and Walsh M. (1972), 'No questions asked': consideration of the History of Criminal Receiving: Mimeograph paper presented to conference on 'Present day implications of the history of violence and other crime'. State University of New York, New York.

Clemmer D. (1958), *The Prison Community,* New York.

Clinard M. and Quinney, R. (1967), *Criminal Behaviour Systems: a Typology*, Hold, Rinehart and Winston, New York.

Clockars Carl (1972), *The fence: caveat emptor, caveat vendor*, Paper presented to the American Society of Criminology Inter-American Conference in Caracas, Venezuela, November 1972 — mimeograph.

Clockars Carl (1974), *The Professional fence*, Free Press, Glencoe, Illinois.

Cohen S. (1971), *Images of Deviance*, Penguin, London.

Cosson J. (1971), *Les Grands Industriels de la Fraude Fiscale*, Seuil, Paris.

Council (1971), *Current trends in Criminological Research*, being vol. VI of *Collected Studies in Criminological Research*, Council of Europe, Strasbourg.

Cressey D. R. (1967), *Paper in Task Force report: Organised crime, Washington. (q.v.)*

Cressy D. R. (1969), *Theft of the Nation*, Harper and Row, New York.

Cressey D. R. (1972), *Criminal Organisation*, Heinemann, London.

Defosse M. (1970), 'Le Procès Guérini', *Revue de Droit Penal et de Criminologie*, vol. 59, pp. 767-78.

Einstadter W. J. (1969), 'The social organisation of armed robbery', *Social Problems*, vol. 17 (Summer), pp. 64-82, New York.

Eysenck H. J. (1964), *Crime and Personality*, Routledge and Kegan Paul, London.

Ferri Enrico (1917), *Criminal Sociology*, [English translation by J. I. Kelly and J. Lisle], Little, Brown, Boston.

Fordham P. (1972), *Inside the Underworld*, Allen and Unwin, London.

Fowler N. (1970), 'Crime in Britain', part 2, *The Times*, London, 7 April 1970, p. 11.

Gage Nicholas (1971), *The Mafia is not an Equal-opportunity Employer*, McGraw-Hill, New York.

Gardiner J. A. (1970), *The politics of corruption: organised crime in an American city*, Russell Sage Foundation, New York.

Geis Gilbert (1968 (ed.), *White-collar Criminal*, Atherton Press, New York.

Gibbons D. C. (1970), *Delinquent Behaviour*, Prenctice-Hall Inc., New York.

Gibbons D. C. and Garrity D. L. (1962), 'Definitions and analysis of certain criminal types, *Journal of Criminal Law, Criminology, and Police Science*, vol. 53 (1962), pp. 28-35; also in Radzinowicz and Wolfgang (1971), pp. 243-53.

Goffmann, E. (1963), *Stigma,* Englewood Cliffs, 1963; also Penguin, London.

Goring C. (1913), *The English Convict,* HMSO, London.

Gould Leroy (1967), Mimeograph, 'The Professional Criminal', prepared for the President's Commission on Law Enforcement etc. (*see* Task Force).

Green T. (1969), *The Smugglers,* Michael Joseph, London.

Greenwood C. (1972), *Firearms Control,* Routledge and Kegan Paul, London.

Gregory J. (1932) (ed.), *Crime from the Inside,* John Long, London.

Hadden T. (1967), *The Development and Administration of the English law of Criminal fraud,* Institute of Criminology Library, University of Cambridge.

Hadden T. (1968), 'The control of Company fraud', Political and Economic Planning, London, vol. XXXIV, no. 503.

Hartung F. (1950), 'White-collar offenses in the wholesale meat industry in Detroit', *American Journal of Sociology,* vol. 56 (July 1950), pp. 25-34.

von Hentig R. (1947), *Crime: Causes and Conditions,* New York, McGraw-Hill (1947).

Hess H. (1973), *Mafia and Mafiosi: the structure of power,* (D. C. Heath, London) (Translated from German: *Mafia: zentrale Herrschaft und Lokale Gegenmacht,* J. C. B. Mohr, Tübingen, 1970).

Hudson W. M. F. (1971), 'R. *v.* Kray and others', *Medico-Legal Journal,* vol. 39, pp. 4-16.

Ianni F. A. J. (1972), *A Family Business,* Routledge and Kegan Paul, London.

Ianni F. A. J. (1974), *The Black Mafia,* Simon and Schuster, New York.

Inciardi J. A. (1972), 'Visibility, societal reaction, and criminal behaviour', Criminology 10, vol. 2, pp. 217-33.

Inciardi J. A. (1974), *Careers in Crime,* New York, Rand McNally.

International criminal police organisation (Interpol) (1968), *Symposium on International Frauds,* 24-26 April, 1968. Final Draft.

Interpol (1971), *IIe Colloque international sur le Crime organisé,* Paris — Saint Cloud.

Jackson R. (1967), *Occupied with Crime,* Harrap, London.

Jackson B. (1969), *A Thief's Primer,* Macmillan, London.

Judges A. V. (1930, 1965), *The Elizabethan Underworld,* London, 1965; 1st edn. 1930.

Lemert E. (1958), 'The behaviour of the systematic check forger', *Social Problems*, vol. 6 (fall), pp. 141-9, New York.

Lewis N. (1964), *The Honoured Society*, G. P. Putnam's Sons, New York.

Lucas Norman (1969), *Britain's Gangland*, Pan Books, London.

McIntosh M. (1971*a*), 'Four varieties of professional crime', mimeograph of paper given to British Sociological Association 1971 Conference, London.

McIntosh M. (1971*b*), 'Changes in the organization of thieving', in S. Cohen (ed.) (1971).

McIntosh M. (1973), 'The growth of racketeering', *Economy and Society*, vol. 2, no. 1, London.

Mack J. A. (1954), Chapter on 'Crime' in A. K. Cairncross (ed.), *The Scottish Economy*, Cambridge University Press, London.

Mack J. A. (1964), 'Full-time miscreants etc.', *The British Journal of Sociology*, vol. XV, pp. 38-53.

Mack J. A. (1970*a*), 'Does the Mafia exist?', *New Society*, no. 409, 7 July 1970, pp. 194-5.

Mack J. A. (1970*b*), Review of Cressey, 1969 (q.v.), *New Society*, no. 423, p. 835.

Mack J. A. (1971), 'Business-type crime on the increase?' Mimeograph, International Centre for Comparative Criminology Symposium, Versailles 1971.

Mack J. A. (1972), 'Carry on slinging' (review of Ianni, 1972), *New Society*, vol. 22, no. 526, pp. 286-7.

Mannheim H. (1960) (ed.). *Pioneers in Criminology*, Stevens & Sons, London.

Mannheim H. (1965), *Comparative Criminology* (2 vols), vol. 2, Routledge and Kegan Paul, London.

Maurer D. W. (1955) (1964), *Whiz mob: a correlation of the technical argot of Pickpockets with their behaviour pattern*, American Dialect Society Publication No. 24, Gainesville, Florida; also College and University Press, New Haven, 1964.

Millen E. (1972), *Specialist in Crime*, Harrap, London.

Mori C. (1933), *The last struggle with the Mafia*, Putnam, London.

Morris Norval and Hawkins Gordon (1970), *The honest politician's guide to crime control*, University of Chicago Press.

McClintock F. H. (1963), 'Criminological aspects of violent Behaviour' (Mimeograph). Paper read to British Association for the Advancement of Science, 1963.

McClintock F. H. and Gibson E. (1961), *Robbery in London*, Macmillan, London.

Pantaleone G. (1966), *The Mafia and Politics,* Coward-McCann Inc., New York.

Parker (1781), *View of Society,* London.

Parker D. B. *et al.* (1973), *Computer Abuse,* California, Stanford Research Institute.

Partridge Eric (1949), *A Dictionary of the Underworld,* Routledge and Kegan Paul, London.

Payne L. (1973), *The Brotherhood,* Michael Joseph, London.

Pearson J. (1972), *The Profession of Violence,* Weidenfeld and Nicolson, London.

Peronaci A. (1971), *Difficultés qu'on rencontre dans la Repression de la Criminalité professionnelle,* Mimeograph 1971, Strasbourg.

Pinatel J. (1957), 'Le Criminel professionel', *La Revue des Sciences Criminelles,* 1957 volume, pp. 909-24.

Pinatel J. (1971), *La Société criminogène,* (Paris: Calmann 1971).

Ploscowe Maurice (1931), 'Some causative factors in criminality', *Reports on the causes of crime,* vol. I, Washington, D.C., National Commission on Law Observance and Enforcement, no. 13, 1931.

Poletti F. (1882), *Del sentimento nella scienza del diritto penale,* Udine, 1882.

Polsky N. (1967), *Hustlers, Beats, and others,* Aldine Publishing Company, Chicago.

Radzinowicz Leon (1971), 'Economic pressures', in L. Radzinowicz and M. E. Wolfgang, *Crime and Justice,* vol. I, *The Criminal in Society,* Basic Books, New York, 1971, pp. 420-42.

Raw C., Page B., and Hodgson G. (1972), *Do you sincerely want to be rich?* Penguin, London.

Robert P., Bombet J. P. and Saudinos D. (1970, 'Le Cout du crime en France', *Annales Internationales de Criminologie,* 9/2, pp. 599-656 (1970).

Sellin T. (1960), 'Enrico Ferri', in Mannheim (1960) (q.v.), pp. 277-300.

Spencer J. (1965), 'White-collar crime', in T. Grygier, H. Jones and J. Spencer (eds.), *Criminology in Transition,* pp. 251-64, Tavistock, London.

Sveri K. and Werner H. (1963), *Safebreakers and Habitual Criminals,* Stockholm, 1963, Criminological Institute of the University of Stockholm, publication no. 2, (in Swedish).

Shover N. (1971) (1972), ' "Supporting elements" and careers in burglary', paper presented to 66th annual meeting of the American Sociological Association, Denver 1971. *See also* 'Structures and careers in burglary', *Journal of Criminal Law, Criminology, and Police Science,* vol. 63, pp. 540-9, 1972.

Gladstone Smith P. (1970), *The Crime Explosion,* Macdonald, London.

Susini J. (1971), 'Mafia', in *L'Encyclopaedia Universalis,* 1971, pp. 284-7.

Sutherland E. H. (1937), *The Professional Thief,* University of Chicago Press, Chicago.

Sutherland E. H. (1949), *White Collar Crime,* Holt, Rinehart and Winston, New York. 1st edn. 1949, later edn. 1961.

Sutherland E. H. and Cressey D. R. (1960), *Principles of Criminology,* 6th edn. J. B. Lippincott, Philadelphia.

Task Force Report on organised crime (1967), The U.S. president's commission on law enforcement and administration of justice, *Task Force Report,* etc., Washington.

Teresa V. (1973), *My Life in the Mafia,* Hart-Davis McGibbon, London.

Tobias J. J. (1968), 'The crime industry', *The British Journal of Criminology,* vol. II, pp. 247-58.

Trasler G. (1962), *The Explanation of Criminality,* Routledge and Kegan Paul, London.

Turner W. (1968), *The Police Establishment,* Putnam, New York.

Vold G. B. (1958), *Theoretical Criminology,* London, Oxford University Press.

Walsh M. and Chappell D. (1973), 'Operational parameters in the stolen property system', paper presented to the 44th National Operations Research Society of America Meeting, November 1973, San Diego, California.

Weatherhead A. D. and Robinson, B. M. (1970), *Firearms in Crime,* Home Office Statistical Division Report, London, HMSO.

Wheatcroft G. S. A. (1972), *Value-Added Tax,* Cassell, London.

Whitehead A. N. (1926), *Science and the modern world,* London, Cambridge University Press.

Wiles P. and McClintock F. H. (1972), 'The security industry in the United Kingdom', paper presented to the Cropwood Round-Table Conference, July 1972. Cambridge, Institute of Criminology, [University of Cambridge 1972].

Wilkins L. T. (1964), *Social Deviance,* Tavistock, London.

Wolf P. (1968), 'Crime and development: an international comparison of crime rates', *Sociological Microjournal,* vol. II, Ficue no. 8, Copenhagen 1968 also, *Scandinavian Studies in Criminology,* vol. III pp. 107-20, 1971 (see Bondeson above).

200

Wolfgang M. E. (1960), 'Cesare Lombroso', in Mannheim (1960) (q.v.), pp. 168-227.

German, Dutch, etc.

van den Aardweg G. J. M. en Dorpmans J. A. M. (1966), *Persoonlijkheidsfaktoren bijk Delinkwenten-recidivisten,* Onderzoeksrapport; 's-Gravenhage: Selectie- en Orientatiecentrum van het Gevangeniswezen.

Achtert H. J. (1969), 'Bandenmässig verübte PKW-Diebstahle', *Kriminalistik* 23, 119-22.

Amelunxen W. (1967), 'Der Zuhalter. Wandlungen eines Tatertyp, *Kriminalistik,* Hamburg.

Aube L. (1958), 'Internationale Trickdiebe'. In: *Bekämpfung von Diebstahl, Einbruch, Raub,* Bundeskriminalamt (Hrsg.), Wiesbaden, pp. 89 ff.

Baan P. A. H. (1969), 'Grundsätzliches zur Therapie von Ruckfallverbrechern'. In *Verbrechen − Schuld oder Schicksal?:* hrsg.v.W. Bitter. Klett, Stuttgart, pp. 73-87.

Bader K. S. (1949), *Soziologie der deutschen Mach-kriegskriminalitat,* J. C. B. Mohr, Tübingen.

Bauer G. (1970), *Raub und Rauber. Ein Kriminalistischer und Kriminologischer Beitrag zur Bekämpfung und Verhutung der Raubkriminalitat,* Steintor-Verlag, Hamburg.

van Bemmelen J. M. (1952), *Criminologie. Leerboek der Misdaadkunde,* 3. druk. Tjeenk-Willink, Zwolle.

Blanek G. und Holzenbecher G. (1970), 'Kfz.-diebe unterhalten Spezialfirma für VW-Verwertung', *Kriminalistik* 24, 446-550.

Brückner C. (1971), *Der Gewohnheitsverbrecher und die Verwahrung in der Schweiz gemäss Artickel 42 STGB − eine statistische Darstellung,* Helbing u. Lichtenhahn, Basel und Stuttgart.

Claessens D., Klönne A. und Tschoppe A. (1965), *Sozialkunde der Bundesrepublik Deutschland,* Diederichs, Düsseldorf − Köln.

Ender K. (1972), 'Sicherheitsproblem Nr.1: die Serientater', *Kriminalistik* 26, pp. 26-9.

Fridberg H. (1970), 'Das Rauschgiftproblem in Schweden', *Kriminalistik* 24, pp. 629-30.

Fürstenberg F. (1967), *Die Sozialstruktur der Bundesrepublik Deutschland. Ein soziologischer Uberblick,* Westdeutscher Verlag, Köln und Opladen.

Gleisner G., Lorenz W., May V. und Schubert D. (1972), *Bankraub in der Bundesrepublik Deutschland* (2. vol), Enke, Stuttgart.

Goedecke W. (1962), *Berufs- und Gewohnheitsverbrecher. Eine Untersuchung zur allgemeinen Charakteristik dieser Tätergruppe*, Schriftenreine des Bundeskriminalamts, Wiesbaden.

Göppinger H. (1971), *Kriminologie. Eine Einfuhrung*, C. H. Beck, München.

Heindl R. (1926), *Der Berufsverbrecher. Ein Beitrag zur Strafrechtsreform*, Pan-Verlag Rolf Heise, Berlin.

Hellmer J. (1961), *Der Gewohnheitsverbrecher und die Sicherungsverwahrung 1934-1945*, Duncker u. Humblot, Berlin.

Hess H. (1970), *Mafia Zentrale Herrschaft und lokale Gegenmacht*, J. C. B. Mohr, Tübingen.

Hoberg L. (1958), 'Ringvereine — Einst und Jetzt', In *Bekämpfung von Diebstahl, Einbruch, Raub*, hrsg. vom Bundeskriminalamt. Reihe des Bundeskriminalamts, Wiesbaden, pp. 143-52.

Hoeveler H. J. (1963), 'Reisescheckbetruger', in *Taschenbuch für Kriminalisten*, Band 13, hrsg. von E. Eschenbach, Verlag Deutsche Polizei, Hamburg.

Hoeveler H. J. (1966), *Internationale Bekämpfung des Verbrechens*, Verlag Deutsche Polizei, Hamburg.

Holle R. (1966), *Diebstahl und Raub im Spiegel der Polizeilichen Kriminalstatistik (1953-1962)*, Schriftenreihe des Bundeskriminalamts, Wiesbaden.

Holle R. (1968), *Die Kriminalität in der Bundesrepublik Deutschland im Vergleich zu Osterreich, Frankreich, den Niederlanden, Dänemark, Schweden, England und Wales und Italien 1955-1964*, Schriftenreihe des Bundeskriminalamts, Wiesbaden.

John A. (1929), *Die Ruckfalldiebe. Eine Untersuchung uber Erscheinungsformen des Verbrechens*, Ernst Wiegandt Verlagsbuchhandlung, Leipzig.

Kaiser G. (1966), 'Entwicklung und Stand der Jugend-kriminalität in Deutschland', in *Kriminalbiologische Gegenwartsfragen*, Heft 7, Enke, Stuttgart, pp. 17-68.

Kaiser G. (1971), *Kriminologie. Eine Einfuhrung in die Grundlagen*, C. F. Müller, Karlsruhe.

Kallenborn J. W. (1960), 'Internationale Munz- und Banknotenfälscher', in *Internationale Verbrechensbekämpfung*, hrsg. vom Bundeskriminalamt. Reihe des Bundeskriminalamts, Wiesbaden, pp. 131-8.

Kerner H. I. (1973), 'Professionelles und organisierte Verbrechen', Schriftenreihe des Bundeskriminalamtes, Wiesbaden.

Landmann H. (1959), 'Ring- und Unterweltvereine als Forderer der Kriminalität', *Kriminalistik* 13, 35-6.

Lindenau (1906), 'Das internationale Verbrechen und seine Bekämpfung', in *Mitteilungen der Internationalen Kriminalistischen Vereinigung,* Band 13 (Berlin), p. 192 ff.

Lissy H. (1970), Kraftfahrzeig-verschiebungen-versuch einer Analyse der Kraftfahrzeugkriminalität des Jahres 1969 im Land Nord-Rhein-Westfalen', *Kriminalistik* 24, 339-42.

Manopoulo A. (1967), 'Die Mafia — Das organisierte Verbrechen', in *Kriminalpolizei und Technik,* hrsg. vom Bundeskriminalamt, Reihe des Bundeskriminalamts, Wiesbaden, pp. 89-109.

Muller H. (1939), *Die Entwicklung und Lebensverhaltnisse von 135 Gewohnheitsverbrechern,* Ernst Wiegandt Verlagsbuchhandlung, Leipzig.

Naucke W. (1962), 'Methodenfragen zum "Typ" des Gewohnheitsverbrechers', *Monatsschrift für Kriminologie und Strafrechtsform,* 45, 84-93.

Palitzsch B. (1926), *Die Bekämpfung des Internationalen Verbrechertums,* Meissner, Hamburg

Polizei-Institut Hiltrup (1969), *Bekämpfung uberortlich Tätiger Räuber- und Einbrecherbanden,* Eigenverlag Polizei-Institut, Hiltrup/Westfalen.

Polizei-Institut Hiltrup (1966), *Bekämpfung von Einbruch und Raub,* Eigenverlag Polizei-Institut, Hiltrup/Westfalen.

Polizei-Institut Hiltrup (1971), *Praxis- und Problematik der Uberwachung von Schwerkriminellen,* Eigenverlag Polizei-Institut, Hiltrup/Westfalen.

Rangol A. J. (1959), 'Gewaltverberechen dies Jugen Fruhcr und IIeute', *Wirtschaft und Statistik,* pp. 365-7.

Rangol A. J. (1960), 'Die Straffälligkeit nach Hauptdeliktsgruppen 1882 bis 1958', *Wirtschaft und Statistik,* pp. 590-6.

Rangol A. J. (1962), 'Die Straffälligkeit nach Hauptdeliktsgruppen und Altersklassen 1884 bis 1958', *Monatsschrift für Kriminologie und Strafrechtsreform* 45, pp. 157-75.

Rangol A. J. (1971*a*), 'Der Diebstahl im Rahmen der Gesamtkriminalität', *Wirtschaft und Statistik,* pp.224-8.

Rangol A. J. (1971*b*), 'Geschlecht und Alter der Diebe und ihre Bestrafung', *Wirtschaft und Statistik,* pp. 344-51.

van Rooy H. (1957), *Criminologisch onderzoek betreffende Rezidivisten en Terbeschikkinggestelden,* Uitgave van het Studie – en Voorlichtingscentrum van het Ministerie van Justitie, 's-Gravenhage.

Schneider H. J. (1972), 'Wirtschaftskriminalität in kriminologischer und Strafrecht licher sicht', *Juristenzeitung* pp. 461-7.
Schröder H. (1970), 'Internationale Diebesbanden, ihre Arbeitsmethoden, Probleme ihrer Bekämpfung', in *Bekämpfung überörtlichtätiger Räuber- und Einbrecherbanden,* hrsg. vom Polizei-Institut Hiltrup. Eigenverlag Polizei-Institut, Hiltrup/Westfalen, pp. 67-96.
Schurich, J. (1930), *Lebensläufe vielfach ruckfalliger Verbrecher,* Ernst Wiegandt Verlagsbuchhandlung, Leipzig.
Steinke R. (1971), 'Die Internationale Zusammenarbeit bei der Bekämpfung von Falschgelddelikten', in *Taschenbuch für Kriminalisten,* Band 21, hrsg. von H. J. Hoeveler, Verlag Deutsche Polizei, Hilden/Rheinland, pp. 237-72.

Tiedemann K. (1972*a*), *Die Verbrechen in der Wirtschaft. 2. Auflage,* C. F. Muller, Karlsruhe.
Tiedemann K. (1972*b*), 'Welche Strafrechtlichen mittel empfehlen sich für eine Wirksame Bekämpfung der Wirtschaftskriminalität?' *Gutachten c. zum 49.* Deutschen Juristentag. C. H. Beck, München.

Weidermann O. (1969), 'Berufmässige tatbegehung', *Kriminologische Schriftenreihe,* Band 44. Kriminalistik Hamburg.
Wend J. (1936), *Untersuchungen and Straflisten Vielfach Ruckfälliger verbrecher,* Ernst Wiegandt Verlagsbuchhandlung, Leipzig.
Wetterich P. (1963), *Erscheinungsformen Gefährlicher Gewohnheitsverbrecher,* Freiburg im Breisgau, Jura Diss.
Wurtenberger Th. und Herren R. (1970), 'Bankraub in der Bundesrepublik', *Kriminalistik,* 24, pp. 475-80.

Zirpins W. und Terstegen O. (1963), *Wirtschaftskriminalität, ihre Erscheinungsformen und ihre Bekämpfung,* Max Schmidt-Romhild, Lübeck.

Subject Index

Author Index